Open Mouth Already a Mistake

Talks by

Zen Master Wu Kwang

Primary Point Press
Cumberland, Rhode Island

First edition, 1997

Cover artwork by Dorota J. Streitfeld
Back cover photograph by Billy Cunningham
Primary Point Press logo by Grazyna Perl, JDPSN

Material on Shakyamuni Buddha in chapter 1 is from:
Transmission of Light, Thomas Cleary, North Point Press,
San Francisco, 1990

Material on Queen Maya in chapter 2 is from:
Flower Ornament Sutra, Thomas Cleary, Shambhala Press, San Francisco

Material on Zen Master Ma Jo (Matsu) in chapter 9 is from:
Sun Face Buddha, Cheng Chien Bhikshu, Asian Humanities Press,
Berkeley, California, 1992

Material on Zen Master Un Mun (Yun Men) in chapter 16 is from:
Master Yunmen, Urs App, Kodansha Int., 1994
Zen & Zen Classics, R. H. Blyth, Vintage Books, 1978

Stories in chapter 17 are from:
Zen and Zen Classics, R.H. Blyth, Vintage Books, 1978
The Gateless Barrier, translated by Robert Aitken, Roshi,
North Point Press, San Francisco, 1991

Stories of Baek Jang (Pai-chang) in chapter 29 are from:
The Sayings and Doings of Pai-chang, translated by T. Cleary,
Zen Center of Los Angeles, 1975

Stories in chapter 30 are from:
Swampland Flowers, translated by Christopher Cleary,
Grove Press, Inc., 1977

Stories about Lin-chi in chapter 32 are from:
The Zen Teaching of Master Lin-chi, Burton Watson,
Shambhala Publications, 1993

ISBN 0-942795-08-3

Dedication:
To Su Bong Soen Sa
and Susan Kimberly Shrobe,
whose leaving this world so soon,
taught us the meaning of the Diamond Sutra's
"Like a dew drop, a flash of lightning…"

Table of Contents

Acknowledgements

ᔪ

First and foremost, I want to thank my teacher, Zen Master Seung Sahn without whose help, support, and teaching this *big mistake* could not have happened! I also want to thank several of the teachers of the Kwan Um School of Zen for their guidance, inspiration, and spiritual friendship during my studies. They are Zen Master Soeng Hyang (Barbara Rhodes), Zen Master Bo Mun (George Bowman), the late Zen Master Su Bong, and especially Linc Rhodes Ji Do Poep Sa Nim, who skillfully guided me during the early days of my assuming teaching responsibilities. Also thanks to my wife, Brenda Phifer-Shrobe, and my many students who supported me in going forward with this work. Special thanks to Sally Kealy who transcribed the original talks, painstakingly typed each revision of the manuscript, and offered many useful suggestions. Also thanks to Pat Morimando who edited the original talks, Alan Davies and Kim Anderson for proofing the final manuscript, and Jan Potemkin for helping with the transliteration of Chinese names.

Foreword

Zen Master Wu Kwang:
An Unsolicited Appreciation

ᔉ

Everyone at Chogye understands what happened
To Bodhidharma's beard.
Universal light fills the Dharma room
Bowing alone, Tuesday, 5:15 AM

Zen Master Wu Kwang doesn't exemplify anything. Prefaces are often an occasion for accolades, but accolades are not ordinary enough for this occasion. Still, because we venerate teachers, it may be important to talk about just what kind of person this Zen Master is.

Richard is an ordinary guy. He lives in an apartment in the East Village, in a complex with thousands of other New Yorkers. He and Brenda have been married for over thirty years. They have three children, one of whom has died. After she died, I asked him how his Zen practice addressed this.

He said, "I've learned two things. One is not to be afraid of my emotions. The other is that everything is impermanent."

They have a granddaughter. She coos. She burps. She crawls. He has a job and works a long week. He talks to a lot of people. Sometimes he walks; sometimes he takes the subway; at other times, he rides his bicycle. He pays his rent. He pays his electric bills. He pays his taxes. We've never discussed who does the laundry in the twenty-one years I've known him. On Saturday mornings, he gives interviews. He talks to a lot of people. Once a month, sometimes twice, he leads retreats. Just one thing after another after another.

In response to a question about the nature of the dharma, an eminent teacher replied, "I have to go make water. What a pity. Even such a trifling matter, I have to attend to myself."

In gratitude,

Ken Kessel, Ji Do Poep Sa Nim
April 26, 1996

Author's Preface

৩

An old Zen poem says:

Sitting quietly in a mountain temple in the quiet night,
Extreme quiet and stillness are original nature.
Why then does the western wind shake the forest?
A single cry of winter geese fills the sky.

If, according to the poem, quiescence and stillness are our original nature, then to be born into this world of coming and going, action and effort, is already a mistake. As the old Zen masters said: "like making waves where there is no wind." Further, Shakyamuni Buddha is reported as having remarked that although he preached for forty-nine years, in reality he had never uttered a word, i.e. never given birth to speech and words. At the time of Buddha's passing on the succession of the Zen lineage to Mahakasyapa, he said, "I have a special transmission outside the doctrinal teachings, not dependent on words, this I give to Mahakasyapa." Centuries later when Bodhidharma took the Zen teaching to China, he spoke similarly of a mind to mind transmission outside the scriptures, not dependent on speech and words. Therefore, the second "mistake" is to open one's mouth and give rise to conceptual frames of reference. However, throughout its history, the Zen tradition has always made use of verbal teaching as part of its method. It is to be noted, however, that there is a distinct difference between using words and speech, rather than depending on words and speech.

In the Zen tradition of selfless action, there is a distinction made between committing a small mistake and living the "big mistake." Down through the ages, when the Zen masters opened their mouths to encourage students to practice, this was termed the "big mistake." The verbal teaching was used as a pointer toward finding the correct "Way," and facilitating the correct approach and attitude toward practice. In 1984, when I was given the responsibility of Zen teaching, I also began to commit the "mistake" of my predecessors, by trying to support the practice efforts of Zen students through giving Dharma talks and answering questions.

The material in this book is derived from talks given during the period of 1990 to 1995. For the most part, these talks were presented at Chogye International Zen Center of New York, although some were given at New

Haven, Providence and Cambridge Zen Centers. The setting varied, i.e. some talks were offered as part of a formal event, during a retreat or ceremony such as the commemoration of Buddha's Enlightenment. Others were talks given at a Zen Center as part of their ongoing program. Stylistically, the material is of three varieties. Some chapters are in the form of questions and answers. These have the flavor of free flowing informal improvisation. Other parts of the material are informal talks on some aspect of Zen practice. The third type is in the form of a formal Dharma speech wherein the opening section challenges the mind of the listener to return to an absolute point before dualistic frames of reference, and then perceive clearly things just as they are. Strictly speaking, the speech is complete at that point, but most often, a discourse follows which ends with a return to the absolute clarity of the opening section.

The beginnings of this book took place several years ago when a student of mine, Sally Kealy, urged me to regularly record my talks with the promise that she would transcribe the material. Over a period of time, we began to accumulate quite a pile of transcripts. These appeared to have the potential of being turned into a book. However, the process of transmuting raw transcripts into written form seemed daunting. Realizing that I had neither the time nor the acumen for this, I consulted a writer and editor friend, Pat Morimando. Pat, although not a Zen student, has a good knowledge of spiritual traditions, and a lot of experience in working with transcribed material and transforming it into readable English. We decided that we would try as best we could, to keep the spoken flavor and aliveness of the original talks, rather than polishing the English too much.

In these talks, I have attempted to move toward an integration of the traditional language of Zen with the cultural milieu of American Zen practitioners. In many instances, I use the teaching stories (kong-ans) of the early Chinese Masters, because in their timelessness, these stories carry the "bone" of Zen teaching in that they transcend culture and form, while simultaneously being applicable to the situation of every person. This is the teaching of Zen as "Everyday Mind." At the same time, you will find within these talks, subjects that are more specifically of current concern to American Zen students; things like the role of emotions in Zen, Zen and psychotherapy, substance abuse and addiction, homelessness, social relationships and responsibility, and how Zen addresses these issues.

The transplantation of a tradition from one cultural soil to another is a slow and cumulative process. This is evident if one looks at the historical movement of Zen from India to China to Korea, Japan, and Viet Nam. What has happened with the movement of Zen to the United States and Europe in the last few decades is further evidence of this process. That Zen has taken root here is by now obvious. Recently a college student came to the Chogye International Zen Center of New York to participate in a retreat.

During his interview with me, he said, "My father is a student of Zen and Tibetan Buddhism. When I was thirteen, he took me to a Zen retreat. I loved it and have been interested in practicing ever since." American Zen, however fragile its roots still are, is now at least second or third generation. When a tradition takes hold in a new cultural setting, an oral and written transmission begins to emerge. That a body of written Zen teaching is already appearing, can be seen by looking at the reference sources in this volume. I find myself quoting and paraphrasing the writings of first generation American teachers such as Suzuki Roshi; Aitken Roshi, and my teacher Seung Sahn Dae Soen Sa Nim, because these writings inspire and support my practice. My hope is that, in some small way, this book will similarly serve American Zen practitioners.

Zen Master Wu Kwang
(Richard Shrobe)
February 1996

Open Mouth
Already A Mistake

Buddha's Enlightenment Day

December 8, 1990

ᕫ

(Hitting the table with his Zen stick)

Sitting under the bodhi tree, mind calm as the vast ocean without waves, attains samadhi.

(Hitting the table)

Sitting under the bodhi tree,
mind calm and serene perceives the morning star,
awakens completely, loses samadhi.

(Hitting the table)

Attains samadhi, loses samadhi, completely awake.
Which one is correct?

KATZ!!!

Today is December 8th, Buddha's Enlightenment Day.

There are many accounts of Buddha's enlightenment experience. Of these, I'm familiar with three. In one account it says that at the moment Buddha perceived the star and had his great awakening he said, "I and all beings together attain enlightenment at the same time." In a second account it says that at the moment that he saw the star he exclaimed, "Now I realize that from the very first, all beings are imbued with the Buddha nature." And in the third account it says that Buddha sat under the tree and did battle with the demonic armies of Mara. As he vanquished them in the first watch of the night he perceived all of his previous lives. And in the third watch of the night, he perceived in deep meditation the chain of cause and effect, starting from ignorance, through desire and clinging, and ending with birth, old age, sickness and death. He perceived these both in their ascending order and in their descending order. And at that moment he was completely liberated.

All three of these accounts come from the story of Buddha's great renunciation and leaving home, which also appears in many forms, and I want to read just one which is very concise:

> Shakyamuni left his palace one night when he was nineteen years old and shaved off his hair. After that he spent six years practicing ascetic exercises. Subsequently, he sat on an indestructible seat, so immobile that there were cobwebs in his brows, a bird's nest on his head, and reeds growing up through his mat. Thus he sat for six years. In his thirtieth year on the eighth day of the twelfth month, when he was suddenly enlightened when the morning star appeared, then he spoke his first lion's roar.

Great story, but a little hard to believe—cobwebs and bird's nests and reeds growing up through the mat. But I suggest that it is absolutely imperative that we believe that story whether it ever happened or not. If you can't believe that story, then how is it going to be possible to exert the effort to get up in the morning, morning after morning after morning, and sit, whether there's a group to support you or whether you are in your own apartment or home? And further, how is it going to be possible to practice Zen when you enter the IRT subway train in New York City or when you get on the California freeway outside of Los Angeles? So, it is most important that we believe it and that our effort comes from that point. When Buddha said, now I see that all beings from the very start are imbued with the Buddha nature, that becomes, in Zen, the point of our original faith and original confidence that already, we too have this awakened nature.

One day Zen Master Un Mun addressing his assembly said, "Within Heaven and Earth, throughout the universe of time and space, there is a jewel hidden in the mountain of form. Pick up the lamp and head straight for the Buddha hall, take the triple gate and carry it on the lamp." That's Un Mun's crazy speech.

Zen practice is based on the recognition that what you ordinarily think of as a lump of coal is already a jewel. It's very important to recognize that point and to practice Buddha's enlightenment. The only way we can practice Buddha's enlightenment is to start from that point of faith.

Un Mun said, "Pick up the lamp." If you have that jewel, it means your mind is brightly shining and you can perceive and function. So he said, "Pick up the lamp and head straight for the Buddha hall." But, where is the Buddha hall? Is this room the Buddha hall? Is the room upstairs the Buddha hall? Is the Buddha hall up the hill at Diamond Hill Zen Monastery? Where is the Buddha hall? Where will we find that hall which contains Buddha? If you have that light then you can perceive the answer.

One time during winter Zen Master Dan Ha was staying at a rustic mountain temple and he was freezing. On the altar were three wooden Buddhas. Dan Ha took one down and set it on fire. The monk who was in charge exclaimed in shock, "Why are you burning my Buddha?" Dan Ha, poking his stick into the fire stirring up the ashes said, "To get the Buddha's shari." For those of you who "don't know" this word "shari," when a saint dies and the body is cremated, it's said that some relics appear, some indestructible diamond-like relics, which in Sanskrit are called "shari." But as Dan Ha poked further, the monk asked, "How is it possible for a wooden Buddha to have shari?" Dan Ha poked further and said, "There's none here, let's burn the other two."

So Un Mun said, "Head straight for the Buddha hall, and pick up the triple gate and carry it on that lamp." In every temple in the Orient there are a series of gates at the entrance. But a gate is a place of entrance, and so if you have that clear light shining from that confidence in your Buddha nature, then the gate of entry of the bodhisattva path is everywhere. At every moment you can extend helping hands to the world, regardless of the specifics of what you do.

The other two versions of Buddha's enlightenment have to do with interdependence and cause and effect. Buddha said at the moment of enlightenment, "I and all beings TOGETHER attain enlightenment." That means enlightenment is like a net. If you pick up one part of the net, all the strands come up at the same time. In some way we are all netted together and not just attaining individual enlightenment. Whatever we do, all beings attain that at the same time. So it behooves us to be careful about what we do in this world because it doesn't just affect us; the whole net arises at one time. It's with that sense of responsibility that we have to proceed, realizing that this world is in our hands.

A woman came to me a few weeks ago and told me a horrendous story of being separated from her children. She was divorced and her ex-husband lived in another country. According to her perception, the husband did things to keep her from visiting the children and having contact with them.

As she talked, she repeatedly said, "He's an evil man, he's an evil man, he's an evil man." Finally, after she had talked for quite some time and gotten a lot out of her system, she said, "Maybe I bring out the evil in him." It's very important for us to see ourselves and our world as always touching one another. If evil is here, in some way it's our evil as well. And if good is here, it's our good as well.

Those things coming from Buddha's enlightenment and his exclamations at that time should encourage us to practice and to try to help this world in whatever way we can.

(Hitting the table)

I and all beings together at the same time attain enlightenment.

(Hitting the table)

From the very first, all beings have the Buddha nature.

(Hitting the table)

Cause and effect are very clear. Which one is the best?

KATZ!!!

Outside, a gray December day, inside many bright faces.

Queen Maya

Buddha's Birthday Celebration Talk

ᛦ

(Hitting the table with his Zen stick)

When Shakyamuni Buddha was conceived in the womb of Queen Maya, already at that time there was one thing complete and perfect, shining in the ten directions.

(Hitting the table)

When Shakyamuni Buddha sprang from the right side of Queen Maya and walked seven steps in each of the directions and then held one finger up and one down and said, "Above heaven and below the earth, I alone am holy," there was one thing which neither moved right nor left and existed before any notion of holy or unholy.

(Hitting the table)

Un Mun Zen Master, commenting on Buddha's birth said, "If I had been there at that time, I would have taken a big stick, hit Buddha, killed him, and fed him to a hungry dog. Then the whole world would have been at peace."

There was one thing before any notion of birth and death. Then what is the one thing already complete, not coming, not going, before birth and death?

KATZ!!!

In the womb of a cow, a horse is born. When the sun comes out, the whole world is bright.

I want to talk about Buddha's birthday not so much from the perspective of Buddha, but from the perspective of Buddha's mother. Buddha's birthday is really a celebration of Mother's Day. And so to mother Buddha is simultaneously to conceive Buddha, to carry Buddha, and to give birth to Buddha moment by moment. In the last book of the Hua-Yen Sutra, there is a long story about a young pilgrim named Sudhana who meets Manjusri Bodhisattva and asks for instruction in how to practice the enlightened wisdom of bodhisattvas. Manjusri sends him on a journey to fifty-two different teachers. Each one gives him some instruction in the practice of bodhisattvahood, or enlightened being, and then sends him on to another teacher. These teachers come in a variety of forms; all are not just monks and nuns glowing with halos. One, for example, is a perfume salesman; another is a sailor; another is a prostitute; and the list goes on. This bodhisattva wisdom comes through a wide range of human experience.

Finally, at some point in his studies, he meets the Buddha's mother, Queen Maya, and asks for instruction from her. I want to tell a little of that story. The flavor of it is very interesting. When he comes to Queen Maya, he bows to her and tells her that the Great Bodhisattva Manjusri has sent him to seek instruction from all enlightened beings. Can she please give him instruction?

She says:

> I have attained an enlightening liberation, a magical manifestation of knowledge of great vows. Imbued with this liberation, I am the mother of all enlightened beings in their final existence in all the worlds in this world ocean where Buddha's miraculous manifestation of birth as an enlightened being in the final existence takes place. All those enlightened beings grow in my belly and come forth from my right side. So hereto in the great city of Kapilavastu as wife of the King Shuddhodana, I became the mother of the enlightened being, Siddhartha.

Then she goes on to describe what it was like at the moment of conception:

> As she looked to the heaven of contentment where the future Buddha was sitting at that time, a great light appeared and came down and infiltrated every pore in her body, and then came into her womb. When the light came inside, she had a vision of all of the Buddhas of the past, present, and future in all the ten directions existing here, and she saw them all making their initial vows, she saw them all sitting under the bodhi tree and attaining enlightenment, she saw them all turning the wheel of dharma teaching, and then she saw their final nirvana.

She continues:

> When those rays of light of the Enlightened Being entered my

body, my body outreached all worlds, and my belly became as vast as space, and yet did not go beyond the human physical size. The supernal manifestations of the enlightened beings' abode in the womb everywhere in the ten directions all appeared in my body.

Upon this appearance of the bodhisattva coming into her, many, many, many, many, many, many, many bodhisattvas appeared. Actually, as many as atoms in ten Buddha lands. (Now that's a lot of bodhisattvas!)

All with the same Great Vows, all entered my belly, and all entered my belly with their entire retinue. Once all of them were in my belly, they walked around in strides as big as a billion-world universe, even as big as worlds as numerous as atoms in untold Buddha lands. Also, all of the untold congregations of Enlightened Beings at the feet of all Buddhas in all worlds in the ten directions entered my belly in every moment of thought to see the miracle of the Enlightened Beings dwelling in my womb. The chief gods of all the heavens also came to the Enlightened Being in my womb to see and honor him, to listen to the teaching, and to hear his discourse.

Now here comes a very important sentence; important because it normalizes and humanizes what at first appears miraculous:

Yet even though it took in all of those multitudes, my belly was not enlarged, nor did this body of mine become any more than a human body. Just as I received the Enlightened Being in my belly in this world, so did I likewise do so in all worlds in the billion-world universe, and with this miraculous manifestation; yet, this body of mine is neither dual nor non-dual, neither single nor multiple; this is because of the development of the Enlightened Liberation of the magic of knowledge of Great Vows. And just as I was the mother of this Buddha Vairocana, so was I the mother of infinite Buddhas before. Whenever an Enlightened Being was spontaneously born in the calyx of a lotus, there I became the Lotus-Pond Goddess and received the Enlightened Being, and the world recognized me as the progenitrix of Enlightened Beings.

In Korean temples on Buddha's birthday, lanterns shaped like lotus flowers are made. The lotus flower has its roots in the mud. The stem comes up through the water, and the flower appears. In some way we have to recognize that our practice is rooted in the mud. I recently talked to two people who had been in rather unusual circumstances. One is a senior dharma teacher at Chogye International Zen Center of New York, Ruth Forero. Ruth is a Social Worker who counsels crime and rape victims. The International Red Cross in conjunction with Ms. Magazine sponsored Ruth and a few other people to go to Croatia to train local health professionals in how to interact with rape victims within the Muslim community. She told me that the more violence she witnessed, the more she had to remind herself not to hate the inflictor of the violence, as well as to recognize that violence exists in all of us. She said that was very hard practice.

The other person is a friend of mine who I hadn't seen for about twenty years. His parents were concentration camp survivors, and he was born in the refugee camps in Cypress right after the Second World War. The family moved to Israel, and he lived there until he was about fourteen, at which time he came to this country. This past summer he went back to Israel for the first time, and traveled around for five weeks. He told me that one of the things he noticed was that people within their own community can be very loving and caring and respectful toward each other, but when they look across the street to the other community, those people are seen as less than human. That is a very amazing issue: Human beings can be loving within their own circle, and then outside of that circle they have the most non-human attitudes and reactions toward others.

So, we have a lot of work to do! And it is good that we all recognize that our roots are in the mud, and that to conceive Buddha, to carry Buddha, and to give birth to Buddha is our non-stop ongoing path.

(Hitting the table)

At this point how will you find Buddha's conception?

(Hitting the table)

At this point, how will you find Buddha's birth?

(Hitting the table)

At this point, how do you find Buddha's teaching?

KATZ!!!

One kind action gives birth to infinite Buddhas. After lunch, please enjoy the cake and ice cream.

Wearing the Iron Collar with No Hole

The Zen Tradition

§

For those of you who are very new to this whole business, I'll give some general information. The Zen tradition as we know it arose in China. Its roots lie in India and came to China via a semi-historical Buddhist figure, Bodhidharma, who became the first Zen patriarch in China. Every Zen center has a picture of Bodhidharma, and he always looks ferocious or unusual. The succession of teaching passed down from Bodhidharma through five patriarchs. By the time the Sixth Patriarch appeared, the Zen tradition had taken on pretty much of a Chinese character, and was free of some of its prior Indian Buddhist colorations. The Sixth Patriarch's teaching method ushered in a style quite different from the Indian Buddhist style. He used a questioning approach, the language and imagery of which was very down to earth. In one of his teachings he says to a monk, "Sit down. Don't make good and bad. At that time or at that moment, what is your original face before your parents were born?" This question has become one of the kongans (a question given to the student by the Zen Master to open the non-discursive mind) used in almost every Zen school.

After the Sixth Patriarch, the succession of teaching broadened and five different Zen schools appeared in China over the next couple of centuries. During the time of great Zen Master Ma Jo, slightly before the appearance of the five schools, some Korean Buddhist monks went to China and studied with Chinese Zen Masters, then returned to Korea. A little later on, Zen also went into Japan. Gradually, over hundreds of years, the five schools collapsed one into the other. There now remain two main teaching lines. In Japan they are called the Soto line and Rinzai line. Rinzai is the Japanese pronunciation of Zen Master Lin Chi's name. Lin Chi was one of the great Zen Masters during the T'ang period in China (700–1000 AD, approximately). The Korean school of Zen has some of its roots in the Lin Chi tradition as well as in the earlier teachings of Ma Jo.

When Buddhism and Zen migrated to other Asian countries, the teaching took on certain local color and cultural aspects, but the bone or heart of the teaching remains similar. So, for example, Korean Zen has a slightly different flavor from Japanese Zen, and Japanese Zen has a slightly different flavor from the Zen practiced in Vietnam. And, of course, the Zen practiced in the United States will gradually emerge with its own flavor. For example, at one point Zen became colored by the Samurai tradition in Japan. So, sometimes, the character of Japanese Rinzai Zen has a military flavor—SIT STRAIGHT! DON'T MOVE!—with some guy running up and down the aisles with a stick ready to whack anyone who isn't sitting straight! That's an exaggeration of the Rinzai spirit, although not too much of an exaggeration!

The Korean tradition is a lot looser. In Korea, the Zen monks were mostly illiterate farmers. Since they were not nobility, Korean Zen has an earthy flavor to it. Also, the Korean tradition uses the questioning approach, or the kong-an approach. (The Japanese say *koan* and the Chinese word is *kung-an*.) Kong-an literally means "a case of public record." So, the kong-an usually is taken from an interchange between a teacher and a student. And, within that interchange is an essential point. For example, there's an old Zen story about a great Zen teacher named P'ang. P'ang was not a monk; he was a lay person with a family. There are many stories about Layman P'ang and his family, who were all said to be Zen adepts. In one short interchange between P'ang, his wife and daughter, Layman P'ang says, "Difficult, difficult, like trying to pierce a mustard seed with a needle." Mrs. P'ang says, "Easy, easy like touching your nose in the morning after getting out of bed." And the daughter says, "Neither difficult nor easy; on the tips of a hundred blades of grass are the Zen Masters' meaning." A question may be, "What is it that is neither difficult nor easy?" That would be the question that you would grab hold of. Or, when Layman P'ang's daughter says that the patriarchs' meaning is clear on a hundred tips of grass, what does she mean? That would be a kong-an.

There are various kinds of kong-ans, but, in practicing, one sticks to one main kong-an which is referred to in Korean as hwadu. Hwadu means "question" or "word's head." So, the words of the kong-an are called the "question's tail." The mind state that the words or tail of the question points you towards is called the "hwadu," or the question-head or word-head. For example, take a big, essential question such as the Sixth Patriarch's question, "What is your original face before your parents were born?" Your body's face came from your parents. What is your original face before your parents were even born? This is just another way of saying: What is your essential nature? What is your true self before any idea appears, before any conditioning appears, before any history appears, what are you? So the words "What am I" are the question's tail. The mind state that results from asking that is hwadu (Stuck! No words or speech; the mind before thinking.) That state of mind is called "don't know."

Essentially, when you open your mouth and say, "don't know," that's not the fundamental "don't know." But, the words "don't know" will help you to tune yourself to this essentially wordless "don't know." "don't know" is the state of mind when the question becomes complete. At that time, there's no sense of "I." What am I? No "I"; no "other." No "inside"; no "outside." No "subject"; no "object." Then: What? *(Hitting the table—Whack!)* Maybe that! When that becomes clear, then the patriarchs' meaning "on a hundred blades of grass" is right in front of your face! The kong-an is used in that kind of way to bring your mind to the moment of no thought. Before thinking; before your parents were even born—what is that?

In the Korean tradition, first and foremost, they make use of one big question. And, some Korean Zen Masters will only use that one question. Just one question a monk or a nun may sit with for years. And even if they have some awakenings along the way, still they keep using that one big question. Other kong-ans are used to test the student's clarity.

In Korea until recently, Zen existed mostly as a monastic tradition; most of the practice went on in mountain monasteries. The monks and the nuns sat two ninety-day communal retreats each year: a winter retreat for three months, and a summer retreat for three months. Between retreats, either they stayed in a monastery and kept practicing on a more relaxed schedule or traveled to call on other teachers. During the ninety-day retreat, the Zen Master came into the meditation hall usually twice a month to give a formal talk. During his talk he might throw out a challenge. (This also is the style that existed in China originally.) He might say, "Layman P'ang's daughter said 'Neither difficult nor easy!' If someone can say something on that matter, stand up and speak NOW!!" Now, if you've got enough heart, you'll stand up and say something, or you'll stand up and knock him off his seat, or some other crazy thing! (When you've been sitting many weeks, one's state of mind gets to be rather unusual!)

That's one style of interaction between the Zen Master and the students that are sitting. During the daily sitting practice, the Zen Master stays in a small cottage near the meditation hall. If one of the monks or nuns wants to go and see the Zen Master with a question or some experience that they want to validate, they can go and check in with him. That's a little different from the Japanese Rinzai style where, during a retreat, there are several formal interviews every day where everyone lines up, the bell is rung, and one-by-one the students go into the Zen Master's room and are quickly tested on whatever kong-an they are using, and then are rung out of the room!

When Zen Master Seung Sahn came to this country from Korea in the early 70's, he didn't want to stick too strictly with the Korean monastic tradition. He mostly taught lay students on short retreats and in daily practice. These were people who either lived in a Zen center with outside jobs, or people who came in just to practice and then went back to their homes. Our basic style evolved out of the monastic Korean style and we use the one big question method. We also use other kong-ans as a way of digesting and clarifying the teaching. So, that's the approach in our school, the Kwan Um School of Zen.

Certain traditional Korean monks have at times taken issue with our approach! For example, there are a few American guys who went to Korea and studied with some Master there. But when their Master died, they came back to the United States. By that time, my teacher had made his appearance here. So, these guys came around and said, "What is this? That is not Korean Zen!" But, that's already missing the fundamental point! That's holding some "idea" of what Korean Zen is, or what Zen "should" be. Zen is always evolving as a form. And when it becomes too stylized, too rigidified in any of its forms, it begins to decline. At the same time, there has to be within Zen practice a certain respect for the traditions that evolved over the centuries.

Our lineage comes through the Lin Chi line, and we can trace it back to one Korean teacher, Taego Pou, who went to China in 1347 and received dharma transmission from Zen Master Shih-Wu, an eighteenth generation successor of Lin Chi.

Spring Comes.
Flowers Bloom Everywhere.

How Zen is Communicated

$\wp$

The tradition of Zen has several ways of being communicated. One of the well-known ways it has been passed along from generation to generation is through the little stories and sayings of the Zen Masters from the earliest times when Buddhist thought came from India into China. A whole folklore and tradition of stories grew up around the interchanges between teachers and students, and after a while they were set down and recorded. These stories are referred to as kong-ans. (In Japanese they are called koans.)

Another way that the Zen tradition has been passed along is through a type of poetry. The Zen stories that had been written down for focusing on or meditating on, inspired some teachers to write verses which were an expression of what had moved them in a particular story. As a result, a whole series of Zen poetry came out of China, Korea, Japan, and other countries where Zen had gone.

When my teacher first came to this country from Korea, he knew very little English. But even with his limited English, he wrote poems. Students would write and ask him a question about their Zen practice, and his response to them would be a short poem. Several years ago, some of these poems were put together in a book called *Bone of Space*. The title itself is a kong-an. What is the bone of space?

I will use one of the poems to illustrate this talk:

A great man goes on a one-hundred day
Retreat. He makes many demons, gods,
Animals, buddhas. One hundred days
Are the same as the time of one breath.

He has brushed off all dust and breathed in
Sky and ground. The Great Path is in the palm
Of his hand, and the Great Freedom at his feet.
Spring comes. Flowers bloom everywhere.

A great man goes on a one-hundred day retreat. In the Zen tradition retreat training is and always has been a part of practice. There are two ways to cultivate practicing. One is daily practice which is done consistently for a short period of time. So you might sit for half an hour every day, or an hour every day, or sit twice a day, or whatever is convenient in terms of your daily schedule. The other way is in the retreat setting which is a longer and more intensive form of meditation practice. A retreat can be done alone or in a group. What interests me in this line about "A great man goes on a one-hundred day retreat," is that it could be 100 days, or it could be one thousand days, or ten thousand days, or ten thousand years. It doesn't make any difference because, in fact, all of us who enter into a path of Zen training and practice are, from that moment, on a sort of retreat! That means we are practicing continuously in some way to cultivate the path. Retreat just means paying attention. So, all of us from the moment we first get interested in this business are on retreat! And that is the Number One Big Mistake—to get interested in this business in the first place! So, realize that you are signing up for the one-hundred YEAR retreat.

He makes many demons, gods, animals, buddhas. He MAKES that! Yesterday we had a retreat, and someone came into the interview room for an interchange. I read this poem to him. When I got to this line "He makes many demons, animals, gods, buddhas," the student said, "He must be very busy!" What does that mean? That is our consciousness! As you're practicing Zen take care not to make good and bad, and not to evaluate what you are doing. Just do it, at that moment. So, if you make good, that is making gods and buddhas. If you make bad, that's making demons. But there is a difference between making good and bad, and perceiving good and bad as it is really connected to any particular situation. If you MAKE good and bad, that is your prior idea being imposed onto the present; coming from your consciousness. On the other hand, if you perceive what is correct or incorrect at any given moment, then that's "good for this situation"; "bad for this situation." You PERCEIVE clearly good and bad. Salt is salty; sugar is sweet. That is just perceiving. But, if you say,"I don't like salt, I like sugar," that's making something. That's your taste, your inclination, your tendency, which you bring to the situation.

When you go on an intensive meditation retreat, or practice a lot of meditation, sometimes something similar to dreaming occurs. You begin to perceive unusual things like gods, and buddhas, and animals, and demons, and lights, and sounds, and strange feelings and other unusual things. You're always perceiving something like that; it's just that you don't recognize it most of the time. One of the functions of meditation practice is to pay attention to how the mind is working. The mind creating something; the mind creating something else, over and over and over again; and the particular feelings attached to all of the notions that are created and made. That is something like a dream.

There is an old Zen saying: "Host and guest, together talked about last night's dream. How regrettable they don't realize that they are in a dream." So, in a certain sense we are all in a dream continuously, and Zen practice is about "wake up"! As you begin to practice and pay attention more and more on this ten thousand year retreat that you and I are all on together, you begin to perceive how you are making gods, buddhas, demons, and various dreams and overlaying the simple fact of what is. When you begin to perceive that, then you aren't pulled around by it so much. And at that moment you begin to settle down and become clear. Your original mind is clear and not colored by all of these things.

One hundred days are the same as the time of one breath. This means that when you are completely in the moment, past, present and future all come together. So, one moment is ten thousand years; ten thousand years is one moment. When you begin to sit meditation, sometimes it feels like a half hour is a long, long time. But, as you begin to enter into it and let go of the notion of time and space, all of a sudden the bell rings (or whatever the signal is), and you realize "Oh, it's over!" It was like one bre'ath. That means you have touched base with *moment mind.* Not the mind that judges things according to progression, but just one moment; one moment; one moment. Each moment then is complete, just like each breath is complete.

This sentence also has a big question in it: *One hundred days are the same as the time of one breath.* We can all understand that philosophically, but what does it really mean? *How* is one hundred days the same as the time of one breath? *What is that?* This is the point in Zen where philosophy ends and question begins.

Zen practice is sometimes divided into three aspects: Theoretical Zen, Tathagata Zen, and Patriarchal Zen. Theoretical Zen means: We hear a line of teaching, and it sounds good to us, but we have not yet really owned or digested it. At a certain point we enter into it sincerely and look at that idea and the philosophy of it, and we recognize: We don't have the foggiest idea what that means! Really! And there is just a big question mark. How? Why? At that point we enter into what is called Tathagata Zen. All ideas fall away. And we are left with a big feeling of uncertainty, or questioning, or perplexity, or, as we say in our school, "don't know."

One Old Zen Master said, "When you say *"don't know"* you are closest to it." That doesn't mean when you say "don't know" with your mouth, but when you completely enter into it and experience the sense of not knowing, you are closest to it—to the true reality of what is. At that time you aren't coloring anything, not holding anything, not making anything. There is just openness. Clear and open mind like space.

There is a famous story about the difference between theoretical understanding and going beyond the theoretical into the actual. One day Zen

Master Soel Bong addressed his assembly. He said, "If you want to understand this matter of Zen, you should keep your mind like the great round Ancient Mirror. If a Chinese face comes in front of it, it just reflects a Chinese face. If a non-Chinese face comes in front of it, it just reflects a non-Chinese face." So, that is a very good teaching. Keep your mind like an empty clear mirror. A great round equalizing mirror. Everything is reflected in it clearly. Red comes, it's just red. White comes, it's just white. Gods come, it's just Gods. Demons come, it's just demons. So, when a Chinese face comes, the mirror makes no judgments. No coloring anything, no evaluating anything. Just sees what is. Just reflects a Chinese face.

Soel Bong's disciples liked that teaching. But the head monk had a question. In Soel Bong's assembly, the head monk was almost equal to the Zen Master. They were both very experienced and seasoned dharma brothers. And so sometimes the head monk would give the Zen Master a hard time. The head monk stood up and said, "Zen Master! That's a wonderful teaching. But suppose the mirror is broken! Then what?" Zen Master Soel Bong said, "Then both Chinese face and non-Chinese face all disappear." The head monk looked at him and said, "Old Master Soel Bong's feet still have not landed on the ground," and he walked out. That means that even if you have a wonderful metaphor or image like the Ancient Mirror, when you hold onto that idea or image or metaphor or philosophy, as if it were the *actual thing,* then you are still caught in some way.

So, one hundred years are the same as one breath. One breath is the same as one hundred years. That is the start of a big, big question.

The next line says: *He has brushed off all dust and breathed in sky and ground.* The landscape of your mind, or your mind land, your consciousness, is tainted or colored in some way. The practice of meditation is like cleaning the dust off the mirror over and over and over again. When you sit down and try to keep your meditation point, you lose it but then you come back to it for a minute, and then you lose it again. And after a while your mind begins to get dull, or drowsy, or it begins to race around with a million different ideas. And then you come back again. That's all referred to as *dust.* It means your mind is not clear and centered. Here it says *he has brushed off all dust.* His mind is completely clear.

There are two ideas about this clearing in the Zen tradition. One is of gradualness, the other is of suddenness. Even to have the idea that you have to clean the mirror over and over again is itself a kind of dust! Because originally, your mind is not pure or impure. Not tainted, not pure, as it says in the Heart Sutra. Doesn't increase or decrease. Does not appear or disappear. From the most radical perspective, you have to realize that your original mind is never dusty or unclear. That recognition is itself "cleaning dust."

As you practice, if you have some expectation about what kind of condition you should establish yourself in, that moves you away from the actuality of the moment. Over and over again, we train ourselves to come back to the moment just as it is. Perceiving things just as they are is termed Patriarchal Zen. In doing that we come back home to our original place. And the more we are able to establish ourselves in that, the more able we are to be with people, and things, and situations, as they truly are. We are more able to respond to situations as they truly are. A sense of being able to interact and be compassionate starts from that point of being clear. If you are clear, then you're not holding any idea. If you're not holding any idea, then you are responsive to the situation at hand. That is letting go of our dust.

> *The Great Path is in the palm*
> *Of his hand, and the Great Freedom at his feet.*

We all have some moments in practice where we get an experience of that. Where, for a moment or two, we see we are not our thoughts, we are not our concepts, we are not ideas, we are not the identity we hold onto so much of the time. At that moment when you let go and open up your hand rather than holding so tightly, then it's as if the Great Path is in the palm of your hand. It's right there! And the Great Freedom is at your feet. So it's important to watch your step. If you watch your step, and feel that it is right in front of you, then the last line is very clear:

> *Spring comes. Flowers bloom everywhere.*

Don't Know is Closest to It

For those of you who are new to our style of practice and Zen practice in general, I will now introduce you to the practice of "not knowing." Usually, people want to learn something, to know something. Zen practice actually moves in the opposite direction: from knowing to not knowing.

This not knowing is represented in the classical Zen literature by a famous story about Zen Master Poep An. Poep An was one of the main figures of Chinese Zen during the T'ang dynasty, which was the Golden Age of Zen in China. He lived around 900 AD. At the time this story takes place, Poep An was not yet a Zen Master but a monk traveling from one Zen center to another. Making a Zen pilgrimage didn't mean the same thing as traveling means to us today because, of course, there were no airplanes, trains, or buses, just ox carts or foot travel, for the most part. And most of the main centers of Zen activity were in the mountains. So, the journey to call on the various Zen Masters was a rather arduous one. In and of itself, the hardship of traveling hundreds of miles over every kind of terrain, not knowing where you would sleep that night, or where you would find food, was a practice in facing oneself. This was a practice, as the old Zen Masters say, in "putting it all down."

Poep An came to a particular monastery and greeted Master Ji Jang, who was to become his final teacher. Ji Jang asked Poep An, "You're traveling all around China; what's the meaning of your pilgrimage?" Initially, Poep An felt stuck, and momentarily all thinking stopped. Then he said, "don't know." Ji Jang responded, "Not knowing is most intimate." Sometimes you'll see this phrase translated as: "Not knowing is closest to it." So, Poep An decided: I'd better stay here and see what this guy has to offer.

After spending some time at the monastery being introduced into this "don't know," Poep An decided he would continue on his pilgrimage. He told the Master, "Tomorrow I'll be leaving here to become a wandering monk again." Ji Jang said, "Oh, do you think you're ready?" Poep An said, "Certainly!" "Then, let me ask you a question," said Ji Jang. "You are fond of the saying that 'the whole universe is created by mind alone.' So, you see those big boulders over there in the rock garden? Are they inside your mind or outside?" Poep An said, "They're inside my mind. How could anything be outside it?" The Zen Master said, "Oh, well, then you'd better get a good night's sleep because it's going to be hard traveling with all those rocks inside your mind!" Poep An was undone and taken aback, and stayed there with this Master, and finally attained great awakening.

This one sentence, "don't know" or "Not knowing is most intimate," is very much at the heart of our practice. The word intimacy is also quite interesting. Closeness. Becoming one with something. Really being able to fathom something. And, of course, many of our difficulties come about by holding on to some conception of knowing, or some opinion, or some dualistic attitude that separates us from our experience. So, as we cultivate and enter into this attitude of not knowing, true intimacy becomes a possibility, true at-oneness with our own experience and with the world that we find ourselves in.

In Zen practice we're not looking to retreat into some inner blissful recess where there is no problem, no trouble, no feeling. As wonderful as that might sound, somehow that doesn't get us too far. The purpose of Zen practice is to find our center and be able to move with the fluctuations of life while at the same time never losing that primary point of "don't know." Zen practice is aimed at that, and cultivates it over and over. If you have the attitude of "don't know," then your mind opens up and becomes clear and vibrantly radiant. If you're in that clarity of mind, clear like a mirror, when red comes, the mirror is just red. If white comes, the mirror is just white.

Layman P'ang, one of the old Zen Masters, said, "My miraculous meditation power is 'When I'm hungry, I eat. When I'm tired, I sleep.'" We could add one more: If someone else is hungry, then I feed him.

So, a final point of Zen practice is just that: To feed. And, of course, there are all kinds of hungers. Physical hunger, emotional hunger, spiritual hunger, etc. These days this world is a very, very hungry place. Zen practice is not just for ourselves; it also is about being responsive to what is in front of us. It's as if each situation we encounter presents a teacher who says, "Respond!" If you are not stable and not clear, then your response will be colored by what you're holding—by your ideas, your opinions, your limiting of the situation by the conditions that you're holding onto. "don't know" is not just "don't know" in a sitting meditative position. "don't know" means being responsive to the world that you find yourself in.

Q: It takes a lot of work to get rid of the concept of "I."

A: Obviously. Yet, Zen never says, "Get rid of I." An idea that some people take from Zen reading is that you should kill the ego. That's a distortion of teaching. One has to see clearly, perceive clearly, what the correct function of ego is in the totality of one's being. If you see that, then you can use that. But, if your "I" is very limited, if it's possessive in some way, then you have to become clear about it. There are many kinds of "I."

Q: Something like multi-faceted, perhaps?

A: Yeah, there's an "I" that arises with each moment! But, if you don't understand that, then you'll try to reestablish over and over again the same kind of "I-ness." That's a problem, because you become inflexible and rigid, bound by a particular image of "I."

Q: Why would one want to get involved in Zen when there's nothing to get?

A: You have to "get" nothing to get! It's easy to say, "There's nothing to get." But, to really perceive "nothing to get," that's a different matter. In the Heart Sutra, after everything is taken away—no eyes, no ears, no nose, no tongue, no body, no mind, no color, going on and on taking everything away—the final line is: And no attainment with nothing to attain. But, you have to attain "no attainment with nothing to attain!"

Q: Would you say that one of the lessons of Zen is that we might not necessarily have to have as much as we think we ought to have or need to have, and that we still have all the essentials that are necessary?

A: People come to a retreat who have been practicing Zen for a while because they want to deepen their practice. At the retreat, everything is very sparse and regimented. All the creature comforts that you are used to and attached to are not there. The retreat also is conducted in silence, so you can't even open your mouth anymore! And, usually, you are away from what's familiar, you don't have your bed, and you end up sleeping on the floor or on some mats or something like that. Everything is very sparse and different, it's mostly all been taken away. But, most people who have gone through that kind of training will tell you that in the sparseness they discover a certain kind of self-support and richness within, which cannot be compared to anything. So, certainly, one aspect of Zen training is about that. However, Zen training is not interested only in promoting sparseness or asceticism. That is a particular technique to help someone see something more fundamental than the usual things we all attach to. And that's what it's about.

Q: When I walk around New York City, I see a lot of people to give to. Is that compassion?

A: Maybe not giving is compassion.

Q: How's that?

A: One time I remember talking to someone who fancied herself a radical Marxist. Her thing was "If you give someone a quarter or a dollar or whatever, you're only doing that to make yourself feel good. You're not really helping." She said that what is needed is a more radical transformation of the whole social-political set-up. There are all kinds of ways of seeing this situation. The way things are in New York these days, it's impossible to give money to each person you see. The best you can give them all is your best wishes. There's a guy I see in the morning sometimes when I come over to the Zen Center for 5:30 a.m. practice. I also see this guy at other times of the day at various locales around the neighborhood. He always says, "Can you help me? I'm hungry." At one time, he had a crutch. Then another time I saw him walking from one of his locations to another carrying the crutch under his arm! I realized at that point the crutch was a stage prop. I also thought that perhaps he was an addict of some kind. If I give him something, is that compassion? Or am I giving into something I don't really feel comfortable supporting? I don't want to personally be a contributor to someone's addiction. I don't see that as compassionate activity. I feel they would be better off going to a hospital detox ward. And if they have enough difficulty and cannot support their habit, then they might have to go to the hospital. I would rather see that happen than help someone to buy heroin or crack. Responsibility means to have the ability to respond. Perceiving the situation means responding effectively in that situation.

Thread of Spiritualit

ᵹᴑ

Q: A lot of us got religious fervor at one point in our lives which got some of us into religious practice. Why do we look for it here rather than going back to a Jewish temple or a church that we grew up in?

A: Why is that an important question for you?

Q: It would seem logical to go back to where you started from.

A: People who have been through a particular religious training as children sometimes later find it becomes unsatisfactory. They experienced a structured ritual, the meaning of which was not understood or grasped.

I happened to be watching a video of the movie "Gandhi" the other day, and at one point Gandhi is sitting by the Indian Ocean talking with a reporter about the town where he grew up. He's reminiscing and telling the reporter about the temple he attended as a child. There was a song he'd learned, and Gandhi sang it for the reporter. "Of course, as a boy I sang the words not really knowing what they meant," Gandhi said. "I was just going through the action. But somewhere they must have penetrated in some way."

When we go through a ritualized practice such as going to church or synagogue, at a certain point the meaning or form of it may become something that we no longer relate to. And yet, in some way, some kernel within that tradition or practice may trigger something in us that later prompts us to seek answers to the same basic questions in another form of practice. In doing that, we pick up the thread of spirituality that was in our childhood religion but which was lost sight of earlier. I think that's why we come to something a little different.

If you enter into Zen practice deeply and consistently, you will recognize that the essence of Zen is experiencing your original, clear and empty mind—before thinking, before conditioning, before opinions, and before limiting concepts narrow us down. With that mind you can practice Christianity, or Judaism, or Islam, or Buddhism—you can practice anything because you understand what all of these things are either directly or indirectly pointing at! And that is something in human beings and in all of existence which is before name, before form, before speech, but which takes the form of color, sound, and words moment by moment in whatever we do.

It doesn't matter whether you go into a church, or a synagogue or the park. You can practice anywhere. It's all one fabric.

Q: I know there are different kinds of Yoga. Is the core of them meditation practice?

A: The various forms of Yoga meditation depend upon whether they ๆe analytically oriented or emotionally oriented meditation exercises. The root of the Sanskrit word for Yoga has a meaning that's connected with harnessing, like the word "yoke." To put a yoke on an ox comes from that root. The idea behind Yoga is to harness the various mind/body energies to bring them together in a unified form. Essentially, that's what meditation practice is.

In the Zen tradition, there are different kinds of meditations: Outer Path Zen, Inner Path Zen, Action Zen, and so forth. Tai Chi, for example, is a physical exercise practiced as part of the Chinese Taoist Yoga. Through the movements of the exercise one begins to harness their energy and begins to experience "chi," which is their inner vitality or power. That's one way of centering. The main object of any of these practices is to be able to sit still and steady and comfortably. If your body is stiff and if you have a lot of energy blocks in different places, then Yoga exercises will help you to establish this kind of posture. Most of the exercises in Indian Yoga, from a real traditional standpoint—postures, breathing exercises—are seen as aids and help toward establishing the steady sitting posture.

Many Zen practitioners use exercises as aids in establishing meditation practice. If you just sit down, however, and pay attention, you are already harnessing all of your various energies! If you sit still and return to your original center, then mind and body come together, inside and outside all become one. There's no thinking inside versus outside, subject versus object, correct versus incorrect. When all that settles to one still centered point, there is, at least momentarily, an experience of completeness. At that point you regain the ability to act spontaneously in a situation. When you're not thinking about what you should do, you are able to respond to a situation with what you have at your disposal. Zen practice is not limited to the sitting posture but, instead, involves the USE of this clear mind in our moment-by-moment every-day dealings with people, places, and things. At that point, you harness yourself to the whole universe! So, that's a Big Ox-cart!

Q: What is Outer Path Zen?

A: That means it doesn't have the essential direction of Buddhist Zen. For example, if you do martial arts, that might be considered Outer Path Zen practice because it is a practice that develops centeredness and one-mindedness and concentration. Usually, when reference is made to Outer Path, they are talking about developing concentration power, but the practice may not have the direction or intention of developing compassion as its essence. To develop concentration or artistry doesn't necessarily lead to dropping egotism and self-centeredness. So, something like Karate, or Tai Kwan Do, or Kung Fu, or maybe the Japanese Tea Ceremony, or flower arranging, or any of those allied Zen-like arts are sometimes referred to as Outer Path Zen.

Remember, though, that those practices don't necessarily have to be "outer path." As I said before, if you understand the true direction, then many of those things can be used as correct or complete forms of practice. Correct practice means: Become clear mind and be responsive, moment by moment. So, the direction of correct practice is: How may I help this world? In order to help, you have to let go of small "I" first! Anything that facilitates letting go of small "I" is correct Zen, correct Inner Path Zen, whether you formally know anything about Buddhism or not!

Q: Do people ever get to a point where the legs don't hurt while sitting meditation?

A: That depends on how many hours a day they're sitting!

Q: Do monks whose lives are dedicated to this have pain in their legs?

A: In our style of practice we tell people that if it's so painful that it's distracting, stand up! Don't keep sitting at that point. Continue your meditation in a standing position, because this is not an endurance test. You can even gain a degree of competence in sitting, and still there will come a point where you'll have pain in your legs. However, if you've sat enough years, you know how to use that pain as a moment of mindfulness! Pain becomes worse if you try to get away from it because there is a tensing up around the pain. You wish that there was something else at that moment than what there is! If you can let go of that and really sit into it, then it becomes a different kind of experience. It doesn't mean that it necessarily goes away though.

There's a famous kong-an: "This whole universe is on fire. Through what kind of miraculous meditation power can you escape being burned? Through what kind of samadhi can you escape being burned?" You're sitting on your cushion, and the first five minutes are fine, wonderful; you're breezing along and it just feels calm and your breath is easy, and ten minutes later you start to get some pain in your legs. After a while it feels like the whole universe is on fire! At that time, that's your whole universe!

There's a story about Dong Sahn, a great Zen Master in China during the T'ang dynasty. One day, a monk approached him and asked, "When hot and cold come, how can we be free of them?" It's the same question you're asking about pain. "Hey you guys. You have shaved your head and you've been sitting for ten years. Are you free from pain in your legs?" Dong Sahn says, "Why don't you go to the place where there's no hot and no cold?" Why don't you go to that place where there's no pain in your legs? No opposites. The monk says, "Oh, where is it?" And Dong Sahn very quickly retorts, "When hot, heat kills you! When cold, cold kills you!"

Sometimes people get this idea that if you attain some degree of maturity in Zen practice, then everything will be the same to you. Well, that's one side of it, but you still might have your preferences. For example, Zen Master Seung Sahn might rather eat Korean food than eat oatmeal. He could probably eat Korean food three times a day: white rice, kimchi, and miso soup. But, if he's with us it's not a problem to eat oatmeal; the preference might be for Korean food, but something else is okay, too.

When you're sitting with pain, you might prefer that there be no pain. But, if there's pain, then you can sit into it and experience that. That's why the kong-an says, "This whole universe is on fire!" That means there's no choice! The WHOLE universe is on fire, so through what kind of meditation can you escape being burned? If you're faced with a situation where a person is dying for example, there is no choice! The whole universe is only filled with dying at that time for you. Either you deny it and try to get away from it in some way, or you face it, as it is, and embrace it as a part of life, which it is!

Sitting many periods in a row develops the ability to be with many different kinds of experiences: pain in your legs, all kinds of thinking, feelings, and so on. This helps to develop equanimity: To be with hot when it's hot, to be with cold when it's cold. To be with something happy when it's happy, to be with sadness when it's sad. You might prefer to be in the sunshine rather than in the rain, but if you're in the rain, it's okay. You can be with that, and find something meaningful in that because you're not fighting to get away from it.

So, for example, if you're with extreme sadness, then you'll have extreme sadness the same as everyone else in the same situation. This is illustrated in many Zen stories. The scene may be at a funeral. The Zen Master's crying! BIG crying!!! And a student says, "You're a great Zen Master. You already understand that there's no life and no death. So why are you crying?" Suddenly the Zen Master may begin to laugh. Or, he may give a quick retort: "You don't understand my crying? You don't truly understand no life, no death. Because if you *truly* understood that, you would understand my crying."

The goal in Zen practice is not to get to some state where there is no emotion. If you have no emotion, you can't have any compassion. That would be an Outer Path Zen: No emotion. To become just still, just silent. It would be attachment to some state where there is no emotion. So, you've missed the boat at that point, you've missed becoming a complete human being. If you don't become a complete human being, you can't do a human being's job.

Like a Ball on Swift Flowing Water

Non-clinging and Going With the Flow

§𝒫

Q: What is a typical day in the practice of Zen?

A: That would depend upon your life.

Q: Assuming a nine-to-five life.

A: If you're a new practitioner, working a nine-to-five regular kind of job, then you would be able to practice a little bit in the morning, and perhaps a little bit in the evening. You might start with fifteen minutes to a half hour sitting meditation. Try to keep that meditative awareness throughout the day by paying attention to what you're doing moment by moment. That's a way to handle it.

Q: I assume there is a dogma associated with the practice.

A: I hope not! But I'm sure it sneaks in.

Q: What then is the didactic instruction?

A: The spirit of Zen is letting go of concepts and returning to your original, pure and simple mind—before ideas, before concepts, before opinions, before the dichotomy of duality. First and foremost is the establishing of yourself in some practice where you can get a taste of that original, simple mind. With that original, simple mind, you can practice many things. You may practice studying some sutra or scripture; you can practice chanting; you may practice some sitting meditation; you may practice some action meditation; and you may do your daily job and carry on relationships, etc. But, essentially, Zen training tries to let go of anything that smacks of dogma, and instead, emphasizes returning to that original point which is a point of openness and clarity.

For example, Zen stresses over and over again the attitude of "don't know." Now, you can say that's "don't know" dogma, but there's not much dogma sticking to "don't know"!

When you enter into that "don't know" mind your awareness opens up. An old Zen Master said, "Clear like space." That "clear like space" means clear like a mirror. Perceiving your exact situation, your exact relationship, and how you should be functioning moment by moment according to circumstances, is implied in the metaphor of "clear like a mirror." When a mirror is not reflecting anything it's just empty. But, if red comes, the mirror reflects red; if white comes, it reflects white. At the same time that the mirror reflects red, it does not cease to be a mirror. It becomes one with red, but doesn't lose its integrity. And when red goes away, it's again "empty mirror." If you're in a red situation, then become red! If you're in a white situation, then become white. If you're in a difficult situation, just become difficult. If you're in an easy situation, then just become easy. You'll hear this in Zen rhetoric: Don't make easy; don't make difficult. The key word is "make." There's a difference between something being of its own nature difficult, and MAKING something difficult. So, if your mind has that mirror-like quality to it—and by mind I don't just mean cognition, I also mean the feeling aspect—then it can be responsive to a situation, whether difficult or easy—and situation includes relationship. In any situation, we are always in relationship to something or somebody.

The direction of Zen practice is always towards: How do I completely fall into THIS world? How do I become one with my situation moment by moment rather than standing aloof and apart? That involves listening; perceiving clearly. To listen and perceive clearly means to be responsive to the situation, which has in it both the aspect of wisdom (seeing or hearing clearly just what's there), and the aspect of compassionate responsiveness to the situation. If the situation is red, you become red; if it's white, white. If you're hungry, you eat. If you're tired, you sleep. If someone else is hungry, then you also have the ability to offer food.

A very simple type of instruction about Zen mindedness is "Don't make anything; don't hold anything; don't attach to anything." It's very simple; there's not even a technique there yet! Just an attitude: Don't make anything. All the time we're making, making, making, making something in our mind. Some kind of evaluative structure is always forming based on what we know from our previous experience. That is valuable up to a point because it informs our movement in the world. But if we are caught in that, and don't recognize that we're making that at a particular time, then it becomes a problem. So, don't make anything. Don't hold onto anything. The experience is momentary, and then …Gone! Next.

Here's an old Zen story: Zen Master Joju and a monk were talking, and the monk asked Joju, "Does a baby have mind?" Joju said, "Like a ball thrown on swift-flowing water." You see a beach ball thrown on swift flowing water, it's gone! The monk didn't quite understand him, so he called on Zen Master Tu Ja and he told him the story. He asked Tu Ja, "What's the meaning of a ball thrown on swift-flowing water?" Tu Ja said, "Thoughts, thoughts, non-stop thinking." But, if you're not holding on to them, then it's no problem. Thinking, no-thinking, it doesn't make any difference. It's just here and gone.

So, don't make anything; don't hold anything; don't attach to anything; don't cling onto something. But, of course, we're always clinging to something; trying to secure our ground every moment, trying to secure our identity every moment.

There is a short poem that is part of a kong-an. Kong-ans typically are interchanges between a Zen Master and a student. They are used in Zen training as a focusing device, and as a way of helping you to see into the inherent non-meaning of words. The poem says:

> *Walk on sword's edge,*
> *Run on ice ridge,*
> *Not stepping on stairs or ladder,*
> *Release your grip on the cliff!*

The first line, "Walk on sword's edge, run on ice ridge" is a very dangerous kind of procedure. Be very careful. Not stepping on stairs or ladder means not to take a gradual approach. It's not like one step after the other, or climbing up a ladder one rung after the other, but "Let go of your grip on the cliff!" Before we let it happen, we imagine it to be like falling off a cliff, but in reality, it's just "falling" into things as they are. Moment by moment; moment by moment. Then, that's one moment of enlightenment; one moment of enlightenment; one moment of enlightenment; endlessly! Thoughts, thoughts, non-stop thoughts.

More important than some particular technique is the direction of the practice. To keep that direction, and not just to talk about it, requires doing some sitting and some training, and looking into your attitudes—what you're holding, and what you're making over and over again—and processing them. Bull shit makes good fertilizer.

Q: I've never been exposed to any of this before, and I guess going with the flow is not something I consciously think of, but when things get hectic around me, I can calm myself down. But, are you saying even that's too much thinking?

A: There's a difference, of course, between being pulled along by the flow and being able to flow with it like a ball thrown on swift-flowing water. When you flow with it, you feel like the whole universe is your home. Most of us are pulled along by our thinking, by our attitudes, by our emotions, etc.

In the beginning of Zen practice, it's absolutely necessary to settle down and to begin to unattach yourself from your thinking mind. That's why we emphasize things like sitting still and letting your mind rest in your belly. If you let your mind rest in your belly, you will settle down after a while. The belly is the energy center. If you keep your attention in your head, there's a tendency to be pulled along by the stream of your thoughts. If you keep your attention in your heart, there's the tendency to be pulled along by the stream of your emotions. But, if you keep your attention focused just below the navel, then everything will settle down little by little. Think of a glass of cloudy water, the way it sometimes comes out of the tap. You set it down and watch it for a while and, little by little, it clears. Sit still and let your mind gently rest in your belly and breathe slowly. If you let your breath come from the belly area, your breath will become rhythmic. That rhythmic breathing has an effect on your thinking. Thoughts, emotions, and breathing are all interconnected and interdependent.

In this exercise, your breathing settles down, your center of gravity settles, and little by little your mind becomes steady and comes to one point. At that moment you're not clinging to your ideas. So, that's a moment of not being pulled along by your thinking. You have to practice that over and over again. And you begin to get a taste of that mind that's like clear water in Autumn. Cool, clear and pure. If you develop that, then going with the flow is possible and a reality.

There's a story which I tell quite often about my teacher's great-grand teacher Kyong Ho Sunim. He was a Korean Zen Master of a big temple in the late 1800's, early 1900's.

One time he decided to go on a trip to visit somebody. As he walked along on foot over the countryside, he passed through a small village. He noticed that there were no people in the plaza, but he kept going. It began to seem stranger and stranger to him that there was no one around. Finally, he went up to one small house and knocked on the door. When no one answered, he pushed the door open and saw the whole family inside, dead. He went back out, and then he saw a sign in the street that said: CHOLERA. IF YOU VALUE YOUR LIFE, RUN!

At that moment, his heart started beating very fast. He was very frightened, and he ran. But, when he got to the edge of the village, he stopped for a minute. And he thought to himself: The Buddhist scriptures that I teach talk about no birth, no death. I teach this to my students. And yet, here I am standing here, my heart beating like anything, and I'm scared to death of dying! So, my training is not complete.

He returned to his temple and dismissed all his students, saying, "I can't teach you anymore. Go to some other temple and find another Sutra Master." He kept one monk as his attendant, and he sat night and day in his room practicing meditation. He had no teacher, but he had read in a book an ancient kong-an which said, "Before the donkey has left, the horse has already arrived." He sat there contemplating this and asked himself: "What's the meaning? Before the donkey has left, the horse has arrived." Once a day, the attendant came in and gave him food. Sitting, lying down, eating, always keeping that question: What's the meaning? Big perplexity.

This went on for several months. One day, the attendant went to town to get some provisions and ran into a layman named Mr. Lee. Mr. Lee is somewhat of an enigmatic Zen figure himself because he plays a very crucial role in this story. Mr. Lee was a friend of Kyong Ho Sunim's, and he asked the attendant, "What is your Master doing these days?" (He had heard that the Master had dismissed all of his students.) The attendant said, "These days my Master is practicing very hard. He only sleeps, sits, eats, and lies down." Mr. Lee said, "If your Master only sits, eats, sleeps and lies down, he will be reborn as a cow!" The attendant got pissed off! He said, "My Master Kyong Ho Sunim is one of the greatest monks in all of Korea. It's not correct to speak of him that way." So, Mr. Lee said, "No, no. That's not the way to respond to that kind of statement." The attendant was very perplexed. "How should I respond?" Mr. Lee said, "You say the same thing to me, and I'll show you." So, the attendant repeated Mr. Lee's words, "If your Master only sits, eats, sleeps and lies down, he'll be reborn as a cow." So, Mr. Lee said without hesitation, "If Kyong Ho Sunim is born as a cow, it will be a cow with no nostrils." So now the attendant is even more perplexed. "I "don't know" what you're talking about." Mr Lee said, "You go back and ask Kyong Ho Sunim what that means." All the way back the attendant had his energy up. He went to Kyong Ho Sunim's room. "Oh, I saw Mr. Lee in town." "What did Mr. Lee say?" "Mr. Lee said…" and he told his Master the whole story. When he got to the line, "will be reborn as a cow with no nostrils," Kyong Ho Sunim's face lit up. He stood up, and walked out of the room. In that moment, his training had reached completion. Then he wrote his enlightenment poem:

> *I heard about the cow with no nostrils*
> *And suddenly the whole universe is my home.*
> *Yon Am Mountain lies flat under the road*
> *A farmer, at the end of his work, is singing.*

Why did I go on at length with that story? In Asian countries, an ox or a cow is used to help plow the fields for the rice. They harness the animal with a ring through the nostrils. That's a very easy way of controlling an ox or a cow. When you pull the ring a little bit this way, the cow goes this way! If you pull it that way, the cow goes that way. Suppose you have no nostrils. Which way do you go?

We're being pulled by our thinking all the time. Is this good? Is this bad? Being pulled around by the nose. Consequently, we lose our original center. So, a "cow with no nostrils" means being free from that kind of pull. The mind which is no-mind. If you have that mirror-like open state—not being pulled by anything—then you can go with the flow. Thinking is no problem; feeling is no problem. A difficult situation is no problem. An easy situation is no problem. Everything is no problem. It doesn't mean that there's no difficulty, it just means that there's no problem! There's a difference between difficulty and problem. A problem is what you *make* psychologically out of something. Difficult is: "Something is difficult."

To go with the flow, first you have to sit still and become not-moving mind. The cow that has no nostrils. If you find that, then going with the flow is possible.

Like Painting Feet on a Snake

ℰ

Q: Should I accept all of my thoughts when they're happening?
A: The basic attitude of Zen practice is keeping non-interfering awareness. That means, don't try to get rid of anything that comes into your mind, and don't hold onto or cling to any particular state of mind that suddenly develops. If thoughts come, just let them come. They're like clouds passing in front of the moon. Whether the clouds are in front of the moon or not, the moon still remains there.

You have to sit with that kind of attitude. Trying to get rid of thoughts is another kind of thought! You are fighting with yourself at that moment, and you're divided. It's like the old Zen Master who said, "That's like putting another head on top of your head." Or, like "painting feet on a snake"! The snake is already complete as it is. It doesn't need your painted-on feet. So, don't try to get rid of thinking; just let it be. Let it come; let it go. And, if you have a moment of clarity, or good feeling, or some particularly unusual state of mind, don't try to grab hold of it and keep it. Just let it be and let it unfold.

Thinking is what you know. What you know is based either on your own past experience, which may not be relevant to the present moment, or it's based on something that somebody told you (your mother or your father or your teacher). That's what you know.

When you come to not knowing, then your attachment to all of that falls away. Even when it comes back, you see it from a different angle. In a way, when you practice Zen, time goes from present to past instead of from past to present. It's like this: Here you are in the present, at this moment. At this very moment before thinking, all of a sudden some thought comes in that's connected with your past. Here's the present, and now you go to the past. When you recognize that, you wake up to the present! So in Zen we wake up over and over again from this dream that we are involved in most of the time. Our practice is to wake up. In fact, the word *Buddha* comes from the Sanskrit root of the idea of "awake." So a Buddha is one who has awakened.

Buddha's Pure Meditation

Zen Master Ma Jo's Faith Mind

ᛒ

(Hitting the table with his Zen stick)

If you believe in that,
that's already a mistake.

(Hitting the table)

If you do not believe in that,
that's also a mistake.

(Hitting the table)

Believing in this; not believing in this.
What is it that is not a mistake?

KATZ!!!

When the sun comes up, the sky is blue.
When the moon comes up, the sky is dark.

I'd like to talk a little bit about two things: the teachings of Zen Master Ma Jo, and the attitude of faith as it relates to Zen practice. Zen Master Ma Jo—whom the Chinese call Matsu and the Japanese call Basho (but not the Basho who wrote all the Haiku poems; he comes much later)—lived around 700 AD in China and was a successor of a student of the Sixth Patriarch. The Korean tradition of our Zen Center has a strong affiliation with Zen Master Ma Jo. A number of Korean monks went to China at that time and became disciples of Ma Jo's successors. They were given authority to teach on their own, and went back to Korea and started the Nine Mountain Schools. Ma Jo's Zen predates the breaking up of Zen tradition in China into five different schools. It is a very early and non-sectarian practice.

Ma Jo is also known for a few other things. One is his use of unusual methods, including an emphasis on a sudden approach to his students. Ma Jo used techniques such as shouts, hitting with the Zen stick, and various other unorthodox approaches that served to shake the students out of their normal point of view and frame of reference.

There are three stories about Ma Jo and his students that give the flavor of his style. When a monk named Wu-yeh first came to call on Zen Master Ma Jo, Ma Jo noticed immediately that he had a very unusual appearance, and that his voice was like a deep, deep bell. Ma Jo said to him, "What an imposing Buddha hall, but no Buddha in it!" Wu-yeh knelt down respectfully and said to Zen Master Ma Jo, "I've studied quite a bit of the teaching of the Three Vehicles of Buddhism, and these teachings I roughly understand. I have also heard many times the teaching of the Zen School which says that 'Mind itself is Buddha.' This I don't yet understand." Ma Jo immediately said, "This very mind that does not understand, is it!!!! There is no other thing!" Ma Jo was calling for faith in "don't know," which is at the root of our tradition; this very mind which at this moment does not understand is it. There is no other thing. But Wu-yeh looked not quite settled with that, and he gathered himself together and asked, "The secret transmission that the first patriarch Bodhidharma brought from India to China, what is that?" Ma Jo looked at him and said, "Venerable Wu-yeh looks a little disturbed right now. So, you should withdraw and come another time and ask." Wu-yeh bowed down and moved to leave the dharma hall; but just as he got to the door and turned his back, Ma Jo yelled out, "Venerable Wu-yeh!!!!" The monk turned his head and Ma Jo said, "What is it????" And the story goes that at that moment Wu-yeh had an awakening. He bowed down to Ma Jo, who said, "This stupid fellow, what is all this bowing about?"

When the monk Shui-lao first came to call on Ma Jo, he asked the Master, "What is the meaning of Bodhidharma's coming from the West?" Ma Jo said, "Bow down." As Shui-lao was bowing down, Ma Jo suddenly kicked him; Shui-lao fell to the ground and had a very great awakening. He stood up laughing loudly and clapping his hands and said, "Great Joy! The source of thousands and thousands of subtle meditations and meanings can all be found on the tip of a single hair." Then he expressed his gratitude to Ma Jo and left. Later (probably years later), he addressed the assembly and said, "Since the day that Zen Master Ma Jo kicked me, I haven't stopped laughing." (This means that the impression of his realization had remained steady).

The last story is about a day the monks in Zen Master Ma Jo's monastery were all working in the field. Yin-feng, one of the monks, was pushing a cart filled with dirt. As he went down the path, he came across Zen Master Ma Jo sitting on the ground with his legs stretched out across the path. Yin-feng said, "Master, please move your legs." Ma Jo said, "That which has been unfolded, cannot be brought back." Yin-feng looked at him and said, "That being the case, that which has already been set in motion cannot be stopped!" He pushed the cart forward, running over Ma Jo's legs and hurting him quite badly. Later that day, Ma Jo came into the dharma hall carrying a big axe. He looked at the assembly and said, "Where is the one who earlier today hurt this old monk's feet? Let him come forward." Yin-feng stood up, went forward in front of Ma Jo, and extended his neck. Ma Jo put the axe down. In those days, the old monks used unusual and spirited action in their encounters with each other.

When Ma Jo was still a student and not yet a Zen Master, he practiced meditation in a temple that was associated with Zen Master Huai-jang, who was the successor of the Sixth Patriarch. Huai-jang saw a lot of potential in Ma Jo. So, one day, he came to the little hermitage where Ma Jo practiced his intense meditation and said to Ma Jo, "Why are you sitting in meditation?" Why are you sitting practicing? That is an important question not just for Ma Jo, but for here and now. It means, what is the direction of your practice? What is the motivation that underlies the actual activity of meditation? What is it directed towards? Ma Jo said, "I am practicing meditation because I want to become a Buddha." Huai-jang picked up a brick in front of the hermitage and began polishing it. After a while, Ma Jo said, "Why are you polishing that brick?" Huai-jang said, "Because I want to make a mirror." Ma Jo asked, "How can you ever turn a brick into a mirror?" Huai-jang replied, "If I cannot turn this brick into a mirror, then how will you ever become a Buddha by sitting in meditation?"

That is a very, very important point about a certain attitude in practicing. When we practice, we often have the notion that we are practicing to purify something; to rub away something; to eliminate something; and that that will then transform us into something else. Like a brick turning into a mirror. And, of course, a mirror in the old Zen poetry represents the clear mind of wisdom. Totally reflective. So, likewise, to sit in meditation, to want to *become* a Buddha, or to want to *become* anything for that matter, sets a certain kind of obstacle in the road of practice. Something like Ma Jo's legs unfolded across the path. When Huai-jang said to Ma Jo, "If I can't make this brick into a mirror, then how will you become a Buddha by sitting in meditation?" Ma Jo said, "Then what should I do?" Huai-jang then said, "If an ox-cart stops moving, do you hit the cart or do you hit the ox?" Ma Jo had no answer. Huai-jang proceeded further. "Are you practicing to sit in meditation, or are you practicing to sit like a Buddha? If you're practicing to sit in meditation, then you should know that meditation is fundamentally neither sitting nor lying down. If you're practicing to sit like a Buddha, then you should know that the Buddha has no form. In the non-abiding dharma, one should neither reject anything nor grasp anything. If you want to practice to sit like a Buddha, then you are only killing the Buddha; if you attach to the form of meditation, then you will miss the essence of meditation." The story says that when Ma Jo heard this, he felt like he had tasted nectar and his whole attitude and approach toward practice shifted radically at that point.

Later, when he was teaching, a monk asked him, "How should I cultivate the way?" Ma Jo said, "The way does not belong to cultivation." If you talk about cultivation based on attainment, then whatever you get you can also lose just as easily. And that's the way of the small vehicle. The monk said to him, "Then what is the correct understanding that I should have towards practice?" Ma Jo said, "Originally self nature is pure and clear, just as it is. If you don't get hindered by either good or bad things, then that is cultivation." He also said, "It exists here and now, independent of cultivation or sitting in meditation. Not sitting and not cultivating is the Buddha's pure meditation."

In this teaching there is a certain attitude of faith emphasized. Faith of a very particular kind. And a certain emphasis on being very clear about the fundamental direction of practice. Going back to the interchange between Ma Jo and Huai-jang: "If an ox-cart stops moving, do you hit the cart or do you hit the ox?" (The ox often is used to represent the original clear mind, as seen in the famous Ten Ox-herding pictures which use the representation of the ox and person to symbolize aspects of practicing.) This means that if you are not striving towards attaining something, then what should you do? What should be the attitude? Primarily, the attitude should be that you hit this moment. Moment, by moment, by moment.

In the Soto tradition in Japan, they talk about the practice of shikantaza, which means *just to sit*, and this means just to sit and hit the world of opposites, or to let go of dualistic thinking. To just sit and hit the world of opposites is the direction of our practice moment by moment by moment. To become clear about what is.

It's very important not to interpret or think that the teaching in a story like this is that you should take sitting practice and throw it out the window. That it is all irrelevant. That is not what is being said. When Huai-jang says to Ma Jo, "Are you practicing to sit in meditation, or are you practicing to sit like a Buddha? If you're practicing to sit in meditation, then you should know that meditation is fundamentally neither sitting nor lying down," that doesn't mean that sitting meditation is irrelevant. It means that your *attitude* towards sitting meditation should be clear. If you're sitting like Buddha, you should know that the Buddha has no fixed form, and what you should direct yourself toward is the attitude of not grasping and not rejecting. Again, it doesn't mean that you should not practice sitting meditation.

This teaching of not rejecting and not clinging is an essential aspect of Zen practice. The seed or root of compassionate activity comes from this attitude. There is a familiar saying, *charity begins at home.* Likewise, compassion begins at home. If you can observe the comings and goings of your own mind without rejecting anything and without grasping anything, then that is the essential attitude of the bodhisattva's compassion; it is warm and open and accepting of what is. And if you begin by practicing that with yourself,

then you can bring that to your encounters with others. You begin to bring
to situations the attitude of neither trying to get rid of, nor trying to grasp
and manipulate in a particular way. As Huai-jang said, in the nonabiding
dharma (in the dharma where you don't hold onto anything or try to find a
fixed place of staying) one should practice neither grasping nor pushing away.

So, Ma Jo's teaching says the Buddha's meditation is not cultivating;
not sitting. What is that not cultivating? Not sitting? Is this not sitting *(points
to posture)*? Yes, this is sitting. So, when does this sitting become not sitting?
When does practice become not practice? The essential point of faith here is
in this one sentence in which Ma Jo says, "Originally, the self nature is complete." Irrespective of any kind of practice, any kind of cultivation, any kind
of refinement; the self nature is originally complete. If you practice something informed by that basic attitude, then sitting is not sitting; cultivating
is not cultivating. In the Zen tradition, having a certain confidence in this
aspect of "originally the self nature is complete" is called the faith of the Zen
patriarchs. This is contrasted with a faith based in some idea of gradually
purifying yourself over and over again with the purpose of becoming something or other. Why are you practicing meditation? Sitting to become a Buddha is a big mistake. Huai-jang should have hit him at that moment!

Regardless of the technique used—whether you sit with some question, or whether you sit with some mantra, or you sit with only bare attention—if your basic attitude of practice is rooted in *originally the self nature is
complete*, then your practice is not trying to get to some place other than
where you already are. This is why the old Zen Masters said again and again,
it has already appeared, it is already apparent in all things.

When I was at Providence Zen Center, I happened to pick up a copy
of the Kwan Um School of Zen journal, *Primary Point*. It contained a talk by
Zen Master Ko Bong, who was a Zen Master in Korea and was our teacher's
teacher. There are very few of his teachings translated into English. So, I'd
like to read it to you. The title is "How to Meditate."

> Meditation is not special. There are three poisons: Greed, an-
> ger, and ignorance. If you put these down, then your Buddha
> nature appears like a clear mirror, clear ice, an Autumn sky, or a
> very clear lake. The whole universe is in your center. Then your
> body/mind will calm down and you will be at peace. Your heart
> will be like a fresh Autumn wind. Not competitive. If you at-
> tain this level you are one half of a Zen monk [or a Zen stu-
> dent]. But if you are merely satisfied with this, you are still ig-
> norant of the ways of Buddhas and patriarchs. This is a big
> mistake because demons will soon drag you to their lair. [That's
> the way they talk in Korea; Korea is rooted in a shamanistic
> tradition which is pre-Buddhist, so a lot of demons and moun-

tain gods are talked about.] Meditation is originally nothing special. Just keep a strong practice mind. [That's it! Nothing special. Just keep a strong practice mind!] If you want to get rid of distraction, and get enlightenment, this too is a mistake. Throw away this kind of thinking. Only keep a strong mind and practice. Then you will gradually enter *just do it.*

The original phrase in Chinese for the sentence *then you will gradually enter just do it,* is "wu-wei," which literally means "not doing." So, if you throw away wanting to get rid of distraction and get enlightenment, then you will gradually enter *not doing.* But *not doing* is *just doing it.* If you *just do it* without wanting something to come out of it, then that doing IS *not doing.* That is "just sitting," which is "not sitting."
One more paragraph:

Everybody wants meditation. But they think about it in terms of medicine and disease. However, don't be afraid of what you *think of* as disease. [That is a very warm, open attitude.] Only be afraid of going too slow. [That means, "Well maybe tomorrow I'll practice."] Someday you will get enlightenment.

That is Ko Bong Sunim's teaching on meditation.
One day when Ma Jo was an old man, he was walking with his attendant in the mountains. They came to a cave that was very flat and level, and he said to the attendant, "One month from now please return my body to this place." He then came down from the mountain, and shortly after began to get ill. One day the head monk came into Ma Jo's room and said, "How is the Venerable Zen Master's health today?" And Ma Jo said, "Sun Faced Buddha; Moon Faced Buddha." This comes from a sutra called the "Scripture of Buddha's Names." It mentions all of the different Buddhas. And Sun Faced Buddha is said to live for one thousand eight hundred years. A Moon Faced Buddha only lives one day and one night. Shortly after Ma Jo said, "Sun Faced Buddha; Moon Faced Buddha," he passed away sitting in meditation.

Falling Back Into This World

Down-to-Earth Practice

℘

In Zen the word *practice* is used in the same way that we talk about the practice of medicine or the practice of law. It is not practicing to get somewhere, it is a practice which is a way of being and of living.

So, everyday mind is the path! When a monk asked Zen Master Joju, "Master! I've just entered your monastery. Please give me your teaching!" Joju said, "Did you eat breakfast?" The monk said, "Yes, I did." Joju said, "Then wash your bowl!" The monk had an enlightenment experience.

That's a very down-to-earth kind of teaching. Imagine, expecting something profound and hearing, "Did you eat breakfast? Then wash your bowl." Everyday mind is Zen, and Zen is everyday mind. Just be clear about what you're doing. Washing your bowl is enlightenment; enlightenment is washing your bowl.

In our form of meditation practice there are a few simple things we emphasize and rely on. It is not very complicated. We emphasize sitting straight so that you support yourself and keep mindful of your actual sitting position. We emphasize breathing so this area in the lower belly opens up. And then we emphasize some basic looking into ourselves, some questioning attitude, some awareness: What am I? What is this? That is not very complicated.

Also, simple down-to-earth practice asks, "How compassionate is my movement in the world as compared with how self-centered it may be?" This is more important than any particular experience. And, of course it comes from perceiving essentially *what is my basic nature?* If you perceive what your basic nature is, you perceive that in some way you're interrelated with all beings! So, out of that comes a kind of action which has a compassionate connection with all beings.

If you perceive clearly then that means you have basic, enlightened mind. The word for enlightenment is called *kensho* in Japanese, which means to see or perceive true nature. In reality, however, just seeing *is* nature! So, if you are *just seeing* and not making opposites, then you experience true nature. Very simple! Just hearing, just seeing, just being, just acting, just washing your bowls. So, various experiences may come and go, but far more important is our way of being.

It is something that is very down to earth, very practical. So, that is our basic direction in Zen practice.

Q: What is the emphasis on energy in Zen?

A: There is a poem which says:

When you hear the wooden chicken crow in the evening,
you will know the country where your mind was born.
Outside my house, in the garden,
the willow is green, the flower is red.

Wooden chickens don't crow! So, when you hear the wooden chicken crowing, that is something extraordinary! It points to an unusual energy.

Find the place where your mind is born. That's a basic Zen attitude: Where is my mind born? What is my mind? Ma Jo Zen Master used an essential teaching that said over and over again: *Mind is Buddha; Buddha is mind.* There is no Buddha outside of mind; there is no mind outside of Buddha. So, find the place where your mind is born. What is that?

Ma Jo had a student whose name was Tae Mae. When Tae Mae heard this teaching that "Mind is Buddha and Buddha is mind," he had some awakening experience. He left Ma Jo's temple and went to practice for many years on a mountaintop. *"Mind is Buddha, Buddha is mind,"* solidly, over and over again on the mountaintop. After some time passed, Ma Jo told one of his students to call on Tae Mae and see how his practice was going.

The monk made his way to the mountaintop where Tae Mae was practicing and asked, "How is your practice going these days?" Tae Mae said, "I only keep 'Mind is Buddha; Buddha is mind.'" The monk said "OH! But these days Ma Jo Zen Master's teaching is very different." Tae Mae said, "What is he teaching these days"? The monk said, "No mind; No Buddha." Tae Mae said, "That old rascal is making a lot of trouble." The monk went back to Ma Jo and told him this story.

Tae Mae's name in Chinese is Ta-Mei. The word *Ta* means *Great, Mei* means *Plum,* so his name was Great Plum. When Ma Jo heard of Tae Mae's response he said, "Oh, the plum is ripe!"

So, where is mind? If you look into your mind at any moment, you see thoughts appearing, thoughts appearing, thoughts appearing, and you ask yourself, "All of this comes from where?" What is mind? That's a big question. And it leaves you clear like space, in a place before thinking, before color. Pure and clear like a crystal. Just *don't know.* If your mind is like that, it may then enter totally into each and every thing.

The last two lines of the poem signal it is time to fall back *into this world! Completely!* And this is the last word of Zen. Completely perceive just now; what it is. If you perceive this without holding anything, then energy is already there! It is not made. If you are not holding anything, not making anything, not making some limitation, then the willow is green, the flower is red.

Traditionally, Zen meditation is done first thing in the morning upon arising, and in the evening after you have finished your daily activities. Anytime, of course, is okay depending on what your schedule is. It is best to keep to the same time every day; but again, that depends upon your situation.

It helps to make a pact with yourself, that at practice time, no matter what happens, you won't let it interrupt! So, if the phone rings, you have to make up your mind that you're not getting into that at that moment. The establishing of a basic daily practice is very important.

It can be difficult to sustain a daily practice completely on one's own. It can be helpful to come to a group practice periodically. Usually, people start out with a lot of zeal, but after a while the energy can run down. Practicing with other people who are also trying provides a mutual support system. Even if you don't say a word to anyone in the room, there is a communality that encourages you to continue your practice.

Also, it is helpful to have contact with a teacher periodically. As your practice develops, you may want some feedback as to what you're doing, and a teacher can point you in the correct direction. In Buddhism, one of the traditional names for the meditation teacher is *Kalumitra,* which literally means *spiritual friend.* So, a teacher may become a spiritual friend in helping with your meditation practice.

Poor and Destitute

Practice and Relationships

ᚖ

Q: I've been back and forth with Zen practice many times. I need the support of a community. Can you talk about that?

A: It's very difficult to maintain a regularity of practice strictly on one's own. It's possible, but it's difficult. When you sit to practice Zen meditation, nothing happens. Zen meditation is: Nothing is happening. It's boring. In fact, Zen meditation may be viewed as an exercise in boredom! It's very difficult to face boredom day in, day out on one's own. Yet, paradoxically, the road to freedom or the road to experiencing one's self is through boredom.

There's a form in traditional Buddhism called the Three-Fold Refuge. People who consider themselves Buddhists in a formal sense will recite this daily: I take refuge in the Buddha; I take refuge in the dharma; I take refuge in the sangha. The original Sanskrit word for refuge is *namah,* which means to become one with. To take refuge in this sense means to become one with, to become intimate with. To become one or intimate with the Buddha means to become intimate with Buddha's enlightenment or Buddha's mind.

Buddha's enlightenment experience, according to the story, happened this way: Buddha sat under the bodhi tree and said he would not get up again until he attained enlightenment or realized his true self. One morning as dawn was breaking, his mind had become very calm, very serene, very open, very wide. At that moment, he perceived the morning star as it was in the sky. The openness of his mind and the star came together, and he exclaimed in his awakening: "Now I perceive that all beings from the very start are imbued with the awakened nature, with Buddha nature."

"Buddha" just means awakened, so a Buddha is someone who has awakened and does not live in a dream. Buddha is one who perceives clearly what is. So, to take refuge in the Buddha means to take refuge in that mind which is awakened, and which, historically, goes back to that point.

Dharma means teaching, or way. To take refuge in the dharma means to take refuge in the truth of this awakened teaching.

Sangha means community. In its original sense, it meant the community of monks and nuns who were the immediate students and disciples of

Buddha. In a wider sense, sangha means the community of all beings. In a more narrow sense, sangha means the community of people who practice together and support one another in this endeavor of practice. To facilitate this kind of practice, most people need some interconnectedness with other people who are making the same effort. When your practice gets shaky, you can come together with some other people and gain some strength from their practice. This is why we sit in a group rather than sit alone.

Zen practice traditionally is done in a communal setting. There are occasions when people go off on a solo retreat, but usually the practice of meditation is done in a group setting because of the support it gives.

Unless we conceive of ourselves as supermen and superwomen, we should take refuge in the mutual support of a group practice. Some people can't go every day to a group practice, so it's recommended that they go as regularly as possible so that it nurtures and supports their individual practice. If they don't do that, then they will practice in fits and starts.

Practicing in fits and starts is something like planting carrot seeds in the ground. You see a few little green leaves come up, so you think, "Well, let me see then how it's doing." So, you pull it up, but you only have the rudiments of a carrot there. You've disturbed it at that point and it hasn't really taken deep root and become a full vegetable!

Practicing in fits and starts is like that, but of course the beginning process of practicing *is* in fits and starts. At first you may practice, and then there's a break in practice, and you give it up, and then come back to practicing if you're lucky. You may have come back many times to practicing, and that means you have a very sincere and strong determination to practice. If not, you would have thrown it out the window a long time ago, gotten discouraged and said: This is not for me, goodbye.

You have to respect your sincerity and effort to try and to keep going. There's an old Zen saying: Fall down seven times; get up eight times. That doesn't just mean fall down seven times, get up eight times. That means fall down seven thousand times; get up seven thousand and one times!

Q: Can you talk about intimacy and relationships?

A: Yes, and I'm reminded of a story that won't give much more than an idea of it. But sometimes, traditional Zen stories allude to many things through just one episode. It's like a small particle or atom represents something quite a bit bigger than it appears. There is a story about Zen Master Cho Sahn, one of the early Chinese Zen Masters. He and his teacher, Dong Sahn, were the founders of one of the original Zen Schools in China during the T'ang dynasty, Ts'ao-Tung School, or Soto line, which still exists in Japan. In Japan the two lines which continue are the Lin Chi, or Rinzai line, and the Soto line. In China during the T'ang dynasty, there were five main lines, but they gradually converged into two by slowly dying out, or by the teaching of one line being taken over by another line. Cho Sahn was one of the main teachers of this Soto line.

One day a monk named Cheong Sae called on Cho Sahn. In those stories when it says a monk "called on" a Zen Master, that usually means he had traveled hundreds of miles across mountains and valleys, probably in not the best travelling conditions, through highway robbers, to "call" on the Master! Cheong Sae called on Zen Master Cho Sahn and said, "Master! I am poor and destitute. Please help me." Cho Sahn just said: "Cheong Sae!!" The monk responded, "Yes!!" Cho Sahn said, "It's as if you have already drunk three bottles of the best vintage wine in China, and yet you say that you haven't even wet your lips!"

How is this story about intimate relationships? About problems in relationships? The monk says, "Master, I am poor and destitute. Please help me." Sometimes you enter a relationship hoping that the other person will in some way fulfill you. You then devise all kinds of strategies about how you are going to get this to work. And, of course, it doesn't work! Maybe in accepting that it doesn't work, it actually begins to work. So, "I am poor and destitute" has that implied in it. I am empty, please give me something. But, at the same time, I am poor and destitute, from a Zen standpoint means: I am poor and destitute, holding nothing. No ideas; no conceptions; no opinions; no idea of anything. Totally zero. Empty. I've come back to my original mind.

Zen Master Ma Jo always taught, "Mind is Buddha. Buddha is mind." He was famous for this teaching. Everyone expected to hear him say it. But one day he said, "No mind; no Buddha." If you think mind and Buddha, you still have something, some subtle concept. This "no Buddha mind" is being totally poor; totally destitute; not relying on any support, even the support of some idea of mind, or some idea of Buddha. Even "I take refuge in the Buddha" is still some idea! What is *no refuge Buddha?* What is the mind of no mind? So, that day, he said, "No mind; no Buddha," and that is being poor and destitute in the fundamental sense. Totally empty; the mirror is not holding anything. No dust.

But, if you think: I am poor and destitute; I have no idea; no conception; no opinion; I am totally zero point, you still have something. You're still making something. Years ago, there was a student in our group who had been practicing for quite a while. He had become a little disenchanted with the whole rigamarole that we had going. Zen Master Seung Sahn came to New York to give a talk. During the question and answer period, this student said to Zen Master Seung Sahn: "Suppose we take all this business of Zen, the robes and the sitting, and throw it out the window. Then what?" And Zen Master Seung Sahn said, "You still have window!!" So, if you think, *I have nothing*, then you are making something. Making empty. Making nothing, or attached to "Nothing." Making poor and destitute.

Cho Sahn at that moment, perceiving this monk's mind, immediately called out his name, "Cheong Sae!!" And the monk, without thinking anything now—REALLY not thinking poor, destitute, full, empty, form, ANYTHING, just said, "Yes, Master!!" At that moment, *real* intimate relationship had occurred!!! No idea; no taint of spirituality. No nothing; not even making nothing. Just call and response. "Cheong Sae!" "Yes, Master!" So, Cho Sahn said, "It's as if you have drunk three bottles of the best vintage wine in China." Meaning, you have it already, you're quite full and intoxicated with the fullness of this wonderful ever-present spiritual light, and yet, you act as if it has not wet your lips. So, that's a Zen example of intimate relationship.

What creates difficulty in intimate relationships is the holding on to some idea. Even the idea of nothing. Whatever the idea, it gets in the way! It's as if you had a bomb with a long fuse, and the fuse burned down 99% of the way but, at that point, it went out. Even if you've gotten 99% of the way there, still the contact has not really been made. And that is the problem with all of us with relationship and intimacy issues.

This calling/answering interchange is seen in many of the Zen stories. There's another similar story. Ananda, who was one of the first disciples of the Buddha, actually a cousin of the Buddha, was Buddha's attendant. All the years that Buddha went around teaching in India, Ananda accompanied him. He was said to have a photographic memory, so he could remember all of Buddha's discourses. He also was very sharp philosophically. So, he would remember the discourses and then philosophize about them. But, because he was so bright and so philosophical, he never let go of it all. So, during Buddha's lifetime, he never awakened to Buddha's fundamental teaching. After Buddha passed on, Mahakashyapa became Buddha's successor, the second patriarch in the line. One time Ananda came to Mahakashyapa and said, "Besides the brocade robe and the bowl [which were the signs of transmission which Buddha passed on to him], did the Buddha transmit anything else to you, Mahakashyapa?" Mahakashyapa called out, "Ananda!" Ananda, without thinking, said, "Yes, sir!" Mahakashyapa said, "Take down the flag pole from the gate." At that time in India when there was some kind of religious discourse being given or dharma speech, a pendant was raised in front of the temple gate. When the spiritual discourse was over, it was taken down. So, when Mahakashyapa told Ananda to "Take down the flag pole from the gate!" that meant, "You've already received the whole teaching just in my calling and in your answer."

Zen training and Zen meditation are basically that—just sitting and experiencing responsiveness. It's not possible to be responsive when you are holding on to your own agenda. Zen meditation, regardless of the technique, is about fundamental attitude. The fundamental attitude is: *Don't make anything; don't hold anything; don't attach to anything!* If you don't do these things, then you have the ability to be responsive to what is! So, when you're sitting, and you're not holding anything, and you just hear the raindrops, you can respond to that moment.

In your daily life, if you're not holding anything, not making anything, not attaching to anything, when someone calls on you in some particular way, you can respond simply and appropriately without self-consciousness. Without narrowing down to some self-centered hopes. Zen practice emphasizes this over and over again: Let go of self-centered hopes and become Big Mind. Big Mind is the whole universe! It's difficult, but difficult or easy, it doesn't make any difference. Just try, over and over and over again. Just try.

It's not that somehow we find some idealistic place where we never make mistakes or move to one side or the other. If that were the case, then we would become like a wall. Life is not like that. But, in losing our balance, we have to know where the center is, and come back to that. If you don't understand what a mistake is, then compassion is not possible. If you don't understand what suffering is like, then compassion is not possible. If you don't understand what making an absolute fool out of yourself is like, then compassion is not possible. So, a mistake is not a mistake; it's very good fertilizer for practice. Without mistakes, it's all too rarefied.

At one time all of the Buddhas of the ten directions gathered together in some heaven to have a conference. Manjusri, who is the Bodhisattva of Primal Wisdom, appeared there. According to the myth, Manjusri could not come into the conference at first, but he saw from the doorway that a woman sat very close to the Buddha. She sat in deep meditation, in samadhi. When all of the Buddhas of the ten directions returned to their original places, Manjusri came in and said to Shakyamuni Buddha, "How come this woman can sit so close to you, and I couldn't come right in?" At that time in India, there was a very strong sexist bias. Even today in Asia at the monk's assemblies, monks sit in the first row and nuns sit behind them. Buddha said to Manjusri, "You wake her up from her deep meditation and ask her!" Manjusri walked around the woman three times and snapped his fingers, but nothing happened. He took her in the palm of his hands and went up to some transcendental realm, and tried to use his great mystical power to awaken her, but still she would not awaken from the deep meditation. He then returned to Buddha. Buddha said to Manjusri, "Even if ten thousand Manjusris appeared here, still they couldn't awaken this woman from her deep meditation. But, down below, beyond thousands and thousands of worlds, is Ma Myung Bodhisattva." Ma Myung means "from the earth." This earthly bodhisattva, Ma Myung, can awaken the woman, but not the celestial Manjusri! Just at that moment, out of the ground appeared Ma Myung. Ma Myung walked up to the woman and walked around her three times and snapped his fingers. The woman awakened! So, that's the myth. What's the meaning of it?

Manjusri represents this very rarefied Primal Wisdom which means a recognition of equality; that everything is one. This one is before name, before form. But it doesn't take into account the recognition of the particulars of each and every thing *as it is.* Ma Myung represents the recognition of particulars: woman is woman; man is man. And so, the story is an example of how we have to use our human nature with all of its characteristics, mistakes, and all of those things as a device for perceiving.

We have sadness, we have mistakes, we have humiliation, we have shame, and we have all of these various things that go on in human existence. Those are the food of practice; that is the fertilizer of practice.

Cow-Dung Mirror

Three Forms of Practice

ℰ

Q: How do you deal with competitiveness in Zen? Like who has the straightest back, who walks the best, and so on?

A: My teacher came from Korea and his English was very limited. He took a crash course in English as a Second Language at Harvard University one summer after arriving here, so he had a few words that he worked with! His instruction for Zen practice at that time consisted of three lines: Don't check yourself. Only go straight. Don't know. "Don't check" means don't evaluate your practice or make the categories of "good and bad." Only pay attention in the moment. If you follow that, where is competition?

Traditionally, there are three ways to practice. The first way is to practice in a solitary situation. In the old days some monks and nuns went off to the mountains, found a cave or a little hermitage and practiced there all alone.

There is a famous story about solitary practice. Zen Master Soeng Am Eon once practiced as a hermit. Every day he would stand in front of his little hut and yell out, "Master!" Then he would answer, "Yes?" "Keep clear!" "Yes!" "Don't be deceived by others any place, any time!" "Yes, yes!" This was Soeng Am's practice. Since he practiced as a hermit, he called himself and answered himself.

The second form of practice is with a group in a specialized setting, a center or temple or a monastery, some place where there is a community of practitioners. In Asian countries, traditionally that is a monastic setting, especially in the old days. In that kind of situation, the schedule for practice is clearly delineated and defined. At a certain time early in the morning, a bell is rung or a drum is hit and everyone knows that this is the time to get up. Everyone gets up, folds their bedding, puts it away, comes into the meditation hall and sits. Then the head teacher signals and everyone gets up and walks. Meal time is specified, next practice is specified, work time is specified. Everything is regimented. What this means is that you aren't running your own show! There is a certain benefit to that in terms of not having so many options open to you. Because everybody is doing the same thing, if you are not doing the same thing, they will tell you before long, "You shouldn't

be here, please leave by the gate which is over there!" Whereas, if you practice alone, you might decide, "I think I'll sleep for another half hour before
I get up to practice!"

The third type of practice is practicing in the world. This means practice goes on in your everyday circumstances. In that type of situation, you
may find some time to formally sit and practice, but, additionally, your everyday life situation is the focus of awareness. Every moment something
presents itself to you, and either you are awake to it or you are asleep in some
way, or falling into delusion.

These are the three styles of practice. One is not necessarily better
than the other. But, each has its place and its time and its function as a
therapeutic medicinal.

(Hitting the floor.) This is a simple demonstration of original energy
point before thinking. Community practice can act as a mirror. You begin to
see your competitiveness, your checking, your evaluations, and things of
that sort come up. So, that becomes awareness practice. You see your mind
in the mirror of the situation. Zen practice is "perceive your mind." That
doesn't mean only your good mind or your holy or your spiritual mind!
Perceive your mind!

Cow dung makes good fertilizer. You can grow many good things in
it. That is one of the benefits of group practice. In a certain sense, as odd as
it may sound, you have to have a feeling of gratitude towards that mirror
which lets you see yourself. All it is doing is showing your conditioning.
Even in a situation where the activity is so simple, your conditioning becomes apparent. To see that is in some sense, to not be caught by it all the
time like an ox tethered with a ring in its nose. Your conditioning pulls you
around this way and the other. So you have to find your point which is
before condition, before situation, before any idea.

Nothing is Better than a Good Thing

ℰ

Nothing, or *no-thing*, does not mean blankness. Nothing means not holding onto something as if it is a solid or substantial existence.

Nothing means everything is in process, and everything depends on everything else. So, to see that is to see through things. That's why in the Heart Sutra it is said, "When the bodhisattva perceives that all formations are empty, then the mind is no hindrance!" That doesn't mean he makes his mind a blank piece of nothing. When he perceives that all formations are empty, "empty" means empty of self-nature! Empty of self sufficiency. Nothing exists on its own. This is a cup. But this cup is not a cup in the sense that it's not going to exist on its own forever and ever. If you look into this cup, you also will see all of the non-cup things that are in it. The potter, the clay, the earth where it came from, the potter's teacher who trained him how to be a potter, and so on. It goes on and on and on all the way to the rain that fell on the ground where the clay was formed. This cup is *empty* of self-sufficiency! It is inter-dependent with many things. This is an ecological view. Everything is part of a vast network.

In the Heart Sutra it says, "When the bodhisattva perceives that all formations are empty, then the mind is no hindrance! Without any hindrance no fears exist." That is another important point. Without any mental hindrance no fears exist.

Competitiveness is based in fear. Not necessarily the same exact fear for every person in every competitive situation, but there is some fear underlying competitiveness. So, when you perceive the true nature of being, which is inter-being, then the mind is no hindrance—then your thinking is no hindrance. Your ideas are no hindrance. You can see a thing clearly for what it is and not get caught by it. Your conditioning doesn't pull you.

This is why when we practice we are interested in just perceiving moment by moment: Thinking is coming, thinking is going. Little by little it becomes clear. That is why we emphasize this attitude of *don't know*. If you "don't know," then where is right and wrong? Where is good and bad? Where is better and worse?

You don't know! Because what are you going to weigh it with? Which scale? There is a famous story about the Sixth Patriarch of Chinese Zen. The Sixth Patriarch said to a monk, "Don't make good and bad. At that moment, what is your original face before your parents were even born?" The monk heard that and had an awakening.

That is an interesting three-line teaching. Don't make good and bad is the first line. That means don't make dualistic thinking. This doesn't mean Zen is amoral. A lot of people misunderstand this kind of teaching. It does not mean there is no right and wrong or correct or incorrect. But if you are *making* good and bad, that is conditioned by somebody else's view. You are not perceiving your relationship to a particular situation.

Second line: So, at that moment, what is your original face? Your body's face is not your original face! Your original face is maybe as big as the universe! Something like that last scene in The Wizard of Oz where the wizard is hiding behind a curtain, and there is this huge face filling up the whole room! So, what is your original face? What is your true or original self before thinking?

Third line: Before your parents were even born? Where was I before my mother was even born? If you really think about it for a second, you cannot get a hold on it. So, you hit a stuck point! That cuts off all attachment to thinking. Also, there's a psychological point here that the Sixth Patriarch understood umpteen centuries ago in China. Good and bad, your whole system of should and should nots, all of your conditioning comes from a learned set of things that are pumped into you. And the people that pump it into you are your mother, your father, and other significant adults in your early upbringing—your teachers, your peers and so on.

The Hindus say your first guru (teacher) is your mother. So, what is your original face before your parents were even born? That means you can't use "My mother said this was good, or not so good." There is nothing to lean back on there! No support for good and bad, right and wrong, because that is before any of that. In that moment, all conditioning is cut off. It doesn't mean it won't come back. It comes back over and over again. That is what training and practice are about.

Sometimes you may get a moment of insight into your original self before all of that conditioning. But then, ongoing cultivation is necessary to support that moment of insight, and to let it permeate your everyday life.

Chanting Practice, Structure, Freedom

℘

Chanting is a helpful practice because it gives you something concrete to focus on. Because of this, it is easier than sitting meditation. We use the sound and words and vibration as a mindfulness device. The Heart Sutra obviously has a meaning and a philosophy, but as we chant we are concerned more with just perceiving the sound. If you perceive the sound and become clear, the chant will be absorbed, and at some time in the future the meaning will appear!

The language of Buddhism originally is from India. When Zen went from India into China, the Indian Zen monks brought with them their chanting. The Chinese couldn't pronounce some of the Sanskrit sounds, so they found the closest equivalent sound to them. Our school of Zen comes from a Korean lineage. Zen went from China into Korea, Vietnam and then to Japan. Koreans pronounce the Chinese characters in their own way. So, a chant sounds a little different in Korea than it does in China or in India. And even though Korean people may practice a particular chant every day, they may not have the foggiest idea what the meaning is!

The primary purpose of chanting in Zen is actually to have clear perception of the sound, and only secondarily to understand the meaning.

One of the things that comes up as a result of the structured environment in the Zen school is resistance to the various practices and forms. This can present a problem in the beginning. Something gets triggered in these situations in terms of your mind's reaction.

The actual purpose of the structure is to find one's sense of freedom. There is freedom from something, meaning you want to get away from something. And then there is finding freedom in something. We are always confronted with some situation in life. The direction of Zen practice is to find freedom within the context of the situation. In order to find your freedom within the context of the situation that you are in, you have to have the ability to let go of emotional and intellectual constructions. As the old Zen Masters would say, "Let go of like and dislike. Don't make like and dislike. Don't make good and bad. If you don't make good and bad or like and dislike, then you perceive your original, clear mind." And, your clear mind unites with the situation and functions freely within the context of that situation.

So, one of the purposes of the chanting form in Zen practice is to find your sense of freedom within the routine. At first, some people may react with: "Why do we have to chant all these strange sounds? Why, why, why?" For others it is not a problem. In fact, they actually find the structure to be helpful. They don't have to think about what they should do. An attitude of "just do it" begins to develop. In Zen retreats, for example, you don't have to concern yourself with should I do this, shouldn't I do this? When *should* and *shouldn't* drop away, you perceive clearly the simplicity of the situation, whether it's chanting or bowing or sitting etc.

It is always interesting and helpful to see how we make something out of what inherently is not problematic! The grey robe we wear is not good or bad. But, we can make it "like" or "dislike." You need to see what you make in terms of your construction. See what you hold on to. What you attach to. What you have an aversion to.

One of the basic attitudes in meditation practice is the correct attitude of mind. That is, not trying to get rid of anything or holding onto anything that is in your mind at the moment. A classical example in the Zen texts is, your thinking and your emotional mind are like clouds floating in the sky. They come and go. You need not push them away or bring them in. If you have that attitude of non-interference, then little by little you return to your original center. It is something like a glass of water: If you try to clarify it in some way, you usually stir it up more. If you set it down and just let it settle by itself, gradually you will have a glass of clear water. Zen meditation is about becoming clear. As you do that you perceive what comes up, and what kind of world you are making at that moment. What kind of *I* am I making at that moment? What kind of *I* am I constructing? *I* is a construction. We are using *I* all day long. I this; I that. What is it that the word "I" is referring to?

The old Zen teachers asked, "I" comes from where? If you try an experiment, and just repeat the word "I" over and over again, after a while it floats in the space of your mind. You get a sense of what is around the edges of this word "I." The true *I* is not this construction "I." In fact, self-image, self-concept and the fear of some particular view being challenged is how we ordinarily live. Zen practice keeps looking into this construction, and begins to see more and more clearly that that is simply what "*I*" is—a construction! None of this is the fundamental, basic I.

It is not so easy, of course, to let go of our constructions, those feelings that we all suffer from—embarrassment, self-consciousness, humiliation, self concepts, but we have to try, try, try non-stop for ten thousand years.

Grist for the Mill

Karma

℘

Q: I don't believe I've ever heard you talk about karma.

A: The word karma comes from the Sanskrit root kri, which implies action, work, energy. Karma means action and reaction, cause and effect. You can see that in a very simple, linear, one-dimensional way in the game of pool. After hitting the cue ball, the nine ball may go into the pocket. That's cause and effect, and the effect in turn becomes the cause of another effect.

But things are not always that simple. In Buddhism, there is the idea of primary cause, and then numerous secondary conditions within which this cause operates. According to the interaction of primary cause and the secondary conditions, some set of effects will be set in motion. This means that in all of our activity, what's occurring is not occurring haphazardly or randomly or by chance. It's following some law, some order. Sometimes you may see that order apparently and immediately. Sometimes you cannot see it for a long time. Sometimes you look back on ten years and you can see from that vantage point that there was some meaning to what happened at the time. But then you were wondering: Why the hell am I doing this? Sometimes the meaning and order can't be seen in a lifetime.

But, the basic idea is, there is some law or order that operates throughout the universe, that things do not happen randomly. You plant corn seed, corn will come up. Something good will arise out of that. But not necessarily immediately! It's not as simple as corn seed. You do something not so good, then something not so good will result sooner or later. *When* the seed of that action unfolds depends upon the condition, upon the type of soil that is there.

There is a notion that when you do something, a certain kind of tendency or seed of that lingers on in your mind in the storehouse consciousness. The Indian word for that idea means to *perfume*. Perfume leaves a scent, and, at some time in the future, your perfumed consciousness will come forth and bear its result.

One kong-an in the *Mu Mun Kwan* collection is a fable-like story about cause and effect and how it's related to Zen practice.

In this kong-an an interchange takes place between Zen Master Baek

Jang and an old man about cause and effect. Initially Baek Jang asked him, "Who are you?" The old man said, "I am not a human being." A very interesting statement: I am not a human being. The old man continued: "In the ancient past in the days of Kashyapa Buddha, I was the Zen Master on this mountain. Someone asked me, 'Does a Zen Master come under the law of cause and effect or not?' And I said, 'He does not.' For that I was reborn as a fox for five hundred generations."

The old man then asked, "You please give me a turning word to free me of my fox's body." A turning word means to say something that causes a revolution at the basis of consciousness where all unconscious tendencies reside. Baek Jang said, "You ask me the same question." The old man asked, "Does a Zen Master fall under cause and effect or not?" Baek Jang responded, "Cause and effect are clear." Some translations say, "Cause and effect are not obscured."

There are a couple of essential points here. The first is cause and effect are not obscured; cause and effect are clear. No matter what kind of great enlightenment you may or may not have, still cause and effect is there throughout the universe. There is a story about this: One of Buddha's disciples had a vision that the kingdom was going to be decimated in a petty war between kingdoms. He told the Buddha! Buddha said, "Merited karma cannot be taken away."

The disciple couldn't accept what the Buddha told him. According to the story, the disciple magically shrank the kingdom and put it in a teacup. Then he put the saucer on top of the cup to protect the miniature kingdom, and then rose up to some high celestial place and stayed there past the time of the prediction of the calamity. When he returned to earth to Buddha's assembly, he lifted the saucer off the cup and saw that the teacup had undergone a miniature war, resulting in a miniature decimation. So, cause and effect are clear.

The second point of interest in the story of the fox and old man is found in a statement that Hwang Beok, Baek Jang's disciple makes at the end of the story. He said, "This old man made one mistake [a single mistake, he opened his mouth wrong once] and was reborn as a fox for five hundred generations. Suppose the mistake had never been made, then what?" What's a mistake? What's not a mistake? What's correct? What's incorrect? If you perceive moment by moment your correct function, correct situation, correct relationship, then moment by moment by moment there is no cause, no effect. No birth, no death. You enter the eternal at that moment. But, eternal is different from everlasting. Everlasting means a long time, but eternal is no time: not born. So, if you perceive this moment, there is no birth, no death, no appearing, no disappearing. It's like one complete snapshot.

So, from one perspective, cause and effect are nonstop. From another perspective, there's no cause and effect. There is just what is.

Q: Is what you've been saying the same as the idea of personal karma?
A: Personal karma is never strictly personal karma. The primary cause may be personal, but conditions go beyond just one person. The German philosopher Schopenhauer made an interesting statement when he was in his sixties. It goes something like this: When you look back at things that have gone on in your life, you can see that they were a marvelous dream, but you can also see within the dream that each and every person has their own dream.

Think about how expansive that becomes, your dream, and each person in the dream having a dream, and those dreams include other dreams. The idea of the dream in which each person in the dream has a dream is similar to imagery found in the Hua-Yen Sutra. The sutra says: "If you want to understand all the Buddhas, you should view the nature of the universe as being made by mind alone." The idea that within my dream every character has their own dream evokes the image of vast, vast mind.

But, if you perceive momentariness, you perceive this moment as "unborn." For example, if someone you care about has died, you can have an experience of remembering that person in a situation where you were in intimate contact, and you feel a moment of timelessness. In that sense, the person is still with you. But, if you can't also open yourself to the intense pain of loss within the sphere of your particular "dream" world, then trying to re-capture that eternal moment becomes a denial of that loss. You have to see both. This is a very important point in terms of not ignoring cause and effect.

Similarly, when you watch a river flowing, it's flowing, flowing, flowing, nonstop. The water that is here now almost instantaneously is gone. It's like the kong-an about Joju. He and another Zen Master were having an interchange. His companion said, "Does a baby have mind consciousness?" Joju says, "Like a ball thrown on swift-flowing water." When a ball is thrown on swift-flowing water it's gone! That's impermanence. Transiency. The Diamond Sutra says it's like a dewdrop, very quickly evaporated. At the same time, if you were to take one moment's worth of an aerial view of that river, it's complete. One complete moment like one frame in a film strip. That's birthlessness. This is not just poetry! It's not just a good idea or image. It's living your life from the poetic, not from intellectualization.

Q: I remember a saying in reference to Zen that it is a teaching outside the sutras not dependent on words or speech, yet still, in study groups here, we study sutras. What is the distinction between Zen practice and Mahayana study of sutras, chanting, and the other forms?
A: The form doesn't make the difference. You could, for example, read the sutra, chant the sutra and study the sutra, and have it be Zen practice. You could chant the Buddha's name as they do in the Pure Land sect of Buddhism, and still have it be Zen practice. You could chant some mantras,

as they do in the Tantric practices, and still it can be Zen practice. You could do breathing exercises and bowing exercises, and still it can be Zen practice. One of the key differences has to do with faith.

Karma is the equivalent of God's will in a god-oriented religion. This is the law of cause and effect that says, if you purify yourself and do good actions through the practices of various paramitas (giving, discipline, energy, patience, meditation, wisdom) and keep the precepts, then you will become Buddha. Mahayana sutras say everyone has the Buddha nature. But this is understood as everyone having the *seed* of Buddha nature, or the potential of Buddha nature. If you practice making good causes, good causes, good causes, good causes, gradually you will refine yourself. It's something like refining gold and getting rid of all the impurities until you are finally shining! The basic teaching of karma instills the faith that if one practices over eon, and eon, and eon, and eon, and lifetimes, and lifetimes, and lifetimes, and lifetimes, one will gradually go through all the stages of the bodhisattva and ultimately attain Buddhahood.

The teaching "outside the sutras" is a reference to a statement by Bodhidharma. The teaching of cause and effect, holiness, and gradually purifying oneself, was very strong in Southern China in 500 AD when Bodhidharma arrived. The emperor at that time asked Bodhidharma, "I have built many temples, many pagodas, supported many monks and many nuns; what is the merit I have earned?" Bodhidharma answered, "None!" That was a radical turning of the tables! The teachings at that time said: Do good works and you'll earn merit, and if you keep it up, eventually you will become Buddha because you have nourished the Buddha seed, the Buddha potentiality.

But, Bodhidharma proclaimed there was no merit in that. The emperor was shocked. He said to Bodhidharma, "What is the highest meaning of the holy truths?" and Bodhidharma said, "Emptiness, no holiness." The emperor then said, "Who is this standing before me?" Bodhidharma said, "Don't know."

That's radical Zen teaching. The point is, there are two views of faith. The Mahayana view of faith is: I believe I have the potentiality of Buddhahood; so I should practice, and gradually, gradually, gradually refine myself until I become Buddha. This is a "betterment campaign" which is not bad. It's better to do something good than something bad! The attitude of faith expressed here is one of a gradual "heading toward something" which is idealized in the future. But, the more you try to get toward something in the future, in a certain sense the farther away it gets. That's okay if it's pushed to its extreme, because if it gets totally away, then you realize it isn't the goal but each step on the journey that's important. At that point, your faith flips over to a more radical kind of faith, which is Zen practice.

The radical attitude of faith in Zen practice is that *from the beginning* you are *already* Buddha. This is why you see such statements in Zen literature as: Without cultivation you are already Buddha. If you can accept that kind of faith, have a moment of that kind of faith, that moment is called *giving rise to the enlightened mind.* Within that moment of faith there is no separation. Each step of the journey is complete just as it is. The basic idea in Zen faith is: *Already complete.*

The interaction between teacher and student in Zen practice is mind to mind. The goal is to effect some moment of just seeing, just being, where there is no separation between subject and object, inside and outside. Mahayana Buddhism is a more gradual process. For example, in Pure Land practice, the idea behind the chanting of the name of the Buddha over and over is that you will connect with the power of the great vows of Amita Buddha, and you will be taken to his paradise and there achieve great happiness and enlightenment. However, you'll find some teachers even within the Pure Land traditions who sound like Zen teachers. These teachers will say, similarly to a Zen Master: This very moment, this very mind before thought, is already the Pure Land. That's a different kind of faith than imagining a paradise somewhere that is going to be your salvation. Also, in Zen, "Question" is a part of faith. For example, to sincerely recognize that along with the faith already one is complete, there is a doubt experientially about what that really means. That is faith and question interfused.

Q: That reminds me of the story in the Bible about Job, who goes through terrible misfortunes, and physical agonies, yet never loses his faith in God. But, he kept asking: WHY is this happening to me?

A: Stephen Mitchell who edited Zen Master Seung Sahn's book, *Dropping Ashes on the Buddha*, recently did a translation of the Book of Job, and a lot of people are raving about it. He probably picked the Book of Job because it has that flavor of faith/doubt. That's very important. The faith to doubt. Sometimes the doubt side gets strong; sometimes the faith side gets strong, but if they are both there, the question becomes more and more profound. That may occur because basically the essence of our life is ungraspable. "What is it?" So, if you think you have it, still you don't have it! There's always some questioning aspect occurring because it is ungraspable. "What is it?"

Of course when someone is struggling with practice, there are all kinds of emotionally based and personal kinds of questions that also come up. Practice is not necessarily going to eliminate those things so much as it may help you to find a more meaningful orientation toward emotions and personal issues. At the beginning someone may think that practice will eliminate those things, and sometimes for a while it appears as though they have been eliminated. But, in fact, they resurrect themselves according to the particular tendencies you are still carrying. That's all grist for the mill.

Shallow/Deep

Zen Master Un Mun and Renunciation

႟

(Hitting the table with his Zen stick)

Look and listen. The red tongue of the
Zen patriarchs has a bone.

(Hitting the table)

Look and listen. The red tongue of the
Zen patriarchs has no bone.

(Hitting the table)

Tongue with a bone; tongue with no bone.
Which one is a mistake?

KATZ!!!

Last weekend we all sat a silent retreat.
This weekend there is non-stop talking at the Zen Center.

For those of you who have never seen this kind of Zen theater before,
strictly speaking the dharma speech is now complete!

A while ago we decided that we should get together some kind of
memorial service to be used upon the death of a family member of a student,
or when a member of our sangha dies. We agreed that we would get the
Korean memorial service transcribed, and we got someone who could translate the original Chinese characters. When it came back to us, it was many,
many, many pages long. I asked the translator—a Korean monk named Do
Kwan Sunim—what we could cut so American students would not feel over-
whelmed by its lengthiness. He said, "Well, one time when I was in Korea
with Zen Master Seung Sahn, our teacher, it was during the time of the
memorial service for his teacher, Ko Bong Sunim. They were in Hwa Gae
Sah temple in Seoul, which was the temple that Ko Bong Sunim was the
Zen Master of when he was alive. They went into the chanting hall to have
the memorial service for the Master, and Zen Master Seung Sahn took the

chugpi and hit it three times. All the monks bowed. He then said, 'The memorial service for Great Zen Master Ko Bong Sunim is now complete.'"

Tonight I want to talk about Un Mun Zen Master. A monk came to Un Mun and said, "It's said that when one's parents won't give permission to leave home, then one should not leave home." To leave home, in this context, means to become a monk or to renounce the world. The monk asked Un Mun, "What then should one do to leave home?" And Un Mun said, "Shallow." The monk said, "I don't understand." And Un Mun said, "Deep."

Before I go further into the story I'd like to say a little bit more about Un Mun's style of teaching. Un Mun lived in China around 800-900 AD. He was one of the great, great Zen Masters in China during that period. The Un Mun school rose up around him and lasted for several generations. He is famous for a number of things, but two things stand out in his style.

One was his crude style of answer, and the other was the style of answer that was sometimes called Un Mun's one-word Zen or Un Mun's short-answer Zen.

An example of his crude, cutting style would be his comment on the scriptural reference on Buddha's birth. Buddha sprang from his mother's right side (he didn't have a normal birth), took seven steps in each direction, and then raised up one finger to the heaven and pointed one finger of the other hand down to the ground, and proclaimed, "Above the heavens and below the earth, I alone am the most holy." Un Mun, commenting on that piece of business said, "If I had been there at that time, I would have taken a stick and hit him and killed him. Then the whole world would be at peace."

In a Buddhist country, to talk about hitting the Buddha and killing him with a stick is pretty rough speech!

Another example of Un Mun's rough style is recounted in the story of his first meeting with his future successor, Dong Sahn. Un Mun said, "Where are you coming from?" The question has a hook in it; it's a Zen question. It can be related to from a Zen viewpoint or from an ordinary standpoint. Dong Sahn said, "From Sah Do Temple, Master." Un Mun said, "Oh, and where did you sit the summer retreat last year?" "Oh, at Bo Ja Temple in Hoe Nam, Master." "And, on what day did you leave there?" "Oh, on the twenty-fifth day of August, Master." Un Mun said, "I give you sixty blows with my stick!" Dong Sahn was taken aback, and went away and sat up all night wondering: Where was my mistake? I answered all of his questions, and yet he said, "I'll give you sixty blows with my stick." So, Dong Sahn came back the next day, bowed to Un Mun, and said, "Master, yesterday you gave me sixty blows with your stick. But I don't understand. Where is my mistake?" Un Mun said, "You rice bag, why have you been prowling around Kang Soe and Hoe Nam?" All of a sudden Dong Sahn had an enlightenment experience. (Rice bag in Chinese means all you are good for is eating rice, in other words, you're good for nothing.)

Un Mun's short-answer style is a little different, and sometimes they overlap. For example, many of them are one-word answers. A monk once asked Un Mun, "What is Buddha?" Un Mun said, "Shit stick." That is both one-word answer and crude style. Another time someone asked Un Mun, "What is it that goes beyond the Buddha and the patriarchs?" Un Mun said, "Cake." Another monk asked Un Mun, "What is my original face?" Un Mun said, "Sightseeing amongst the mountains and valleys." On another occasion someone asked Un Mun, "When the chick is pecking out, and the hen is pecking in, how is it?" Un Mun said, "Echo." So, Un Mun always adjusted his answer to his student's mind at the time even though the answer didn't make logical sense. With his short answers, he awakened many students.

Un Mun's own story is interesting. He decided he would practice Zen after being a monk and studying for some time in a formal style with which he was not satisfied. He made a pilgrimage to a mountain where Zen Master Muk Ju was living as a hermit. When Muk Ju saw Un Mun coming, he closed the door to his hut. When Un Mun knocked on the door, Muk Ju said roughly, "Who is it?" "It's me, Un Mun." "What do you want?" "I still am not clear about this matter of myself. Please give me some teaching." So Muk Ju opened the door and then slammed the door. This went on for three days. Same question, same answer. On the third day, before Muk Ju could close the door, Un Mun stuck his leg in the doorway as if he was going to force his way in, and Muk Ju closed the door. Some translations say that Un Mun's leg was broken, and others say he hurt his leg, but at that moment of closing the door, he had an awakening. Then Muk Ju said to him, "You should now go and study with Zen Master Soel Bong." Un Mun made the journey to Soel Bong's temple. When he got to the village at the foot of the mountain of the temple, he met another monk and asked him, "Venerable friend, will you be climbing the mountain to Soel Bong's temple?" "Yes," was the reply. Un Mun said, "I want you to give a message to the Zen Master, but don't say it came from me, say it as though this is your message. When you enter the hall and the Zen Master comes in, at that time you should stand in front of him, clasp your hands, and say to him, 'Master, when will you take the yoke off your neck?' Say this to him and see what he says. The monk climbed the mountain, entered the hall; Soel Bong came in and the monk said, "Master, when will you take the yoke off your neck?" Soel Bong immediately came down from the podium, grabbed the monk, shook him, and said, "Speak, speak!!!" The monk did not know what to say at that point, so Soel Bong said, "These words are not yours, whose are they?" "Mine," said the monk. Soel Bong said, "Attendant, bring some rope and big sticks." At this point the monk admitted that these words were not his. "These words are the words of a monk that I met in the village." Soel Bong said, "Go to the village and greet the Master of five hundred monks."

Un Mun came up the hill and submitted himself to Soel Bong's teaching. He stayed with the Master for several years, and Soel Bong finally gave him dharma transmission. Un Mun became a Zen Master.

Un Mun did not teach right away. He tried to remain anonymous and traveled to many temples in China. Finally he came to the temple of Lingshu, where Zen Master Rumin was the abbot. Un Mun didn't know at that time that he had come to the temple in fulfillment of a prophecy. In the twenty or thirty years that Rumin had been abbot of this temple, he had never appointed a head monk. In Zen temples there is a Zen Master and a head monk. The head monk always presides over the retreat hall where the monks sit meditation for ninety days. The head monk is a very important figure in the temple, but this Zen Master had never appointed one. Every so often he would make some cryptic remark such as "Oh, now the head monk is being born," or, "The head monk is tending cattle," or "Now the head monk is traveling on foot." Then one day, all of a sudden, he told his attendant, "Go ring the temple bell, the head monk has now come." Just then Un Mun came to the first gate of the temple. Un Mun was given the head monk's seat in the hall. When Rumin died, Un Mun became Zen Master of that temple. This is where the stories of Un Mun's one-word Zen began.

Returning to the story of the monk who asked Un Mun, "If your parents do not give permission, one should not leave home. What, then, should one do?" Un Mun said, "Shallow." The monk, confused, said, "I don't understand." Un Mun said, "Deep." Here is Un Mun's one-word style of Zen. The question that the monk asks has something to do with becoming a monk as well as with the spirit of renunciation, or what he calls "leaving home." At the core of any spiritual practice is this matter of renunciation. If there's no renunciation or spirit of renunciation then meditation practice by itself is not complete meditation practice. Being a monk is just a job like any other job. A policeman puts on a police uniform; a fireman puts on a fireman's uniform; and a monk puts on a monk's uniform. It is just a job. The spirit of renunciation may or may not be there.

Connected with this notion of renunciation, there is the idea of non-attachment. Non-attachment and renunciation are two words for the same kind of attitude. The monk's question to Un Mun, of course, is about social protocol. In China at that time, and perhaps still today, filial piety and honoring one's parents is a central issue. The notion of your parents not giving permission for you to leave home is really a question of how to do what you want to do when it is not in accordance with the rules of the social structure. And, of course, Un Mun replies very quickly, "Shallow." As long as we operate on the level of thinking about things in terms of appropriateness or inappropriateness or right or wrong, then we operate on a shallow level. But, the monk gets perplexed and says he does not understand. Un Mun then replies, "Deep." This not understanding is at that moment deep and deeply penetrating of this whole matter of non-attachment and renunciation. Essentially, renunciation is not about giving up anything in an external sense. It's really about letting go of rigid mind structures that we all create for ourselves—holding onto ideas, opinions, and concepts, making them into something very solid and giving them an existence of their own. When we arrive at "don't know" or "Don't Understand," at that moment we take a step beyond all of that. Suzuki Roshi in his book *Zen Mind, Beginner's Mind*, talks about non-attachment and quotes from Japanese Zen Master Dogen Zenji: "That we like flowers and we don't like weeds is also Buddha's activity." Suzuki Roshi says that in love there should be hate, and in hate there should be love. What he means by that is that in love there should be non-attachment, and in not liking something (or hate) there should be acceptance of what is. Essentially, the spirit of renunciation is the acceptance of what is. Zen meditation practice is primarily concerned with seeing things as they are and letting things be as they are. Letting things come and go and clearly seeing them. Thus, the spirit of not-knowing or not understanding is to renounce or let go of all ideas and judgments and manipulation of what is. Dogen further said, "Even though we love flowers, still they will fall, and even though we don't like weeds, still they will grow up." That is, whatever we think is beautiful and wonderful is so in this moment, but in some sense it will also fall or pass. To be able to keep centered and live with that fact is true non-attachment. Those things which we don't like will still emerge, and to be with that without trying to fight it or get rid of it, and to see the truth in that, that is true renunciation, or truly "leaving home." To leave home means to let go of that small-minded attitude.

In Buddhist practice, when someone takes the five precepts they are given a cloth called the kasa, which is a small version of the original monk's robe in India. It has different strips of cloth sewn into it. At that time in India, the monks used discarded pieces of cloth the people gave them, which they sewed together and made a large robe to wrap themselves in. These strips in the kasa are representative of those pieces of cloth. The kasa has four points and a middle point. This signifies all the directions, or carrying the entire world. So, when the monk puts on his patchwork robe, he is saying in essence that he has wrapped himself in the entire world, and the entire world has become his family. Regardless of what our outside job is, still our inner job is represented by this: Our spirit of compassion, which comes out of seeing things as they are and accepting things as they come and go, should gradually extend itself to the entire world.

(Hits table three times with Zen stick)

Are there any questions?
Q: How do the precepts relate to Zen?
A: In the five precepts ceremony, there is a line that says "Know when

the precepts are open, and when they are closed; when to keep them, and when to break them." That is the Zen spirit of precepts, which is different from the more Orthodox approach or spirit of precepts. In some forms of Buddhism, you should never break the precepts in your behavior. In other forms of Buddhism, it's said that even if you think in your mind of breaking the precepts, then you have already broken them. A monk asked Un Mun, "What is Buddhism?" Un Mun said, "Wide." The precepts can also become a yoke around one's neck. The essential precept is compassionate activity based on a perception that everyone is part of one family. Everyone has something in common or shared. Any other precept should come out of that spirit. If it violates that spirit then it violates the fundamental precept. Sometimes a Zen Master may do outrageous things. The question is, "For whom?" Is it for himself or as a teaching device?

Q: Why take the precepts at all if you know that when you take them you are taking them in the spirit of sometimes keeping them and sometimes breaking them. It seems revisionist or weak-kneed, and apologetic to say "we are doing this, but we are doing it in the spirit of compassion." It doesn't seem compelling to me.

A: I wonder where you heard an apology there.

Q: To the world at large, maybe.

A: Have you now spoken for the world at large?

Q: I listen for it.

A: Yes, but through what kind of filter? The precepts have become a dilemma for you and cannot be related to strictly in a rational, straightforward manner. So the precepts themselves become a kong-an for you. In some traditions, each precept is used as a kong-an. If you say you are not going to lie, then you should firmly hold on to that. But if telling the truth results in the loss of a life, then at that moment telling a lie is the truth. A simplistic example would be: You are walking in the woods and a rabbit comes running by followed by two hunters. You have already taken the precepts. The first precept says "Don't take life." That also means, don't make yourself a party to taking any life. The two hunters did not see which way the rabbit ran. They ask you, "Did you see a rabbit? Which way did he go?" If you tell them which way, you keep the precept of truthfulness, but if they kill the rabbit, then you violate the precept of not taking life. Which one is correct?

Q: That's splitting hairs!! *(Laughter)*

A: The precepts are a guide or a road map. When Buddha was about to die, the monks asked him, "When you're gone, who will be our guide?" He said, "The precepts will be your guide." They point. Depending on how much you need that particular pointer, and in what way you need that pointer, and according to the situation, the time, the place, and the particular relationship of that moment, the precepts will be a guide. There is no absolute right or wrong from the Buddhist standpoint. Right and wrong are always based on time, place, and situation. What is right for one kind of place is wrong for another kind of place. If you can return to your original mind before thinking, then you can respond clearly to what is in front of you, and out of that responsiveness comes the appropriate keeping of precepts. Taking them is very important. That is a formalization of your commitment and an encouragement to practice.

There are two lines in the precepts ceremony that have made an impression on me and stay with me. One says, "How good it is, the Robe of Liberation, a robe of highest merit." The second talks about the merit of the homeless life outweighing the merit of filling three thousand worlds with stupas of the purest gold.

So, what does "the Robe of Liberation" mean? In a sense, it means that when you take the precepts you are wrapping yourself in Buddha's mind. When someone asked him "After you die, who will be our guide?" he said, "Let the precepts act as your guide." So, the precepts are, in a sense, the Robe of Liberation and function as our guide.

The question is: If this is the Robe of Liberation, what are we liberating ourselves from on the one hand, and what are we liberating ourselves to have the freedom to do, on the other hand?

The precepts act as a guide toward not holding anything, checking anything, attaching to anything; not making anything. Just total freedom. That's the robe of liberation. To be liberated from our own narrow opinions, concepts, our own system of ordering the world as we think it should be. To be liberated from that. That is to clothe ourselves in Buddha's robe. At that moment, then, we can be free to be in the world.

Why take any particular action? Is it "for me" or for something greater than me? For what? How does my action connect with the particular situation at that time? That is an important point. Is it compassion in some way, or is it self-centered? Governing our actions by compassion is the root of the precepts.

The intention of non-killing means to have some kind of positive valuation of everything. You could say all life, but actually it extends beyond all life. Zen Master Seung Sahn sometimes tells the story of a Zen Master who yells at his student who is spilling water on the ground. The Zen Master yells, "Why are you killing water?" The student is not respecting the value of water. He is throwing it away. So, a positive attitude towards the value of each and every existence IS the direction of the non-killing precept: Do not kill, and cherish all life.

Passing the Summer There

Zen As Ordinariness

(Hitting the table with his Zen stick)

If you can make that special, then you're already dwelling in one of the hell realms for a long time.

(Hitting the table)

If you say that that is not special, then you're trapped in a realm of dull, dark metal.

(Hitting the table)

Special, not special. How will you resolve that paradox?

KATZ!!!

Go outside and ask the snowflakes. They'll give you a much better answer than I.

Let me begin by telling three short Zen stories. The first story is about Zen Master Joju. One day, Joju and a friend decided to have a contest. The purpose of this contest was to lose, not to win. The winner, that is the loser, was to supply some fruit as a prize. They began. Joju said, "I'm a donkey." His friend said, "I am the donkey's behind." Joju said, "I am the donkey's dung." Then his friend said, "I am a worm in the donkey's dung." Joju said, "Oh, what are you doing there?" His friend replied, "I'm passing the summer there." Joju said, "You go get the fruit!"

"Passing the summer" has a special meaning. In many of the old Zen stories one monk will ask another, "Where did you pass the winter last year? Where did you pass the summer last year?" In China, at that time, and in Korea today, there are two ninety-day retreats held each year: one in the winter and one in the summer. So, "Where did you pass the summer last year?" means "Where did you sit the summer retreat?"

Joju's friend said, "I'm a worm in the donkey's dung," and went on to say that he was sitting the summer retreat there! That is a very special kind of retreat! Any of you who have sat a retreat, or even just sat Zen on a regular basis day in and day out, know that in the course of sitting you find yourself in many, many unusual places. Within the course of a week's retreat, for example, certainly you may find yourself sitting the retreat as a worm in the donkey's dung, or in any number of other places!

The second story is also about Joju. A monk asked Joju, "What is the Buddha?" Joju answered, "The one in the hall." The monk said, "The one in the hall is only a statue, only a lump of clay or dirt." Joju said, "That's so, that's so." The monk said, "So then, what is the Buddha?" Joju said, "The one in the hall." The commentary on this little story says, "Even the statue of someone who lived a couple of thousand years ago is the Buddha. What isn't the Buddha? Even the Buddha is the Buddha."

The third story is about Joju's teacher, Nam Cheon. One time, Nam Cheon and two monks were on a pilgrimage. While on the road one day, they met an old woman. "Where do you live?" they asked her. She said, "Right here, in this tea house. Come in and have some tea with me." Nam Cheon and the other monks went in and sat down. The old woman prepared a pot of tea and placed it on a table with three cups. She said, "Let the one who has god-like power drink the tea." They all looked at each other, and no one said anything. No one drank the tea. Finally, the old woman said, "Let this silly old woman show you the full extent of HER power." And she quickly drank up the tea and left.

I want to talk tonight about the notion of Zen as ordinariness. Ordinariness is stressed very much in the teachings of the old Zen Masters and their successors.

Zen Master Seung Sahn, the founder of our school, says this repeatedly: "Zen is not special, Zen is not special." There is a couplet in a poem by Layman P'ang that has become well known in Zen: "Supernatural power and marvelous activity. Drawing water, and chopping firewood." And, in another poem of his he says, "Neither a saint nor a sage. Just an ordinary man who has done his work." Over and over again, Zen as ordinariness is found in the teachings of those old Masters.

One of the most well-known examples of this teaching style is in a dialogue between Joju and Nam Cheon. At the time of the story, Joju was a student of Nam Cheon. It is in a collection of Zen kong-ans (literally, a public record) called the *Mu Mun Kwan*. This case title is usually translated "Ordinary Mind is the Way" or "Everyday Mind is the Way [or the Path]." Joju asked Nam Cheon, "What is the true way?" Nam Cheon said, "Everyday mind is the true way." "Should I try to keep it or not?" Joju asked. Nam Cheon said, "If you try to keep it, you are already mistaken." Then Joju said, "If I don't try to keep it, how can I understand the true way?" Nam Cheon said, "The true way is not dependent on understanding or not understanding. Understanding is illusion. Not understanding is blankness. When you completely attain the true way of not thinking, it is like space. Clear and void. So, why do you make right and wrong?" At this, Joju suddenly got enlightenment.

There is a poem at the end of the case:

> *Flowers in springtime; moon in autumn,*
> *Cool breezes in summer; snow in winter.*
> *If you don't make anything in your mind,*
> *Then, for you, it's a good season.*

I have three different translations of this case with me. Not knowing Chinese myself, it's always interesting to look at the way different people translate the same Chinese story. The nuances of it in one translation are different from the nuances of another translation. And if you look at each one, sometimes you can get a fuller experience of what the case is indicating.

Beginning with the case title, the first translation is, "The NORMAL is the Way," with normal all capitalized. The second translation is, "Ordinary Mind is the Tao." (Tao has become a common word in English usage. Originally, in Chinese, Tao means the "Way" and is a reference to some Absolute. So, simultaneously it's the Way and has an Absolute aspect.) The third translation is, "Ordinary Mind is the Way." The translation used in our Kwan Um School of Zen is, "Everyday Mind is the Way."

I looked up the word "ordinary" because I was curious to see what the dictionary had to say. One of the meanings of "ordinary" is something that is recurrent and perpetual. It also had synonyms like normal, commonplace, mundane. Now, one of the biggest disturbances of our time, I think, is a desire to be special. Most of us want to be special. We want to feel that we do something that is special. In and of itself, this might not be a big problem. But there are a lot of us who fear being ordinary or not special. And this fear becomes a certain burdensomeness for us.

I share office space with a number of colleagues, and we have a little kitchen there. Sometimes we go into the kitchen in between appointments to have a cup of tea or to eat something. The other night, I went to the kitchen and ran into one of my colleagues. He was standing at the sink washing dishes. He said to me, "This is my meditation." Now this guy does not practice meditation in the formal sense; it's not his thing. But, he said, "This is my meditation. It's very simple, it's very soothing. I see the result." At that moment he has a taste of clarity. Zen Master Seung Sahn wrote a poem which is in his book, *Dropping Ashes on the Buddha*. Two lines from the poem are:

> *After so much suffering in Nirvana Castles*
> *What a joy to fall back into this world.*

Nirvana literally means to extinguish or blow out, as in to blow out a candle. The connotation is: to extinguish all suffering is nirvana. But, here the poem says after so much suffering in nirvana castles, the realm of nirvana is a very purified realm. The air is very pure there—too pure in fact. For example, when my eldest daughter was selecting colleges, she chose a small, exclusive school in the hills of Massachusetts far away from urban life and its diversity. However, some months after her immersion there, she began to write poetry that expressed a longing for the liveliness of New York City street noises and multi-coloredness. So, after so much suffering in nirvana castles, what a joy to fall back into *this* world. This stands the whole business of suffering and freedom on its head.

Anyway, getting back to Joju and Nam Cheon's story here, in our translation it says "Everyday Mind is the Way." The connotation here is something which is recurrent, and which is perpetual. It is the aspect of momentariness in Zen and Buddhism. The absolute realm is just this moment, completely cut off from any concepts of before and after, coming and going, good and bad, inside and outside, subject and object, and any other kind of opposites that we make. The concept of *momentariness* is that essentially the absolute nature of the universe is a pulsating expression of vivid energy flashing into existence. This pulsating energy is in everything. So, there is nothing special about it. Everyday mind means being in the absolute moment, whether it is getting up in the morning, or lying down in the evening, or eating breakfast, or washing the dishes, or having a conversation with someone. The absolute nature of the universe is in whatever we are doing moment by moment by moment. It is not special. It is what we are already engaged in, and what we are already a part of.

In this sense, I personally like the translation "Everyday Mind is the Way" a little better than "The Normal is the Way" or even "Ordinary Mind is the Tao." If you say "ordinary" then you think of "extraordinary," if you think of "normal" then you think of "abnormal." If you think of "everyday," do you think of holiday? I'm not sure. The dialogue between Joju and Nam Cheon is really the concern of a student. "How should I practice?" And Joju, of course, is very sincere in looking for an answer. So, he's already caught heading in the direction of specialness. What is the true way? As if he didn't already know or as if he hadn't already encountered it. Nam Cheon said, "Everyday Mind is the true way." Now, if Joju had gotten it at that moment, the rest of the dialogue would have been unnecessary. But it's very difficult to just accept that *just as it is.* Everyday mind is IT! There is nothing else beyond that. Zen practice is a path, or ongoing way of being and existing in relationship with everything that surrounds us. The dependence is not on some external deity, but is rather on ourselves walking this path or finding this way in an ongoing practice. A way of being and a way of doing. Nam Cheon said, "Everyday mind is the Way." Then Joju asked, "Should I try to keep it?" Already he wants to do something with that! We all have experienced this in practice. We cannot believe that this simple act of just sitting or just standing up, or just chanting the sutra, or whatever it is we're doing IS enough. So, we begin to try to *do* something with it to get something else out of it. As soon as that state of mind appears, we are very far away from the true way.

This is why Nam Cheon said, "If you try to do something with it, you're already mistaken." You have already missed it at that point. Then, of course, with the sincerity of a really serious student, Joju says, "If I don't try, then how can I understand the true way?" This is very skillful teaching. Step by step, like a wise old Grandmother, Nam Cheon just cuts away Joju's trying to make something. One of these translations is by Aitken Roshi with his commentary on the case. Aitken Roshi says:

> When I read this case years ago, I thought that it was a little conceptual. And I wondered, how is Joju ever going to get enlightenment out of this kind of dialogue? Nam Cheon should give him some teaching like "three pounds of flax" or "dry shit on a stick" or "the cypress tree in the garden." With that you can get shocked into enlightenment. But here, I used to think, how is he going to get enlightenment out of this? It's too conversational.

When Joju asked, "How should I understand it?" Nam Cheon answered, "Your understanding is a complete illusion, and not understanding is just a blank. When you completely attain the true way of not thinking, it's like space. Clear and open. Nothing to grab hold of." This does not mean it's space. It is *like* space. Space has certain qualities to it. To say it's *like* space means that this mind has certain qualities like that: it has openness and is clear. You can't grab empty space. So when you attain the way of no thinking, it's like space: clear and open. Nam Cheon asked Joju, "Why then do you make right and wrong?" (Some of these translations say: "Why do you affirm or deny?") At that Joju got enlightenment. Aitken Roshi must have been very surprised.

The translations of the poem are interesting too. This one says:

> *Spring comes with flowers; autumn with the moon.*
> *Summer with breeze; winter with snow.*
> *When idle concerns don't hang in your mind,*
> *That is your best season.*

Another one says:

In spring there are a hundred flowers;
In autumn there is the moon.
In summer there are cool breezes;
In winter there is snow.
If no idle matters hang on your mind,
Then it is a good season in the human world.

They both have the phrase, "If idle matters don't hang in your mind."
The third translation is slightly different:

The spring flowers; the moon in autumn,
The cool breezes of summer; the winter snow.
If idle concerns do not cloud the mind,
This is man's happiest season.

Zen Master Seung Sahn's translation is not as "poetic" as the others:

Flowers in springtime; moon in autumn,
Cool breezes in summer; snow in winter.
If you don't make anything in your mind,
Then, for you, it's a good season.

That's an interesting phrase: "If you don't *make* anything in your mind,"
rather than, "If idle concerns don't cloud the mind." If you don't *make* anything in your mind, then for you it's a good season.

I want to talk a little more about practice in the formal sense and
what's being stressed here. In the years that I've been practicing, whenever
my mind gets too grasping and too greedy towards achieving something in
particular, there are two short chapters in *Dropping Ashes on the Buddha*,
Zen Master Seung Sahn's first book, that I read. One of them is called "The
Moon of Clear Mind," and the other is called "Can You See Your Eyes?" I
recommend these chapters to anyone who has the tendency to want to get
something out of their practice. I "don't know" anyone who doesn't have
that tendency! They are also helpful if you begin to get stale or practice
becomes dry, or you feel like you're travelling in a desert.

I'll just paraphrase these two teachings, which are dialogues between
students and Zen Master Seung Sahn. In "The Moon of Clear Mind," a
student asks, "How can I get past verbalizing the question 'What am I?'"
Zen Master Seung Sahn said, "You want the question to grow. That's very
bad. That is attachment thinking." That's a phrase he uses quite often; sometimes he uses non-attachment thinking. Attachment thinking and non-attachment thinking are not different; they are both thinking. So, attachment
thinking means you are attached to getting somewhere in your practice. He

goes on to say, "It's not important for the question to grow. What is important is the experience of clear mind. If you get that even for a short time then all the rest of the time you may be thinking. That is only your karma. So, even if you get this clear mind for one moment, that's one moment of enlightenment. The rest of the time, that is just your karma coming and going, coming and going. And you should not try to make this clear mind grow; nor should you try to get rid of your karmic thinking. Little by little clear mind will grow on its own, and your karma will gradually come down, come down, come down." Then he makes an analogy which is classical: "The clear mind is the full moon. Sometimes clouds come in front of the moon, but the moon is still there. Sometimes the clouds go away from in front of the moon, and then the moon is shining brightly. Your original clear mind is like that. So don't worry about original clear mind. Clear mind is always there. Thinking is coming; thinking is going. Just don't be attached to the coming and going."

This last point is very important: Let your thinking come and go without in any way being attached to it. That is non-attachment thinking. Then you will be able to use your thinking clearly. In Zen we talk about getting rid of your karma. This does not mean escaping your karma; it means being able to find your correct relationship to your own particular tendencies. If you are attached to certain aspects and repulsed by other aspects, then you cannot have a clear relationship with your own capabilities and capacities. But if you can just be in relationship, coming and going, coming and going, then everything falls into its proper place.

The second chapter is called "Can You See Your Eyes?" In this, a student asks about the difference between two kinds of Zen that are taught in Japan—shikantaza which means just to sit, and kong-an Zen, or practicing with a question. Zen Master Seung Sahn says that in the Soto school they use breathing to cut off thinking and become clear mind. And in the Rinzai school they use the kong-an to cut off thinking and become clear mind. These are essentially two doors into the same room. The essence of both is to let go of attachment thinking and just become clear mind. Then the student asks, "Sometimes you hear of people working with their kong-an for years, and struggling with it and struggling with it. And then finally they give up the struggle. Are you saying that sometimes it's not necessary to struggle with the kong-an?" Zen Master Seung Sahn responds by saying, "If you are using the kong-an to get enlightenment, then that's the wrong approach to using the kong-an. To keep the great question, 'What am I?' means to let go of thinking and become original empty mind. So keeping the question itself is already enlightenment. You're already enlightened but you "don't know" it." That's our situation. So, after a lot of practicing, one day maybe you'll have an experience, and you say, "Oh, this is enlightenment," but it's not something that you didn't already have!

I heard this story one time of Soen Roshi, a well-known Japanese Zen Master and poet who did some teaching in the United States. He had a reputation for being a colorful, eccentric figure. While in this country, Soen Roshi lived in California. He liked going to the park just to sit and observe American life. He was fascinated not just with the people but also with the trees and the birds and the various things one finds in parks. One day, he and a student were sitting in the park and Soen Roshi asked, "How do you call those black birds over there?" The student said, "Blackbird, Roshi." Soen Roshi said, "Yeah, but how do you CALL those black birds?" And the student said, "BLACKBIRD, Roshi." And Soen Roshi said, "Oh, Blackbird!!!" recognizing suddenly that this was the bird's name rather than its description. Okay? That's enlightenment! Oh! Blackbird!

Returning to the second chapter, the question is asked, "Can you see your own eyes?" Obviously, you can't see your own eyes. That doesn't mean that you don't have eyes. You can see that the floor is brown and the wall is white and this indicates that you have eyes. The fact that you hear sounds indicates that you have ears. But the eyes cannot see themselves. Similarly, you cannot understand or grasp your own mind. So, when you raise up a question like "What am I?" that means I is asking I. Can you take out something from your body and hold it in front of you and say "Oh, that's I." It's not possible. The one who is asking is I. So, in that asking, all opposites cease to be. We make opposites not only externally, but also as representations within our minds. So, to hit the world of opposites is to let go of that and enter into the experience of the absolute, moment by moment by moment. And interestingly enough even in the Soto school in Japan, the whole phrase is not just "shikantaza," just to sit, the whole phrase is something like "just to sit and hit." And "hit" here means to hit the world of opposites. Just to sit and hit the world of opposites means to become clear mind. Likewise, if you raise up the question "What am I?" the question itself hits the world of opposites, and it hits your tendency to make or objectify the self. Both of these practices aim at the same essential point. Mainly, somehow we have to find a way of not being too greedy and wanting to get somewhere that we think is more special than where we are at the moment.

There is a very wonderful teaching I'll end with that comes from Kyong Ho Sunim, a Korean Zen Master who lived in the late 1800's into the early 1900's. Kyong Ho Sunim was a reviver of the Zen tradition in Korea, and many Zen Masters came out of his tutelage. One time Kyong Ho Sunim paid a visit to a sutra study temple he'd once attended. (He was originally a scholar monk but gave up all of that.) His visit took place at the time of year when the sutra study ended and the monks went on vacation for a couple of months. So this was like a commencement day at the temple. On this day the Sutra Master got up and said, "You must all study very hard, learn Buddhism, work very hard and become like big trees from which temples are built, and become like great bowls that can hold many good things. The sutras say that water takes the form of whatever you put it in, square or round. Likewise, people become good or bad by the company they keep. So, always keep the Buddha in mind, and keep good friends. Then you can become like great trees, and huge containers of dharma." Then Kyong Ho Sunim came up to the rostrum to give his dharma speech. He was a guest and was well known all over Korea. He said, "All of you are monks, and to be a monk means to be free of petty personal attachments. So, if you want to become a great tree or container of dharma, that will prevent you from being a true teacher. Big trees have big uses, and small trees have small uses. Good and bad bowls each have their place. None are to be discarded. Keep both good and bad friends. Don't reject anyone. My only wish for you is, 'Don't give rise to conceptual thinking.'"

This is a wonderful teaching. I especially like the phrase, "Keep good and bad friends." Out of that grows the attitude of compassionate, great action. Good and bad bowls each have their own place. Don't discard anything. That's an ecological view as well: Don't make junk out of anything. See the absolute value in each and every thing that you encounter.

Kyong Ho Sunim's teaching is very much in line with all of these old Zen birds who lived in China hundreds and hundreds of years ago!

(Hitting the table)

Layman P'ang called on Zen Master Yak Sahn. When he was about to leave, Yak Sahn and ten monks escorted P'ang to the gate. Layman P'ang pointed into the air and he said, "Wonderful snowflakes, they don't fall anywhere else but here." One monk said, "Layman, where do they fall?" Layman P'ang slapped him in the face. The monk said, "Even though you're a layman, you shouldn't be that coarse!" And Layman P'ang slapped him a second time.

(Hitting the table)

Zen Master Hsueh-Tou, commenting on this case, said, "If I had been there, I would have picked up a snowball and thrown it!"

(Hitting the table)

So, how are we to understand Layman P'ang's wonderful snowflakes that don't fall anywhere else but here?

KATZ!!!

The big piles of snow in the street today are melting away to nothing. Please watch your step when you go outside.

When You Hear the Wooden Chicken Crow

The Language of Zen

ᔟ

(Hitting the table with his Zen stick)

Zen Master Ma Jo said, "This very mind is Buddha, and Buddha is this very mind."

(Hitting the table)

On another occasion, Zen Master Ma Jo said, "No mind; no Buddha."

(Hitting the table)

Ma Jo's student, Zen Master Nam Cheon, said, "Not Mind; not Buddha; not things."

Which one of these three sentences hits the mark?

KATZ!!!

Summer's heat has come a little early this year catching us all unprepared.

I would like to start by reading three short poems by Zen Master Seung Sahn from his book Bone of Space, which is a collection of his poetry. The first poem says:

One mind perceives infinite time.
One's all,
Everything's one.
To let go when hanging
Over a cliff is the act of a great man.
Winter
Proceeds north, spring enters from the south.

The second poem is:

Flowers in the spring.
In the summer, cool breezes.
Leaves in the fall,
In winter, pure snow.
Is the world throwing me away?
Am I throwing away the world?
I lie around in the dharma room.
I don't care about anything.
White clouds floating in the sky,
Clear water flowing down the mountain,
The wind through the pagoda:
I surrender my whole life to them.

And the third poem:

Looking over the southern mountain, I
Clap my hands: cumulus clouds transform
Into dog, tiger, man, Buddha, then disperse.
And to my sorrow disappear over the mountain's
Edge in a rush of wind, leaving
The sky blue, the trees green.

These three poems and my opening statements have to do with mind. Zen Masters sometimes borrowed certain Buddhist vocabulary already in China at the time Zen arose there. Within Zen there are three different languages: The language of Buddhism, the language of surprise and unconventional remarks, and the language of nature poetry. The language of philosophy found in Zen, and even in Buddhism in general, is not really philosophy in the true sense of the word. For example, there is the sutra tradition which contains different teaching styles. But the word sutra means, literally, a thread. When you read the sutras, it isn't like reading a philosophy book where a subject is expounded and organized in an academic, philosophical, and logical way. What you find in the sutras are threads of visionary ideas that point toward something. Later on, some of those ideas were taken up and organized into something that looked like philosophy. For example, one philosophical school is the Mind Only or Consciousness Only School.

You find in the sutras sayings like: "If you want to understand all the Buddhas of the past, present, and future, then you should view the nature of the universe as being created by mind alone." Ma Jo took up this teaching style and said, "Mind is Buddha; Buddha is mind." When Shakyamuni Buddha had his enlightenment experience, the traditional account says that he proclaimed, "Now I see that all things are imbued with the Buddha-nature." If mind is Buddha, that means that mind contains all things, and all things are contained in mind. We say in our practice, if you want to find the truth then look into your own mind. If you want to find your true relationship with the universe at large, then look first into your own mind, because essentially the universe is contained in your own mind. Not the mind of everyday thinking, and calculating, and conceptualizing, and discriminating. Although, ultimately, even there you can find everything.

That is a wonderful teaching. But, if you get too attached to that teaching, Ma Jo also said, "No mind; no Buddha." Don't hold onto terms like mind and Buddha because dust in the eyes will blind you. Even gold dust will blind you! So, "Mind is Buddha; Buddha is mind" is like gold dust.

Then Nam Cheon went one step further. He said, "Not mind; not Buddha; not things." Nothing! Now, sometimes people say, "Well. If everything is mind, then that means there is no objective world out here. So if a tree falls in the forest and no one is there to hear it, what is happening there?" But this teaching points toward "perceive the true nature of subject and object," not "everything is some meaningless void and nothing has any reality to it." Take away the usual idea of subject and object, or mind and consciousness and phenomena out here, and perceive the true nature of subject and object, of mind and phenomenon. In everyday language you can say that whatever is perceived by human consciousness is in some way influenced by human consciousness. Subatomic physicists do all kinds of experiments to substantiate that. And, at the same time, any phenomena that is out here also influences human consciousness. So, this is like a two-way street. What you see you influence, and what is seen influences you.

In the old teaching, it is said that the nature of relationship between subject and object or mind and phenomenon has two characteristics to it. One is called simultaneity, and the other is called interchangeability. Both point toward the interdependence of inside and outside, or subject and object. Last year at New Year's time I sent out cards to the membership. The card contained a calligraphy that said, "Full moon makes empty sky." That is the same notion. That means there is never any seeing without something being seen; there is never hearing without something being heard simultaneously. There is never smelling without something being smelled simultaneously. There is never tasting without something being tasted simultaneously. There is never mind without thinking. Those two arise simultaneously and are dependent on each other. So, full moon makes empty sky; empty sky makes full moon. That is simultaneous arising.

The other aspect is interchangeability. When we take the position of seer who is seeing something, we influence what is being seen. We make something at that time, and something is made. That means the act of seeing or experiencing is not clean and clear. We make something, and then that something has a taint on it, or a color of our discriminated egoistic view. We make something, because in some fundamental way we want the world to conform to our particular view of it, and we want the world to confirm our particular view point of it. "Isn't it the truth?"

That is a problem. We usually set up a bunch of markers for ourselves that make us feel a sense of security. We are attracted to some things and repelled by other things, and so we color what is experienced. At the same time, what then comes back to us influences our consciousness. The old Masters said that we color the world, and then the phenomena that we experience perfume our consciousness.

That is a wonderful phrase: "perfume our consciousness." When our consciousness gets perfumed our basic mind is not clear. It carries traces of things that get projected into the world over and over again. Sometimes we act as a cause, and phenomena are then the effect. Simultaneously, the effect that is out here acts as a cause and perfumes or influences our consciousness, which then acts as an effect. So, cause and effect in consciousness are interdependent and interchangeable. But we don't see that clearly, we don't see what we are making and doing all of the time. So, we wind up in a subtly deluded world and our perceptions both of ourselves and our relationships are subtly colored and deluded. That is why Zen Master Seung Sahn gave a very simple teaching: "Don't make anything; don't hold anything; don't attach to anything." But, of course, the first step to not making anything is to perceive clearly that you are making something. In the moment of perceiving that you're making something, that is not making something. You wake up to something: It is what it is. So, this is one aspect of the Mind Only view.

The other aspect is that there is a consciousness beyond the consciousness of the five senses. The mind is a sixth sense or consciousness, and there is a seventh consciousness which is ego consciousness, or our own individual point of reference. All of these seven rest on a basis of something that is referred to in the Mind Only teaching as the storehouse consciousness. The basis of all of our experiencing is rooted in some primal and wide-open storehouse consciousness that holds the seeds of all of these things probably from beginningless time. This basic consciousness either is projecting forth these seeds and coloring the world or being perfumed and influenced by the world in certain ways. But sometimes there is a sudden revolution of consciousness. Sometimes it is called "revolution of the basis of consciousness" or a "turning of the basis of consciousness." Turning or revolution means a re-turning to our original pure, clear mind before any of this other stuff arises. Suddenly, the very basis on which we have structured all of our experiences and our views revolves, or turns around, and everything is suddenly different from before. This is the Zen school teaching of Sudden Enlightenment.

A down-to-earth example of this is Gestalt perceptual drawings. These are drawings of images that are interchangeable; there are two images imbedded in one picture. One that most of you are familiar with is the picture of two faces and one urn. When you look at it in one way, you see an urn. But, if you keep looking at it, the urn switches into a silhouette of two faces, and the images flash back and forth between the dark silhouette of the faces and the white urn. There is another one that is not so commonly seen. It is a drawing of the silhouette of a young woman dressed in evening attire as if she were going to a fancy-dress ball. But looked at from a particular angle, there is the picture of what looks like an old hag with a big nose. But you can't see the old hag easily. My son, who was about 6 or 7 at the time, looked at this picture. He saw the young woman in the evening attire, and he kept looking and kept looking. "I don't see the old hag." Then, all of a sudden, "HAAAAAAAAAA—HHHAAAAAAAAA!!!" That is "revolution of the basis of consciousness." All of a sudden the whole world turns upside down and what was right there in front of your eyes but was not seen is suddenly seen.

Sometimes people get an experience like that and they laugh out loud. This is seen in some of the old Zen poems. Sometimes, though, there can be a feeling of fear that arises. This is because at the moment you perceive that everything you have structured for your security is collapsing, you may suddenly feel as if you're dying. This is why Zen Master Seung Sahn's poem says, "To let go when hanging over a cliff is the act of a great man." In that moment, when the world appears to collapse, and your view of yourself appears to collapse, there is a feeling that everything is disintegrating, or that death is occurring. But, that perception is then infused with a new way of seeing. A kind of light shines forth and you see things in a new way. The other side of the picture emerges! So at that moment you come back to life. In an old kong-an, Zen Master Tu Ja asked Zen Master Joju, "How is it when the man of great death returns to life?" This refers to that kind of experience. Suzuki Roshi in *Zen Mind, Beginner's Mind* says, "To live in the realm of Buddha Nature is to die as a small being moment by moment by moment." All those point to the same thing—the revolution of consciousness.

The notion of simultaneity and interchangeability is hinted at in Zen Master Seung Sahn's other poem where he says, "Is the world throwing me away? Am I throwing away the world?" When the world arises, I arise. If I throw away the world then the world also throws me away. "I lie around in the dharma room. I don't care about anything." This doesn't mean indifference; it means that I have no concern or burden: "The world has thrown me away, and I have thrown away the world." The poem ends, "White clouds floating in the sky, Clear water flowing down the mountain, The wind through the pagoda: I surrender my whole life to them."

We now come to his third poem:

Looking over the southern mountain, I
Clap my hands: cumulus clouds transform
Into dog, tiger, man, Buddha, then disperse.
And to my sorrow disappear over the mountain's
Edge in a rush of wind, leaving
The sky blue, the trees green.

There is some magic going on in the first part of the poem. He looks over the southern mountain and claps his hands. Then the cumulus clouds transform into dogs, tigers, man, and Buddha. That's fantastic. But, the question is: Do I know that I'm doing this or not? Do I know that I'm creating a work of magic, or is it happening and I don't realize I am making it, and then I begin to relate to all of this as if it's the god's honest truth: "Oh, it's a dog." In this poem, he is both the magician and the audience. There are meditations in Tibetan Buddhism that begin with emptiness. Then a Buddha field is visualized and some bodhisattva or Buddha is put in it. This is made on purpose. The person doing the meditation identifies with that, and then little by little the vision is deconstructed until it finally disappears back to emptiness again. So, in the poem, "I clap my hands and clouds transform into dog, tiger, man and Buddha, then disperse."

"And to my sorrow disappear over the mountain's edge in a rush of wind." Now that is an interesting sentence. We might ask, "What are you sad about? It's only clouds, only air, only nothing or emptiness." For some people, this kind of misunderstanding of emptiness teaching is used as a psychological defense mechanism. Everything is just like clouds and sky, it has no substance, therefore, no meaning or feeling. That is like saying, "I don't want to feel any painful emotions, so this philosophy sounds good to me." But here, this Zen Master says, "And to my sorrow, disappear over the mountain's edge in a rush of wind." Rush of wind clears away perfume. There is an interesting point here: As all of this disappears, I have a moment of sorrow. And just like in the transformation there is sometimes a laughing out loud, or sometimes there is a moment of fear because everything is falling away, like falling over a cliff, sometimes there also is a sense of momentary sorrow or loss. Perceiving the transiency of everything has a certain flavor to it.

There is a wonderful story about sadness and sorrow. There was a layman who was a devout student of Ma Jo's. He had a young daughter named Sul, who was even more devout than her father. When her father practiced every day, she practiced along with him, and she accompanied him on his visits to Zen Master Ma Jo.

One day, Ma Jo said to the little girl, "I want to give you a present.

And my present to you are the words, 'Kwan Seum Bosal.' You should repeat these words over and over again everywhere, and then you will find true happiness." (Not that you will create happiness, but that you will find or discover happiness.) Kwan Seum Bosal is the name of the Bodhisattva of Great Compassion. And the words "Kwan Seum Bosal" actually mean "one who perceives the sounds of the world," or "the one who hears the cries of the world." This is the aspect of universal compassion associated with listening. To have the quality of true listening is to enact the quality of great compassion. So, Ma Jo gave this mantra to Sul. When she and her father got home, he gave her a picture of the bodhisattva, who is usually pictured in female form. She put it on her wall above her altar, which contained flowers and the Lotus Sutra and some incense. And every day this little girl practiced. No matter what she was doing, she continually chanted, "Kwan Seum Bosal, Kwan Seum Bosal, Kwan Seum Bosal, Kwan Seum Bosal, Kwan Seum Bosal...." When she was working, "Kwan Seum Bosal...." When she was playing, "Kwan Seum Bosal...." When she was washing the clothes, "Kwan Seum Bosal...." She chanted so constantly that it got to the point where even when she was sleeping, still some part of her mind was repeating "Kwan Seum Bosal, Kwan Seum Bosal, Kwan Seum Bosal...." This is a very important point in terms of our practice: Our practice should not be limited to just sitting on the cushion, but, rather, carried forward into all our activities. Whether you are practicing with a mantra or you're working with a kong-an like "What am I?", carry that forward at all times. If you're just trying to perceive "What is this?", then at all times in all situations perceive clearly what is.

So, Sul practiced like this for several years, and her friends began to think she was a little crazy. But that didn't bother her. She continued with her practice. One day as she was washing clothes in the river, beating the dirt out of them with a washing stick, the big temple bell from Ma Jo's temple rang out: "Boooonnnnnnnnnng." The gong and beating of the clothes with the washing stick came together and her mind opened up. At that moment her experience was that the whole universe was dancing along with Kwan Seum Bosal, Kwan Seum Bosal, Kwan Seum Bosal! This Kwan Seum Bosal was none other than herself. But, not only that, Kwan Seum Bosal was also the sky and the clouds and the trees and the river and the ground and even the heap of dirty clothes next to her. The story says she ran home and never chanted Kwan Seum Bosal again.

But, over the next few days, her behavior began to appear very strange. She was seen having conversations with clouds and trees, and all of a sudden she would start laughing for no particular reason. Sometimes she ran at breakneck speed down the road, which wasn't the way little girls in China behaved at that time. Her father became concerned. One day he peeked in the keyhole of her room to see what she was doing. He could see the altar with the picture of Kwan Seum Bosal and the flowers and the incense, but the Lotus Sutra was not on the altar. He looked a little to the side and he saw Sul sitting facing the wall like a Zen monk, sitting on the Lotus Sutra. He burst into the room. "What are you doing?" he said harshly. "Have you gone crazy? You're sitting on the Lotus Sutra!" Sul said, "So?" He said, "These are the holy words of the Buddha. They contain the truth, and they should be treated with the greatest respect." Sul looked at him very calmly and said, "Can the truth really be contained in words, Father?" Now her father was really perplexed. "Oh, then where do you think the truth is?" She said, "I couldn't explain it to you, but you go ask Zen Master Ma Jo". The father then went to visit Ma Jo and told him everything that had happened. Then he asked Zen Master Ma Jo, "Zen Master, is my daughter crazy?" Ma Jo said,"Your daughter is not crazy, you're crazy! But, don't worry. Take this calligraphy and put it up on her wall and see what happens." The calligraphy said:

> *When you hear the wooden chicken crow in the evening,*
> *Then you will know the country where your mind is born.*
> *Outside of my house in the garden:*
> *The willow is green; the flower is red.*

Wooden chickens don't crow. Wooden chickens are wooden chickens. But if you hear a wooden chicken crow, that's quite unusual. So, we have here a special kind of energy or magic. Sometimes, at the moment when you have this sudden turning of the whole basis of your perception, it feels very unusual and magical and there is a lot of energy that bursts forth. This is like a wooden chicken crowing in the evening. Also, chickens crow in the early morning, and this one crows in the evening. So, when you hear the wooden chicken crowing in the evening, then you will know where your mind is born. You will perceive your true nature.

"Outside of my house in the garden: The willow is green; the flower is red." That means, "Don't stay only in that special magical realm of wooden chickens crowing where everything is just 'Wowwww.'" Also take that mind right out into the garden where the tree is green and the flower is red. Each thing is clear, just as it is. Each thing is not colored by your ideas of it.

When Sul saw this calligraphy on the wall she said, "Oh, Zen Masters are also like that!" And so, she took the Lotus Sutra back to the altar and continued to practice very diligently every day. Sometime later she called on Ma Jo and had an interview with him and another Zen Master who was visiting. Both of them confirmed her attainment.

Sul grew up, got married and raised a large family. She had many children and grandchildren. Her actions in daily life were very ordinary, common lay people's actions. But inside, her mind was always clear and did not cling to anything. Many people came to her for help and for teaching, and she became known as a great Zen Master.

When she was an old woman, one of her grandchildren died suddenly. All through the funeral ceremony and the burial, Sul cried bitterly. When they came back to the house, she still cried bitterly. People began to whisper. Finally one person went over to her and said, "You are a great Zen Master. You already understand that there is no life and no death. Why has your granddaughter's death become a hindrance to your clear mind?" Immediately, Sul stopped crying and said, "You don't understand. These tears are better than any sutras, any teachings, any ceremonies that we might perform. When my granddaughter hears this crying, she will attain nirvana." Then she yelled out to everyone, "Do you all understand that?" But no one understood her.

> *And to my sorrow disappear over the mountain's*
> *Edge in a rush of wind, leaving*
> *The sky blue, the trees green.*

(Hitting the table)

Can you call that mind?

(Hitting the table)

Can you call that Buddha?

(Hitting the table)

Can you call that things?

KATZ!!!

The talk is now over.
Please stay for a cold drink.

Zen and Psychotherapy

Dharma Talk given at Dwight Chapel, Yale University

ℰ

Q: An issue rather than a question has come up lately in discussions about Zen meditation practice and psychotherapy which seems to be a different way of getting at the same things. Do I just sit with something and let it dissolve or is it better to sit and talk about it in a psychotherapy situation?

A: People have often asked me this question. Sometimes in the middle of a retreat, this question has come up. I wondered at first if they were asking just because I'm a psychotherapist. Were they just indulging their intellectual curiosity in the middle of a retreat? It felt counterproductive to me if that was the reason. But I began to realize later on that the question really, in some cases, was: What is the place of my emotional life in Zen practice? Or, is there any place for my emotional life in Zen practice? Of course, practice may have different kinds of leanings or attitudes connected to it. For instance, there is a fierce approach in Zen practice which is about stripping something away and having the courage to have the props knocked out from under you in order to face certain things. This is to fiercely face the rawness of things without any props. On the other hand, some people approach Zen practice from the viewpoint of acceptance, melting, letting go, warm embracing, and appreciation. That has a different flavor and attitude. The direction of the practice is the same in either case, but the nuance is stated differently.

If someone does not have enough confidence in their direction, and in what they need and how they should proceed, they are influenced by messages such as fierceness or openness or warmth. One teacher may say, "Take hold of the big question fiercely and hold it as if your life depended on it. There is nothing more important than this one big question, 'What am I?' or 'Who am I?' Grab hold of that and do not let go." That is the samurai-like attitude of fierceness. On the other hand, another teacher might say, "As soon as you raise the question, already that is enlightened mind." Just let yourself be. What am I? don't know. That is it!

An old Zen Master said, "When you say, 'don't know' you have already hit the nail on the head." That means that you are already enlightened but you do not know it! So let it be, and allow something to emerge.

Zen practice can be therapeutic, but it is not the same as therapy. A lot of therapies deal with shifting around attitudes, whereas Zen practice primarily heads toward wiping everything clean and seeing what is. Sometimes, people need the help of a therapist to talk things out. If what they are holding is very subtle and specific to a "set-up," a specific limiting way of being in the world, then they might need someone fairly skilled in spotting "set-ups" and in helping someone to let go at a pace that is workable and reasonably comfortable. They might also need help in facing why they even feel the need for that set-up! That is what psychotherapy is about. There are many kinds of psychotherapy just as there are many different strains of Zen practice.

Q: In the Kwan Um School of Zen, we emphasize that Zen is everyday mind, nothing special. But there seems to be a style of Zen that tries to encourage profound enlightenment.

Could you comment on the difference?

A: What is profound enlightenment?

Q: I don't know but other schools seem to emphasize finding enlightenment. That I do not understand. Can you comment on it?

A: When you get out of bed and put your foot on the floor, that is the first moment of enlightenment. Then you go to the bathroom, and you look at yourself in the mirror. That is the second moment of enlightenment. (That is what you call a "rude awakening"!) Then there is the brushing your teeth moment of enlightenment. That is, be careful, and polish, polish, polish. At my age the samadhi of tooth brushing becomes very important! But that is no more important than the next step which becomes the samadhi of putting the tea kettle on. I heard that the poet Gary Snyder wanted to visit Japan during the Korean War, and the Japanese officials gave him a hard time. They wanted him to prove that he was an American poet, so he sat down and wrote a poem for the immigration officer:

Making a cup of green tea
I stop the war.

I believe that this poem served as his passport into Japan. So, the samadhi of putting the kettle on, is also very important!

We emphasize the moment of profound enlightenment, but every experience is an opportunity for profound enlightenment. If every experience is profound enlightenment, then why use the word PROFOUND anymore? That is like adding a head on top of your head, or, as the old Chinese Zen Masters used to say, it's like painting feet on a snake. Even though you may think that a snake looks as though it might need feet, it does not! Likewise, the word "profound" originally is not necessary. It is extra.

The Lotus Sutra stresses the point of skillful lying. Throughout its three hundred or more pages, there are several parables in which the main character tells a lie, or tricks the people into doing something that they would not ordinarily do. There is a parable of the skillful physician whose sons took some of his powerful medicine when he was away. When he returned, they were all rolling on the floor poisoned, and he made a remedy. Some of them took the remedy quite readily and returned to normal. His other children refused to take it. "I don't like the smell of it. I don't like the color of it." They are in delusional toxicity! They think that it is important that it smells bad or that they do not like the color! He told them, "Children, I am going to die soon. I am leaving. I have some last business to finish. I leave the remedy here with you." He went away and sent a messenger back who told the children, "Your father has died." He was not dead. So that was a lie and he was breaking one of the five precepts. Hearing this lie about their father's death, they were shocked and in anguish. They felt that they should take the medicine of their father. So, they took it, and then he returned. Likewise, the phrase "profound enlightenment" or "satori" or "kensho," or any of these phrases are big lies. But they are skillful lies. If people are stubborn as a mule, you have to beat them and then they practice! Or if others like candy, candy is offered. "Enlightenment" is only a teaching word. "Enlightenment," that's bull shit. "Profound enlightenment," that's elephant shit! "Deep, profound enlightenment," that's rhinoceros shit! But it helps some people, so it is medicine. The problem is that if you get too attached to the notion of it, or think that practice has to always be fierce and hard and difficult in order to get some moment of profound breakthrough, then that stands in your way like a big iron gate.

In the Zen tradition there are sayings like, "A golden chain still binds," or "Gold dust in the eyes, still blinds you." If you pick up dust off the floor and rub it in your eyes, it will blind you. The same with gold dust; but it's worth a lot of money! The Buddha in our Providence Zen Center is gold leafed. That means that it has gold dust all over it. Someone decided that the Buddha needed to be cleaned and they started to rub it. Some of the gold dust came off. They had to replace it and it was quite expensive. Expensive enlightenment! So gold dust is more valuable than floor dust, but get either of them in your eyes and you still cannot see. If you become too attached to some notion of enlightenment, then that also blinds you.

Sometimes hard training practice is the correct medicine. Sometimes easy does it, or just let it be is the correct medicine. Sometimes not talking about it at all is the correct medicine. Just making a cup of tea to stop the war is the correct medicine. Talk about profound enlightenment is a particular technique. So is telling someone that they have to sit down and dig into the kong-an and experience it. While you may gain something valuable from it, it is a mistake to think that that is the only true way of practice. That can become deeply problematic.

I take as the main keynote of practice the old, old stories in the Zen tradition dating back to the Sixth Patriarch, and the Zen Masters of the T'ang Dynasty. In most of those stories by Zen Masters like Ma Jo, Baek Jang, and Hwang Beok, the teaching revolves around "Why are you making all of this? Why are you constructing all of this? It is already right in front of you. It is already apparent in all things." The famous story of Ma Jo and Huai-jang told earlier illustrates this point. Ma Jo was fiercely sitting Zen every day, and one day Huai-jang strolled by and asked Ma Jo, "Why do you sit Zen?" Ma Jo said, "I sit to become a Buddha." So, Huai-jang picked up a brick and started rubbing it. When Ma Jo asked him why he was rubbing the brick, Huai-jang said, "I am rubbing this tile to turn it into a mirror." Now, we all know that the mirror in Zen imagery has to do with the originally enlightened mind, or clear mind. Ma Jo said, "As much as you polish that brick, it will never become a mirror." Huai-jang said, "As much as you sit Zen, then you will never become Buddha." You will never BECOME Buddha because you are ALREADY from the very start, Buddha. And if your sitting does not proceed from that original point of faith and confidence, then you will never recognize your true self. You will always be reaching for something in front of you. As though perhaps just one more polishing will do it! Perhaps one more sitting will do it! Perhaps one more something will do it! If you practice that way long enough with enough fervor and energy, at a certain point a moment of exhaustion hits you, and you realize the absurdity of it. All at once, the bottom drops out from that kind of practice, and then you laugh out loud! THIS IS THE MOMENT OF PROFOUND ENLIGHTENMENT! You realize that I have been a goddamn ass all of this time! That is a wonderfully refreshing experience. Humility dawns at that moment, and everything appears in the letting go.

Q: Does enlightenment have anything to do with being in touch with your soul?

A: What is it that you are calling your soul?

Q: Your center.

A: The word soul as it is used in Western religions usually has a different meaning from center. The difference is the idea of an entity called "soul." Of course, one of the fundamental points of Buddhism is that essentially there are no entities. When you recognize no entity or no enlightenment, no self or no other, at that point you open up to something which is before any construction that makes things into entities. So, the idea of a soul is not exactly the same as true self in the Zen tradition because soul usually has the connotation of something permanent and fixed that will last forever. That is a little different than the realization of my self being interdependent with the universe.

Q: What do you mean that there is nothing in the Zen tradition that

is permanently fixed or will last forever?
   A: Interdependence is going to last forever. Buddha nature lasts forever. What is Buddha nature? *Just now, sitting here.* But this dharma talk is not going to last forever. That chair that you are sitting on is not going to last forever. Your "behind" in the chair is not going to last forever. None of those elements are going to last forever. They all are existing because of certain causes and certain conditions. This talk exists because you all invited me here. I am talking because of those causes and conditions. You're sitting here and listening because I am here as the speaker, so the cause of your listening is my talking. There are numerous causes and conditions that influence your listening. The chair that you are sitting on exists because of certain causes and conditions: The rain that fed the trees as they were growing, the sun that shines that makes the trees grow, the furniture designer who created it, the carpenter who assembled it, and their mothers and their fathers are all the conditions and the causes for the chair that you are sitting on. When those causes and conditions actually move on, the chair will also gradually move on into something else. At this moment, Buddha nature is "just sitting here listening to you." That is why in our style of Zen practice, with a kong-an like "What is Buddha nature?" the first response is hitting the floor or some other action that demonstrates the same point. Next the challenge—"Only that?" Then a response like—"Just now sitting here, listening to you." Hitting the floor demonstrates something that is before thinking or any particularized description. That is something that cannot be described through names, through speech, through words, and it is not a particular form or condition. It is not a particular entity of any kind. It is something before all of our ideas of anything. Perhaps some primary energy that is the life force of this universe, but already I have said too much. So, the first course is, "What is Buddha nature?" *(Hitting the floor with his Zen stick).* Then, the second course is "Just now sitting here listening to you." This means that this *(hitting the floor)* primary point which is before any description is manifesting itself at this moment as your experience of sitting here listening to me. That is a one-point, at-this-moment perception.
   Most of the time our feelings are going in many different directions. Think of the different conditions that your mind may get into. Sometimes it is racy. Sometimes it is quite dull. And on and on and on. Sometimes you are angry or bored, and when you are pulled by those different emotions, you have no clear perceptual center. The first course is to let them all return to their primary energy point. So, things are moving and the pendulum is swinging but there is a point at which the pendulum is held and upon which its movement is based. From that unmoving point you can perceive the movement without losing the center. Another example is the doll with the weight in its belly. You knock the doll over and it bounces back up. Any way you knock it, it moves. But the weight gives it an unmoving center. If you

have that unmoving center, then you are not being pulled by the various movements of your moment-to-moment experience. That center, though, is not a permanent "entity." It is not entirely separate from the various changes. The Heart Sutra says that form is emptiness, and emptiness is form. If you want to equate emptiness with empty mind, which is not being pulled in any way, then form is essentially emptiness. That means that all of your thoughts, which are essentially different forms, come back to emptiness, or come back to this center point. Form is emptiness. Perceive that and come to center. But, emptiness itself is form. See, don't make some idea of this as being something separate from all of these forms.

There is a case in the *Blue Cliff Record* in which a monk says to Zen Master Joju, "For a long time I have heard of the famous stone bridge of Joju, but now that I'm here I only see an ordinary log bridge." Joju replies, "You only see the log bridge, you don't see the stone bridge." The monk then says, "Oh. What is the stone bridge of Joju?" And Joju quickly responds, "Horses cross; asses cross."

This may need some explanation. In China during the T'ang Dynasty, many of the Zen Masters were called by the name of the place where they taught. Usually it was the name of a mountain. For example, many Zen Masters have the word "shan" in their name, which means mountain. So there was Zen Master Kuei Shan, Zen Master Yang Shan. That means the Zen Master of Mount Kuei or the Zen Master of Mount Yang. This is an interesting point; in some way it says that who you are is never separate from the place where you are. In some particular sense, Zen Master of Yang Shan is the Mount Yang, and vice versa. You are not separate from sitting in the chair in Dwight Chapel of Yale University. You are the listener of Dwight Hall. There is no you that you can abstract from that.

Joju's Chinese name is Chao Chou. So, Chao Chou was the name of a town in China, and this great Zen Master was the Zen Master of Chao Chou. In the town of Chao Chou, there was a famous stone bridge. When the monk came and made his statement to Joju, he was not talking about the stone bridge of the town of Joju. He was referring to the guy standing in front of him who was supposed to be a majestic figure like the stone bridge of the town. "But now that I'm here I only see an ordinary log bridge." Joju was famous for the ordinariness of his style of teaching. He never resorted to dramatic devices like shouting "KATZ!" or saying "I give you thirty blows with a stick!" His Zen later became known as "lips and tongue Zen." He opened his mouth and said something and it had an impact in some way, if you were subtle enough to pick it up. If you weren't it might go past you because it was so conversational. It was something that could easily be missed.

Joju was not to be put off by this "ordinary log bridge." He looked the monk dead in the eye and said, "Yeah, you only see the log bridge. You don't see the stone bridge." That means that "You are caught only by appearances.

You don't see the essential quality." The monk now is not feeling as confident as he was. That is what in dharma combat is called, "Your head is a dragon; but your tail is a snake." This means that your first thrust was pretty strong and came on like a roaring dragon, but the second one disintegrated into a common garden snake. The monk paused and then asked, "Well what IS the stone bridge of Joju?" Now, again, Joju is not going to resort to some dramatic device. He says very simply, "Horses cross; asses cross." This means that all living things cross over from delusion to clarity. All living things cross over here from some dualistic thinking to non-dualism. That means that this stone bridge from the very beginning is not thinking about self and other. It only sees one continuous fabric of all sentient and non-sentient creatures that are one with this moment, or with my self. So, horses cross and asses cross. Everything crosses. That is the great bodhisattva spirit. This spirit carries everything across. Christ said, "Pick up the cross and follow me." That is the same idea. To be like a stone bridge. This means not-moving center. Then everything moving may cross over easily. Thinking crosses; feeling crosses. Seeing crosses; hearing crosses. Everything crosses. Some translations of this story say, "It lets horses cross; it lets asses cross." But, for me, the "it" is a little extra. "Horses cross and asses cross" is a poem in a few words without any taint of separation or duality. This is profound enlightenment! I think I have said much too much, so please hit me thirty times and send me back to New York. Thank you.

Psychotherapy and Zen

Questions & Answers

ᴘ

Q: At Chogye International Zen Center of New York, we have a Zen teacher who is also a psychotherapist. My question relates with both those areas. I don't get it, how you can do both, because it seems that in the therapeutic approach you're encouraged to "go into" certain feelings you have, go into the blocks. And Zen, on the other hand, is about "before conditioning," before "story"—no story. As one works on whatever that story was in therapy, isn't that missing "it"?

A: What's "it"?

Q: Before thought! By bringing your story into "it"—isn't that killing or obscuring "it"?

A: You can never kill the moment. One form of being in the moment is obscuration in varying degrees. There's an old Zen saying, "In the beginning mountains are mountains, rivers are rivers." After practice for some time, "Mountains are not mountains, rivers are not rivers." After that, going further, "Mountains are again mountains, and rivers are again rivers." So, in the beginning your story line is very solid: Who you think you are, the face that you got from your parents is a very substantial and solid edifice. Huge! Made out of granite! How you see yourself and how you see the world and how you see the world in relationship to yourself exists through your story line. So, that's "In the beginning mountains are mountains; rivers are rivers." You take it to be that.

But, words are only designations for something. Unfortunately, we take words as if they really had definite meaning to them. Not just that they are pointers to something. So, when you come to the point of reaching the word's head, then, at that moment, "Mountains are not mountains; rivers are not rivers." So, your story is not your story. There is no story at that point!

But, if you stay at that point, then you're attached to some particular condition, some particular state called "no-story." No mind. Emptiness. There's a lot of Zen jargon for this. The old Zen Masters caution about falling into emptiness and getting stuck there. But, if you go further, mountains are again mountains, rivers are again rivers. If you touch base with your original mind—before thinking, before color, that mind which has no taste—

then you can pick up your story and use it in its appropriate way!

The standard Zen rhetoric is: Your mind is clear like space. Clear like space is clear like a mirror. If red is coming, it's just red. If white is coming, it's just white. Red and white are your story but if you have grasped that mirror-like awareness, then you're not caught by red when red is coming, you're not caught by white when white is coming. You understand red and white, you use red and white instead of red and white using you! Instead of your story pulling you around.

The approach in psychotherapy is different. You're caught in a bunch of negative ideas, let's say—negative feelings about yourself; negative images about yourself, etc. You have to see where you got all of those negative images from. And, you also have to see how you're holding them, and how you're using them. And what your attachment to them is! If you can see that, then you can perhaps experiment with some other view. So, that's the psychotherapeutic approach.

If you're a Zen student, however, you can just let it all fall away and come to your original view. Everyone who has done some sitting knows that all of that stuff keeps coming up. It keeps appearing over and over again! Even after some moment of clarity, some kind of experience of your original face, some kind of awakening or enlightenment, small or large, still there is the pea soup of your personality. It's still around, and so cultivation of ongoing practice sometimes takes a long time. Many of the old Zen stories tell about instant enlightenment and you then assume that the person also is totally transformed. Sometimes there is instant enlightenment and instant cultivation. But, sometimes there is instant enlightenment and gradual cultivation. And sometimes it's like being in a fog; gradually your clothes get permeated with moisture and you realize, "Oh, it's damp!" Sometimes it happens that way.

But, I don't think that the emerging flavor of American Zen is going to be an amalgam of therapeutic and traditional strands. At least, I wouldn't want that to happen. I prefer to see each keep its own integrity.

Zen and Recovery

§

(This talk was originally given as part of a conference at Providence Zen Center on Spirituality and Addictions *co-led by Charles Whitfield, MD and Zen Master Wu Kwang. The question is: Can you please talk on spirituality and recovery, and spiritual and psychological healing?)*

The word *recovery*, according to the dictionary, means the regaining of something that was either stolen or lost. So, the inference is you already have some ownership rights connected with what is being recovered. And, in the most radical spiritual viewpoint, what you recover is your perception of something that you already possess. Your true treasure. From that standpoint, the thief is yourself who distracts your attention from the perception of what you already have.

Case Ten in the *Mu Mun Kwan*, entitled "Cheong Sae is Poor," is a story I often use because it illustrates a variety of points. And, ironically, the symbolism in it is wine and drunkenness. A monk, Cheong Sae, approached Zen Master Cho Sahn and said, "Master! I am poor and destitute. Please help me!" And Zen Master Cho Sahn, without hesitation, called out the monk's name: "Cheong Sae!" And the monk immediately, without thinking, responded, "Yes, sir!" Then, Zen Master Cho Sahn said, "It is as if you have already drunk three bottles of the best vintage wine in China, and yet you act as if you had not even wet your lips."

Among the interesting points in this case is the introduction of the polarity of emptiness/fullness. Which is a very important point in spiritual attitude, as well as looking at things from the emotional and psychological standpoint. There are many different connotations connected with the word *empty*. Here, the monk says, "I am poor and destitute." I have nothing. And so, from one standpoint, I am poor and destitute means: Master, I have emptied myself completely of words, ideas, opinion, and even a feeling of self. So, I am completely empty. In that sense, it is a dharma combat challenge to the Zen Master, as if to say: "So Zen Master, what can you now say in response to my emptiness?"

Many people talk about the *feeling* of emptiness which is associated with depression, despair, and loss of a sense of self or self-esteem. Emptiness is a pre-requisite to an awakening experience, however. For example, at the moment of the poet Basho's awakening, he composed a poem sitting in the garden with the Zen Master. This poem, or haiku, mirrors his experience. He had been presented a question, or kong-an, by the Master and was asked to give something of his own words to it, rather than the words of the Buddhas and patriarchs. Basho was quite stuck and sat there for a long time in stillness, or vacancy. All of a sudden a frog jumped into the pond nearby. And Basho said: "Still pond, Frog jumps in. Splash!" Still pond is this sense of emptiness. But this emptiness comes to life in that momentary perception of: "Splash!" And at that point, emptiness and fullness are like two sides of the same coin.

In Case Ten, the monk says, "I am poor and destitute, please help me!" And Cho Sahn immediately calls out: "Cheong Sae!!!" And the monk responds without thinking, "Yes sir!" From the standpoint of fullness or completeness there is the hearing of the call and the response to the call, which embodies the situation at that moment and the monk's complete functioning without hesitation. So at that point, calling/answering, inside/outside, the universe and myself, all come together in one complete experience of fullness. From a spiritual standpoint, this immediate response is recovery or healing! It is throwing away the last vestige of holding. Because, looked at from another standpoint, when the monk presents himself as poor and destitute, he is still holding one thing—his idea of emptiness. "I am poor and destitute."

If you say that you don't have anything, then even that idea of not having anything has to be dropped. And, it's let go of by just perceiving clearly the sounds of this world moment by moment by moment. That's why the Bodhisattva of Compassion is represented as the one who *hears* the sounds of the world. Compassion is connected with that attitude of hearing with one's whole being without hesitancy, without idea.

People who have a feeling of emptiness attempt to fill it up in some way. In the case of substance abuse or any addictive behavior, the person often is holding on to some internal images of a negative, or bad, or abandoned, or unwanted, or rejected child that has become part of their idea of who they are. And, so, a lot of the current work in recovery programs is about re-parenting the inner child. For example, one of the techniques is to visualize a different kind of inner child, or a different kind of parental relationship with this inner child—one that isn't negligent, or rejecting, or abandoning or what have you.

In psychotherapy work, usually there is a two-pronged approach. One tries to help people heighten their awareness of what they are holding in terms of negative inner images and the feelings connected with those negative inner images. If you're holding an idea of a bad or neglected child or an unwanted child, then there are bad feelings connected with that. So, first some of those images have to be uncovered along with the feelings connected with them.

Then there is a focusing on what might be the person's need to keep holding onto imagery like that. What are they avoiding? Are they avoiding growing beyond that? Because this has its own set of fears. Or, are they avoiding their own uncertainty about whether they can grow beyond that? Or, are they holding onto the idea that a "bad parent or bad family is better than no parent or no family." Re-parenting is an experiment in other ways of being and seeing oneself and supporting oneself.

The AA approach makes use of the paradox of power and powerlessness. It hits at a very fundamental point connected with a sense of arrogance and pride versus shame and self-hatred. In AA and other twelve-step programs there is a statement: I admit my *powerlessness* over alcohol, or drugs, or food, or whatever the addiction happens to be. And, in the admission of powerlessness, and in giving themselves over to a higher power, a certain sense of control or power emerges. Also, a sense of false pride and humiliation is transmuted into a feeling of humility and connectedness to a power greater than oneself. This power can be the group, the community, the sangha, or some more universal principle: God, Buddha Nature, interconnectedness, whatever particular idea or concept the person relates to.

As helpful as all of these approaches are, and they are quite necessary for many people, Zen takes a different way. This is not to say that the Zen approach is better and the others are not as good; in some cases people may need to practice all of them.

The inner child and shame work is, of course, connected with a person's family and childhood. The Sixth Patriarch, in giving instructions to a monk, said, "Don't make good and bad. At that moment, what is your original face before your parents were born?" The last line is an interesting and powerful intervention in healing or recovery: What is your *original* face before your parents were even born? That throws you into a state of mind or attitude which is prior to any ideas, images, or feelings that you may have accumulated. Most of us carry a big burden or baggage on our backs connected with dysfunctional parent/child relationships. But, what is your original face *before your parents were even born?* This big question throws us back to our most primal self at that moment; and if we get a momentary recognition we get one moment's sense of our total freedom uncolored by all of these other things. Of course, to get a sense of that freedom also gives us a vantage point from which to approach these problems. It doesn't mean that one might not need to work through the inner dysfunctional attitudes that one carries around and projects onto relationships with other people. It simply means that one has a vantage point that gives a wonderful sense of centeredness from which to approach all of these problems.

There is the implication in this kong-an that time goes not from past to present to future, but from present to past, psychologically. If you touch that moment where you perceive your original face before your parents were born, then you can also see in the next moment how you then give birth to your parents. If you are having a moment of unencumberedness and then you begin to return to all of the mental and emotional attitudes that are caught up with dualities, at that moment you give birth to a relationship of authority figures and parental edicts. At that moment, you give birth to your parents—whether your biological parents, or little bits and pieces of them which you extracted and which have become undigested bits sitting in your mind-belly, giving you a lot of indigestion!

When you perceive this, you begin to take some responsibility in the present for what you carry around. And this sense of responsibility gives you a tremendous sense of freedom and hopefulness, and a way to work with all of these problems. From a Zen standpoint, we're most interested in what your original face was before your parents were born. Or as Zen Master Cho Sahn said to Cheong Sae: "It's as if you have drunk three cups of the best vintage wine in China, but you say that you haven't yet wet your lips?" So, we all need to be careful that after tasting the best vintage wine in China, we don't slip into acting as if we were poor and destitute, and have not even wet our lips.

The Fitting Game

φ

Q: This question came up for me last week, and I'm still wondering about it. When you do Zen, ideally you let go of all your ideas, opinions, and conditions, and open to your experience as it is. How do you avoid being consumed by situations and events? How do you not lose yourself?

A: That's an important point. Certain people are very "flexible," constantly adjusting and fitting themselves to people's conditions. The most exaggerated form would be the human chameleon. Most of us have some of this capacity. Some of us have it more than others.

This becomes a problem, however, when the person is not really opening and developing. It becomes a problem when they get caught with the idea of giving themselves over to the other person, and taking on something of the other person to please the other person. To do some kind of "adjustment" so that the two appear similar, but in fact are not.

One of the first things that's always emphasized in Zen training is to find your original center. This is a fundamental point. If you don't find your original center, if you don't come together and unify all the divergent energies of your own mind-emotion complex and settle down to a point which is before thinking, then you are like a dog chasing after a bone. You run out toward things, become affected by things, and move out of your center and lose yourself. So, the first step is, over and over again, coming back to that sense of rootedness: What am I?

This is why a classical metaphor used in Zen literature is that of a mirror. A mirror is empty and in a position to be reflective. When red comes, it's red. If white comes, the mirror becomes white. If a dog comes, it reflects a dog. If a cat comes, it reflects a cat. If a blue sky is reflected in it, it becomes blue sky. But, at the same time, that mirror never loses it's own integrity! It becomes one with red at that time, yet still there is an integral mirror there which never loses itself. It has its own center. So, when red goes away, it remains empty. When blue goes away, it's empty.

The one drawback of that metaphor for human beings is that it is a mechanistic image: Red comes, red. Red goes, goodbye. White comes, white. White goes, goodbye. But it doesn't say anything about how we are affected by our interaction with our environment and other people.

Q: Red's easy. What about anger?

A: Anger is red! But, strictly speaking, what comes is not anger. What comes is a situation, and part of our response to that situation is anger. The situation itself does not necessarily bring anger. Situation, condition, and cause are all one in Buddhist philosophy. Primary cause, situation, and condition come together. The condition includes the baggage which you bring to that moment, which evokes a response of anger or pain or any number of things.

The question is: Are you being used by those responses? Are you being used by your anger, your sorrow, your pain, your happiness, your desire? Or, can *you* use anger when it's appropriate to use anger? Can you use something else when it's appropriate to use that? This requires a certain kind of centeredness and non-holding, and a flexibility that adjusts to each moment, moment by moment.

But, if you lose yourself too much in a response, if you become enveloped by it and pulled away from yourself, then it's necessary to come back to zero point and ask: How am I losing myself? In this situation, I become this. How do I get angry? You can't see that unless you have some vantage point. Meditation establishes a vantage point, like an aerial view where you can begin to see thinking coming up, feeling coming up, all these things coming up.

Initially, you train that ability in a very simple environment by sitting on a cushion in silence, pretty much minding your own business at that time, and just paying attention to what comes up for you. If you train yourself to achieve a vantage point awareness, then you are able to see what comes up in other kinds of situations where things move a little quicker than in the meditation hall.

Those of us who have sat many retreats have seen it come up even in a simple situation like this: You sit several periods with some people next to you; somebody down the row decides to blow their nose, and that interrupts you. You were just settling into your big question, and your mind was coming together, and then someone sneezes! And something comes up! And, if the person decides to blow their nose three or four times, then red appears!

Q: Can you elaborate about the vantage point?

A: Suppose you are sitting on a hill looking down at a valley and watching different people, cars, and animals coming and going. Something like a pendulum is fixed above, but the string is hanging and the string is swinging back and forth. So, the vantage point could be here *(points to top of pendulum)*, and things swing here *(points to bottom of pendulum)*.

Another image I like is the one of the doll with the weight in its belly that rocks back and forth and always comes back to sitting up straight. The term "vantage point" isn't accurate with this image, it is more fundamentally connected with a "balance point" and a sense of moving to and fro, always returning to the point of balance. Each metaphor conveys something, but they all have certain limitations in terms of teaching images. The limitation of the visual vantage point is that you can get the idea that you stand back separate from what occurs. If you get into that image too much, you'll be caught. The doll image conveys a sense of being involved in something yet never losing balance completely.

On the other hand, there are some people who always want to please others. It seems like they are being very selfless—not holding anything, not attached to their condition, holding no opinions. But, in fact, they are caught by some idea: "If I do things a certain way, they won't like me," or something like that, and they lose themselves. The same is true of someone who is stand-offish. These are just two opposite ways of being. They're both not yet fully centered.

Essentially, you have to find some point in which to see all of the things that your mind is capable of generating in its interaction with itself, other people, and situations. Then, little by little, you lose yourself less and less. You may lose yourself, but you don't stay out there lost as long! You also lose yourself less intensely. Or, you know how to *use* that losing of yourself.

There's a famous Zen story about Zen Master Duk Sahn. One day, when he was in his eighties, he came down into the Zen hall carrying his bowls as if it were eating time. But the House Master, the cook, saw him and said, "Old Master, where are you going carrying your bowls? The bell hasn't been rung and the drum hasn't been struck yet!" That means that the signal for eating time hasn't occurred. Duk Sahn, without saying a word, just turned around and returned to his room. But, the House Master thought he had gotten one up on the Zen Master that day! So, he told the head monk: "Zen Master Duk Sahn came down carrying his bowls. I said, 'Where are you going carrying your bowls, the bell hasn't been rung, and the drum hasn't been struck.' He just turned around and suddenly went back to his room." The head monk said, "Old Master Duk Sahn doesn't understand the last word!" The "last word" in Zen lingo means the *final truth*, and the head monk was saying that Duk Sahn doesn't have it! Because, if he had it, every moment would be clear in some way, or he would use every moment for teaching.

So now, the whole place is buzzing. All the monks are talking among themselves: The head monk said the Master doesn't understand the last word! Finally, word got back to old Master Duk Sahn that the head monk had said this. So, he spoke with him privately. "Don't you approve of me?" Duk Sahn asked. The head monk whispered something in the Master's ear. Then the Master was relieved. The story doesn't say what was whispered in his ear, all it says is that he was relieved! The next day, when the Zen Master went up to the rostrum to give his speech, it was much different than ever before. The head monk stood up, ran to the front, clapped his hands, and laughed loudly and said, "Great joy! The Old Master has finally grabbed hold of the last word! From now on, no one can 'check' him."

This is a very famous kong-an. Every Zen student has heard it. Sooner or later you come up against that story! The point is that the Old Master is in the wrong place at the wrong time. One version of the story says that on that day the meal was a little late, so he came down expecting a meal, but the signal had not yet occurred. Whatever the case, he didn't lace into the cook: "How come the meal is late? What's going on?" He returned to his room silently. That has some meaning, kind of like ripe cheese, maybe close to rotting! Just turned around silently and went back to his room. That's a kind of teaching. At a certain point, any situation, any response in relationship to the situation can be used as a teaching. That comes with a certain kind of maturity. Before that, there is a lot of groaning, a lot of moaning, and a lot of struggle and adjusting back and forth, back and forth, back and forth. That's why the Path, the training, is non-stop and continuous: a gateless gate, or, goal-less goal. You never get there, but you are already there at every moment, especially if you recognize you don't need to make opposite concepts like getting there or not yet being there.

Q: This reminds me of Dogen Zenji's line: "To study the way is to study the self, to study the self is to forget the self, to forget the self is to be enlightened by all things."

A: Forgetting the self can be a certain kind of neurotic throwing yourself away in order to adjust to a situation. That isn't what Dogen Zenji meant when he said to study the way is to study the self, to study the self is to forget the self; to forget the self is to be enlightened by all things. He later gives some examples in the *Genjo Koan*. What he's talking about is a certain kind of spontaneous adjustment when there is no longer any small self-centeredness. He gives an example such as: A fish doesn't know the water, a bird doesn't know the sky. Self doesn't know self at that time. There's just a complete at-oneness with the environment and situation. It just knows what is occurring without self consciousness. But again, if you are not stable like a mirror, then there's all kinds of ripples. Then it isn't forgetting the self. So, in some way there has to be some stability as a prerequisite.

In the Chinese school of Tien Tai there is a form of meditation called Shamata Vipassana. This school of practice takes its teaching from the Lotus Sutra. The translation of the Chinese characters for Shamata Vipassana is *stopping and seeing*. Shamata means stopping; settling down; stability. "Seeing," or Vipassana, means seeing into, having insight into what is going on. "What is this?" "Stopping" means stopping all the divergent activities, all the ripples and the waves. It doesn't mean stopping by trying to flatten the waves! When you take a glass of water and set it down, little by little the water calms and settles. That's what's meant by stopping. You put it down, put it in one place, and the water becomes clear. Then you can *see* what's on the bottom. Millions of small beings in each drop. That would really be seeing!

My point is, that to forget the self and be awakened by all things means that you have to have that kind of steadiness. That kind of mirror-like quality that cannot lose itself. It can lose it's small self-consciousness, but not basic, original self.

Q: Doesn't someone have to have developed a clear sense of self to be able to forget it?

A: Right, there has to be some sense of an integrated person. And, some insight into the fact that this integrated, individualized person is not the last word!

Q: Most people are not really prepared to look at themselves. When you become a mirror for them, you become a problem. Do you have the answer to that?

A: Yeah, I have an answer; but not *the* answer. I'm sure other people may have an answer also. The direction of Zen practice is compassionate activity, skillful means, practicing loving kindness, and awakening ourselves and others to some kind of wisdom. In that sense, to be a mirror does not necessarily mean to rub someone's nose in shit! It means to have a sense of what is helpful for this person to see at this time. How much can they digest, take in without feeling overloaded? If you have faced many of your own sufferings, then there is as part of clarity the dawning of compassion because you understand what it's like to face sorrow and suffering and loss. And you can have an intuitive sense of how much of that the other person can tolerate. The same with criticism, faults, and millions of other things. Now, obviously, this isn't a perfect science. You will find those who have been practicing for years and years and years, and are teaching and have a following of some kind, who will lose it sometimes. There may be times when they may not be the best kind of mirror for a particular person. What's required is a sincerity on all our parts just to try to be helpful, and to also be able to say I'm sorry when I lose it. If you were just an indiscriminate kind of mirror reflecting everything, everyone would run for the hills! No one wants to see all that stuff at once!

This is similar to the kind of misuse that some people make of psychotherapy. That's my profession, I'm a psychotherapist. Some people go to therapy and begin to experience their feelings, and then they want to talk about feelings all the time. You sit and have coffee with them, and they want to talk about feelings. It's non-stop talk about feelings! Sometimes it's not appropriate or timely to talk about feelings! You might want to talk about the blue sky or how the football scores were this week or whatever. An exclusive focus on feelings eventually feels unbalanced. That's why I've always appreciated Zen Master Seung Sahn's teaching style. He's the Zen Master who founded our school of Zen. He knows when to hit someone between the eyes, and he knows when to go to the movies with them and casually relate in order to create an atmosphere where students can be themselves and gradually develop. He doesn't hesitate to go to the movies with them, nor does he hesitate to say: "What you are doing is no good" when that's fitting!

Q: It seems like there is a trap in Zen practice where one gets caught up in *becoming* rather than *being*. In my case this is what happened in my practice. Isn't this what you're talking about?

A: Sometimes people get a notion, or teachings are imparted which give the notion, or some combination of those two, that some particular ways of being are *better* than some other ways of being. If you are interested in spiritual development but are somewhat naive to the whole business, you begin to adopt some particular *limited* way of being, as if that particular way were better or more spiritual than some other way! One of the dichotomies in the Eastern traditions is that of monk versus lay person. Are you a better Zen student if you become a monk than if you remain a lay person? That question comes up for some people. The teacher may be a monk or a lay person, but if you look up to the teacher as the embodiment of somebody who has developed spiritually, then you think: Oh, that must be the best way. The teacher can even say it doesn't make any difference which way, but you'll think that the teacher isn't telling you the whole truth. And so, you get suspicious. But, that comes from your own thirst, craving, and not seeing the bottom line here, which is basically about finding *your own being*, which is universal!

You can hang a monk's jacket on "It," i.e. your original universal being, you can hang a lay person's jacket on "It," you can hang anything you want on "It" because it flows readily into all forms, but one is not better than the other. They are just different jobs or forms. Monk is a particular kind of job, lay person is another kind of job, nun is another kind of job, married person is another kind of job, single person is another kind of job.

Different people have different inclinations, different tendencies, different personalities, and so different forms may be more advantageous to a particular person than to some other person. One person may have a lot of difficulty practicing in an urban environment. If they have a choice in the matter, it might be more advantageous for them to go to a rural mountain area to practice in a retreat center. Someone else might prefer being alone. I know one guy in our organization who became a Buddhist monk. He spent a number of years in Korea, and lived in many of the mountain temples there. He also traveled on foot all over Korea from one temple to another, and then spent over a year in a hermitage, above Su Dok Sah Monastery, living totally alone. I talked with him shortly after he returned to the U.S., and he said, "I had gone as far as I could go with that kind of practice. I needed to come back into society and interact with people." This was necessary for his development. Now he's running one of our Zen centers on the West Coast and has a lot of headaches in terms of administration of a building and all the day-to-day operations. But he told me, "I needed that." So, at one time he felt he needed one particular style, and another time something else was necessary.

Same thing with being a monk or a nun and being a lay person. Someone might feel that that style of life is advantageous for them at a certain period, and at another point there may be a recognition that this is no longer right for me.

Q: Just because it's all universally the same, that doesn't take the impetus away from us to live our lives with directness, decision-making, and goals and all that.

A: Even though everything from one vantage point is all equal, still white is white and brown is brown. If you only think that it's all equal, but can't see that white is white and brown is brown, and brown is not white, and white is not brown, then you have a problem. And, since that is related to yourself and to what kind of life you're going to lead, that also requires seeing, "Oh, I'm not white, I'm brown." "I'm not brown, I'm white." That's important. Because if you think you should be white when you're brown, then you start doing the "fitting game." Or, if on the other hand, you say, "Well, color doesn't exist in reality. We're all colorless," then this also is not completely clear. Each of us has our own particular dharma, our own particular phenomenological unfolding. Human beings unfold continuously; we are a process, not a mold.

Birds Fly, Feathers Fall
Fish Swim, the Water Gets Muddy

Questions & Answers

℘

Q: I always thought that in the state of non-attachment, you have let go of the past so that you no longer will experience any sense of loss. Will you comment on this?

A: First of all, when you state it that way, you're stating a bunch of ideas about something. So, you're already caught with a picture or an image that you formed in your mind about what non-attachment is, or what great love is, or openness is. So, there's an idea that it should look a particular way.

In each moment, past, present and future coalesce. The idea is not to stop the past or future, but not to be caught by them so that you lose your being in this moment, or lose track of who you are or what you are or the openness of that moment.

The "truth" is in each experience, whether it's a narrow, focused experience or a wide-open experience. Sadness is the truth; happiness is the truth; loss is the truth; grief is the truth. All of these things are truth. They are not apart from the truth. If you want to really understand your human nature, then you have to be willing to enter into all of these aspects of living when they emerge. You don't have to go looking for them; you don't have to seek them out. But if, in the normal course of living, you come face to face with loss and grief, then loss and grief become your friends at that moment. They become your teachers and your partners. The more you try to get rid of them, the more they hang around haunting you.

Many of the old Zen stories and the stories of other traditions deal with the idea of facing whatever is in front of you and entering into it, and becoming one with it. For example, in the Tibetan tradition, there is a well-known story about Milarepa, a famous yogi who lived about 1200 AD in Tibet. One time, Milarepa was going to do a long solo retreat in a cave, as was the custom in Tibet. In that practice, the teacher gave you instructions, sent you off, sealed up the cave, and you were not supposed to come out for however long your retreat was—whether a year, ten years, or whatever. So, Milarepa went to this cave and started his practice. Before long, a demon appeared and began to menace him, harass him, disrupt him, and threaten him. He could not practice! At first he tried ignoring the demon. The more he ignored it, the more ferocious it got. He tried repeating some mantras which were said to have the magical ability to remove demons. It didn't work; the demon just kept getting bigger. Every time he repeated the mantra "om mani padme hum; om mani padme hum," or whatever it was, the demon got even more ferocious! Then he tried repeating some sutras. He figured: The sutras are imbued with very strong power, so, I'll try that! He tried and tried but nothing worked. After exhausting every means that he could think of to get rid of this demon, he finally came to that point we would call in our tradition "don't know." He didn't know what to do. That means at that moment he stopped relating to this being as an object. As long as you're trying to get rid of somebody, or transform them in some way, or shape them, or do something, you're relating to the other being as an object. Manipulation. I want something; I don't want something. At the moment that he totally exhausted all his means, the duality of subject/object was no longer present. Just openness; emptiness, not knowingness. At that moment, he spontaneously jumped up from his meditation seat and ran forward with open arms and embraced the demon. At the moment of embracing the demon, the demon disappeared. And Milarepa continued with his retreat.

That's the Tibetan version. The imagery in the Zen tradition is less colorful and magical. I remember reading an article by Trungpa Rinpoche. Someone asked him what the difference is between Zen and Tibetan Tantra. He said, "Tibetan Tantra is like watching a movie in Technicolor, and Zen practice is like black and white."

The Zen story that I use to represent encountering the moment is about great Zen Master Dong Sahn. A monk approached Dong Sahn one day and said, "Master! When hot and cold come, how can we be free of them?" That's the same thing as when pain comes to your legs, how can you not be bothered by it? When suffering comes in your life, how can you not be bothered by it? When grief appears or loss appears, how can you get rid of it, let go of it? How can you transcend it? How can you go beyond it?

Dong Sahn said to the monk, "Why don't you go to the place where there's no hot and no cold?" So the monk said, "Oh, where is the place of no hot and no cold?" Dong Sahn said, "When hot—heat kills you; when cold—cold kills you." That's the whole teaching right there. Why don't you go to the place where there's no hot and no cold? That may sound like nirvana or heaven. A place of no disturbance. The monk asked, "Please point the way." Dong Sahn said, "When hot—heat kills you; when cold—cold kills you." Again, if you have that mind of questioning at that moment, that is beginner's mind, then you are open to be affected deeply by any event that may be transformative.

Is it through some visualization, through some upholding of mantra, through some blocking out of all thought? Where is it? How can I achieve it? Dong Sahn just said, "When hot, heat kills you; when cold, cold kills you." "You" here means a separate "I-ness," as if it exists independently of your experiences of the moment—of hot and cold, of coming and going, of thinking and not-thinking, of gain and loss. Gain is gain; loss is loss. Form is form; emptiness is emptiness. So, Zen teaching is not so colorful.

You must understand the truth of each moment. Pain of loss is the pain of loss. If you can't cry and feel the sense of loss freely, then you can't affirm the absolute value of who and what that person was, or who and what that relationship was, or who and what that experience was. In fact, at that moment, when you fully enter into it, you affirm the meaning of that person. That becomes the universe at that moment.

Q: What do Zen Buddhists say happens when we die?

A: You go to the cemetery!

Q: I mean in terms of the spirit, not the body.

A: Do you understand spirit?

Q: No.

A: Okay, then you have to understand spirit! What is my true self? What am I? This process of questioning leaves you perplexed. There's only "don't know." If you're having a bunch of ideas about something, then you know something. The moment you recognize that your ideas don't answer the question, then you're in a state of "don't know."

The Sutra we chant says: No appearing; no disappearing; no coming, no going. So that means there is one thing that never appears, never disappears. Never comes, never goes. What is it?

Q: It's your spirit.

A: Yeah, but you only understand the word spirit. You have to understand what that word refers to. That's the beginning of practice, and that's the end of practice, and that's the middle of practice.

According to Buddhist doctrine on reincarnation, we transmigrate in some form from one incarnation to the next, and the next, and the next. So, when your body dies, your energy body leaves and gravitates toward some other incarnation that will help you to unfold your learning of who and what you are. According to the particular tendencies that you cultivate in this life, you will have certain tasks to fulfill in the next life. You will then gravitate toward parents or a situation that will help you to unfold. That's the basic view of Buddhist philosophy.

Zen Buddhism is not so interested in philosophy as it is in experience. What's most important is: What is this spirit that is either going to transmigrate or is not going to transmigrate? What is it? What is my life? What is it that is moving my breath in and out just now? In the most specific and meticulous sense, you are born and die with each breath. When you breathe out, that's it! When you breathe in after that, you're reborn! Each breath is a momentary birth and death. Even more meticulously, each thought-moment comes into being and passes away. Birth and death, from that standpoint, are occurring moment by moment by moment, non-stop.

The emphasis in Zen meditation is: Pay attention, moment by moment by moment. If you really grasp the moment, then that moment has no birth, no death. At the time you are totally in the moment, then there is no coming, no going, no past, no future, no life, no death. Because birth and death, coming and going, are all based on some kind of conceptual framework. So, we look into our minds to see how we are manifesting that moment by moment by moment. And, when we raise up this question: What is it that is coming and going? Or, When I was born, where did I come from, and when I die, where will I go? When we raise up this question, we're left with this mind of not-knowing. We may give ourselves some answers at first, but after a while we may really realize that "I don't really realize what all of that stuff means." I'll tell you the truth: I really "don't know" what all of that stuff about birth and death, and coming and going, and karma and rebirth means! I can console myself with theories, and sometimes that's reassuring! I like it! It sounds like a good idea! But, I don't really know what it means. And, at that moment of really not-knowing what it means, all the props and supports fall away. You're left with just what you are—without idea. So, that really is the starting point of approaching this question of birth and death, coming and going.

Q: How is Zen meditation different from visualization? Is it different?

A: You tell me! If you visualize something, then you're visualizing something. When we sit, we don't visualize anything, except when we drift off to Timbuktu! We don't cultivate the visualized experience in Zen meditation. That is a technique, and each tradition has its own technique. The more important point is, what's the direction or the purpose of the technique? If you understand the direction or purpose of the technique and don't think of it as better or worse, or "this will get me this and the other won't get me this," and if you understand the direction of meditation practice, then any technique will get you to the same place. For example, when you sit Zen style meditation, you sit down and you let go of attachment to ideas and concepts and opinions. That's why we raise up a big, fundamental question: What am I?

So, at that moment, your attention opens up. If you keep that openness of attention and settle down, you begin to see how your mind constructs various little worlds moment by moment. Ideas and concepts, they all appear. And, if you can sit with that openness of attention without clinging to any particular thing or getting stuck anywhere, then you just see things coming and going, coming and going, coming and going—and you come to your clear, perceptive mind before all of that stuff. Your original mind is like blue sky. All the thinking, all the ideas, all the concepts are like clouds coming and going, coming and going. Ultimately, the clouds are not separate from the sky; the sky is not separate from the clouds. But, if you get too involved in just the clouds, you don't experience the whole realm of the sky. So, Zen meditation is something like that. One of the purposes of visualization exercises is that you get a feel of creating something purposefully that you do unawares most of the time. We're always making some imagery in our mind! Making a little world at that moment, with some notion in it of subject and object. Most Buddhist visualization meditations visualize something like a candle flame or a deity. They visualize it first out in front of them, then little by little, they bring it inward to the center of their heart or in the center of their belly, all the while trying to hold the image steady. As the image is held steadily inside, they become one with it until they feel like they are that flame and that flame is them. At a certain point, when they totally become the flame and the flame becomes them, the whole thing dissolves into just openness. At that point, it's the same as in Zen meditation.

You've seen how your mind constructs images and how you can let go of them. Images are not the problem. The problem is getting caught in the imagery. Often we get caught up in either making negative imagery, or creating fantastic, positive images that are far from the reality of our lives. There's a huge gulf between that reality and our expectations. That's a problem. That's a difficulty. When we get to the point where we can create and dissolve imagery, then we're not caught by it. It's not pulling us around by our nose. That's Zen meditation; just being aware moment by moment and letting the clarity of original mind open up. When you're not caught by limiting imagery and dividing your world into some kind of false duality, the possibility of relating in a more meaningful way emerges. Then, loving kindness or compassionate activity or skillful doing what you do in the world becomes a real possibility.

So, any meditation technique is okay. But the question is, what's your purpose, what's your direction, where is it leading you to? Meditation is a way of being. It's an ongoing practice. Like a doctor might say, "I practice medicine." That's what doctors do, ongoingly. The same with meditation. It is not just a technique.

Q: I'd like to ask a question about my experience in meditation today. When you first raised the question about "What am I," I first felt, "I don't know." I wasn't uncomfortable with it, and I had trouble arousing my curiosity. I think maybe I was too peaceful with it, and I want to ask if it is possible to be too peaceful with "I don't know?"

A: Whether it's a burning issue or a subtle issue, or whether you're comfortable with it, is based on your particular life experience at that time. In meditation practice, questioning or curiosity should become more and more subtle as you go along. Let's say that someone has a deep question about life and death. What's it about? Or they have suffered some loss in their life or some disequilibrium. This may be a burning question for them. At that time, the energy of the question will have a certain fervor or fire to it. The old Zen Masters have expressions such as, "It's like swallowing a hot iron ball that gets lodged in your throat; you can't spit it out, and you can't swallow it down and digest it." That's a hyperbolic image which portrays the way certain people may have that kind of questioning energy. It doesn't mean that everybody will have it in that intense way. As one continues to cultivate practice, the sense of questioning or probing or unease with it will get subtler and subtler until there's just this sense of "don't know." And when you're really comfortable with "don't know," your mind simply opens up and you perceive comfortably what is occurring moment by moment by moment. That's the direction of the question. The question points toward a mind which is clear like space. But, if you begin to get drowsy or disinterested or "spaced out," then you don't have quite enough energy in the practice. In certain Zen traditions, there is a practice called "shikantaza" which means "Just to sit." The Soto Zen tradition emphasizes this practice—just to sit. That means, if you just become your sitting, then your awareness opens up. That's the same as, if there's only "don't know," then there's just this openness at that time. At the time that there's 100% "don't know," there's not even a sense of "I" "don't know," or "I" am sitting. "I" and "don't know," or "I" and sitting become a unified experience. The original Chinese phrase for shikantaza is actually "to just sit, and hit the world of opposites." So, to just sit and hit the world of opposites, or to have only "don't know," means at the moment the bell is rung and you're just sitting, there's only the sound of the bell—it is heard without a sense of "I am over here, and the bell is over there." At that point, your practice becomes quite relaxed. But, if there isn't that sense of cutting away the duality of subject and object, of really becoming one, moment by moment, then you're still holding something. There's still some taint, or the mirror isn't totally clean of dust. It doesn't have to be a burning fervor; as a matter of fact, some people burn themselves out with their burning fervor! And then they dislike Zen meditation a lot. That means they are too strong with the questioning. Many of the books on Zen meditation come out of the Japanese tradition of the military samurai spirit, and are colored by that sort of "pushing energy." That kind of spirit may not be suitable for everybody's practice. People sometimes read these books and get the idea that they should be that way and approach practice that way.

In fact, if you really attain some sense of your original natural mind, it's quite relaxed and open. It's not full of angst! But, the question is a way of directing energy towards it.

Q: I have a question about keeping the eyes open during meditation. It's really about the focus being inward with the eyes shut and outward with the eyes open. Is this what happens?

A: Meditation techniques come under two general headings. One is a form and technique involving a quieting down, an indrawing of attention and coming to a point of concentration and stabilization. The other form puts an emphasis on awareness and mindfulness.

For example, in the indrawing form of meditation, a specific focus is used. It can be an idea, a visual image, a light, a religious symbol of some kind like the Buddha, or just a flower, or a mantra. It may be a thought like "what is love," or some particular part of the body like the center of the heart, or, as we do, letting the attention rest in the belly area; some systems use the top of the head. In this form of meditation, you gradually let everything recede and you come to a focal point.

In the systems that put an emphasis on awareness and mindfulness, that emphasis is on perception, or on being mindful and awake to and watching what occurs moment by moment by moment. The attention is left open in a wide way, and attention is paid to whatever is occurring moment by moment. In this approach, attention may be limited to one particular process: For example, the breathing process. Attention is paid not only to the breath coming in, but to the breath as a momentary phenomenon which includes everything that also occurs at that moment. So, as the in breath comes, maybe the air conditioner clicks on; that is also part of your world at that moment. Or, as the breath comes in, if you get a sensation in your ankle, that's part of your experience at that moment. If at the time the breath comes in, some thought comes to your mind, that is also part of your experience at that moment. You don't try to withdraw or recede from it; it's all part of your experience. In this approach, the attention is left open and wide, and the emphasis is on staying present to the process of being and becoming moment by moment.

Now, of course, both methods require a certain degree of stability of attention.

When you withdraw your attention and become concentrated, it's something like taking a vacation. As everyone knows, when you return from a trip and look around your home, you begin to see things that you hadn't noticed before. They have been there the whole time, it's just that your awareness has become dehabituated from what you were used to. If you indraw attention and rest your mind, when you come out it's usually fresher, more vibrant, so increased awareness is a byproduct of concentrated withdrawal.

Keeping the eyes open in Zen meditation facilitates an awakeness and awareness in the present. You do need to be careful, however, not to strain your eyes! When you sit with your eyes open, there is a field, like an oval, around you, and you are in the midst of it. And it isn't just the eyes that are left open. The hearing is also left open, so you hear any sound that occurs. There also is an awareness of any feelings in your body.

In other types of meditation, as you concentrate on your focus there is a sense of leaving the body. You become so concentrated that you forget your body. Zen meditation emphasizes staying grounded in the body, but that is just a matter of emphasis and degree.

The fundamental direction of Zen practice is something we call *everyday mind*. Zen is something special while simultaneously very everydayish and not at all special. The emphasis of Zen practice is not just towards concentration, but is directed more toward perceiving and having insight into this fundamental matter: What am I? What is my existence—before thinking, before ideas, before concepts, before any opinion is formed? Am I and what I perceive two, or one? The old Zen Masters would say, "If you say two, that's a mistake, also if you say one that is a mistake." Not two, not one, then what?

Practice means that the goal is within each footstep, each moment, each experience; at the same time, there is no goal that you will ultimately reach. The aim and the direction are the same—which is to be who you are.

Q: Where does satori fit into Zen practice?

A: Satori, or enlightenment, or awakening, or kensho, or any of those words, just means that experience of your clear, original mind in some particularly vivid moment. The kind of example found in the Zen stories is of someone sweeping the temple compound, and as he's sweeping he hits a pebble with a broom and the pebble goes flying and hits a bamboo tree. Whack! And at that moment, his mind opens and he has kensho, or satori or awakening. That means that this person had some question that went on continuously, whether he was sitting, or sweeping, or eating, or whatever. His questioning mind had become full, complete. When that questioning mind is full, there is a sense of not knowing. There's no more thinking. And at that point, the mind becomes quite wide and spacious. If something happens at that moment, one may get a vivid awakening, a momentary recognition of one's original, beginningless and endless Buddha nature, or awakened nature.

When clouds float back and forth in the sky, sometimes the moon is clearly visible, sometimes it's behind the clouds. The moon still exists even when it is behind the clouds and you can't see it. So is your original before-thinking clear mind; your awakened nature is there at every moment. But, when you get some particular recognition of it, that's what is known in the Zen tradition as satori, enlightenment, or kensho.

If you look for it too intently, then that search becomes a big hindrance. Because, then you have formed some idea about enlightenment and you try to pursue it. If you pursue it, that is already taking it and conceptualizing it. And if you direct yourself too much towards that, you'll never let go and put down all of your thinking and allow it to just emerge.

There is an old Zen poem that says,

> *Good and bad have no self nature.*
> *Enlightened and unenlightened are empty names.*
> *In front of the door is the land of stillness and light.*
> *Spring comes; the grass grows by itself.*

The first line means good exists only in relationship to bad; bad exists only in relationship to good. They don't stand on their own. There is no absolute bad or absolute good. There's good in a particular situation in relationship to bad in that situation, and vice versa. They make each other. All of that comes from thinking.

The second line: *Enlightened and unenlightened are empty names.* This means don't get caught by names and words. That is a number one edict in Zen practice. If you get caught by words and names you're being pulled around by your nose.

The third line: *In front of the door is the land of stillness and light.* That means when you leave here and enter the street, you should perceive the land of stillness and light. "Door" also means the doorway to the senses where you meet the world at each moment. Right before you, moment by moment by moment, is the place of stillness and light. That's not different from the door to the street.

The last line: *Spring comes; the grass grows by itself.* That means natural processes proceed at every moment. Fall comes, the leaves turn colors. Winter, the snow blows. Spring comes, it rains. Summer comes, it's hot. Moment by moment the natural process is occurring. Right here at that very moment is your true teacher or the land of stillness and light.

So, every moment is a moment of enlightened activity. Just let go of making something, holding something, attaching to something. That's why we have one big question: "What am I?" That big question is your direction. Or, it may be "What is this?" At this moment, what is this mind that is perceiving, what is this world that is being perceived. "What is this?" There is awakening. Already complete.

There is a Zen teaching about the mirror image. We say keep your mind clear like space and clear like a mirror, so if red comes it becomes red; if white comes it becomes white. If I'm hungry I eat; if I'm tired I sleep. If someone is sad, then I am sad along with them. If someone is happy, then I am happy along with them. If someone is hungry, then what? Do I just be hungry with them? Obviously, if I have some food, I give it to them. If someone is angry, then what? If they're jumping up and down, do I jump up and down too? Or, do I find some way to intervene? To be soothing or to just be quiet and stand my ground may be the way. But there doesn't seem to be just one way. Sometimes jumping up and down and being more crazy than they are might be the proper medicine. The point is, the less your mind is encumbered with ideas or reactive emotions, you're in a much better position to be responsive in an appropriate way.

A mirror has no emotions. Human beings have emotions. The idea is not to get rid of one's emotions. If the aim of Zen practice is to become fully human, to awaken to your real human nature, then that is not about getting rid of emotions. It means to have some point of clarity, some anchor point that's not reactive.

Once you find that center of gravity, then the correct use of warmth and emotions, and your passions, becomes possible. You're not just being pulled by them, your emotions have a relationship to your world, to the situation, and are not self-centered any more. So, passion becomes compassion. Anger becomes used as a cutting through of delusion and ignorance. Then it becomes the seed of wisdom. For some people, anger might be the most difficult emotion to handle. For others, softness may be the most difficult to manage. It depends upon their temperament and how they use what they have been given.

The story about the two Korean Zen Masters Kyong Ho Sunim and his successor Man Gong Sunim is a good example of passion and desire that goes beyond self-centeredness. In this story, Man Gong Sunim and Kyong Ho Sunim are discussing their individual ways of practice. When Man Gong Sunim asks Kyong Ho Sunim about his practice, Kyong Ho Sunim says, "Sometimes I get a craving to eat garlic." (According to strict Buddhist precepts, garlic is considered an aphrodisiac and is prohibited.) "I go into the village and I buy a couple of bulbs of garlic. Then I come back to the temple, and in the garden I dig a hole and I plant this garlic. Then every day I water it. Little by little it grows up, and then I distribute garlic to everybody who wants it."

This is an example of a simple kind of practice. Kyong Ho is talking about his passion and desire, which goes beyond his self-centeredness. When you are grounded in Zen mind, your passion becomes compassion for all beings and a sharing of yourself. This is the direction of practice. To help all beings, not just myself. That is very important, especially these days.

Thorns on the Old Plum Tree

Questions & Answers

℘

Q: Today my family went to Catholic Mass, and the reading was about Abraham, who was told by God to kill his son. My question is about obedience. There is a stress in Zen practice on autonomy, and yet, in this story about Abraham, great blessings came from his willingness to kill the thing he loved most. Will you talk about that?

A: This story is a real test of obedience because, in fact, Abraham and his wife Sarah had not been able to conceive a son until their old age. There is a magical part to the story because they're both ninety or a hundred years old when, miraculously, Sarah conceives a child, Isaac. When Abraham and Isaac go to the mountain, the boy asks, "Where's the lamb that we're to offer for the sacrifice?" Abraham tells him, "God will provide the lamb." But, when they get there, of course, he puts Isaac on the altar and ties him up, and has the knife at his son's throat when the angel descends and tells him to stop. Of course, this is a test of how much faith he has.

There's a kong-an that says: The National Teacher called to his attendant three times, and the attendant answered three times. [In China, the emperor would award a title to a great master, and this title was National Teacher. So, this guy was a great master.] Then the National Teacher said, "I thought I had deserted you. But now I see that, originally, you deserted me!" There are various points in this story that are interesting. There's the use of the word "deserted." If you look at various translations of that kong-an, you will see slight differences in the word translated as "deserted." *Deserted* has the connotation of leaving behind.

At the moment of calling, one is completely unified in the activity of calling. Completeness! If you just call out with no evaluative consciousness, and you are 100% in that, with that, of that, being that calling at that time, then you are in a sense *completely alone.* You have left everything else behind. If you look at the etymology or derivation of the word *alone,* you will see that it comes from two Old English words that mean *all one.*

At that moment it's of all one substance embodied in the activity of just calling out: "Attendant!" The Master said, "I thought I had deserted you." But see, the attendant just said, "Yes, Master!" And, three times! Now, think if ordinarily I said, "Willie!" By the third time, would you just patiently and completely respond "Yes?"

I read a new translation of the *Mu Mun Kwan* which is where this case comes from. This new translation is by Robert Aitken Roshi, a teacher in Hawaii. In his commentary on this kong-an he said: Imagine being in a restaurant and doing that to the waiter. You call the waiter, "Waiter!" He comes running, and you don't say anything. "Oh, I'm sorry," he may say, and withdraws. And then you say, "Waiter!" and he comes running again. By the third time, a different relationship may develop depending on what kind of waiter he is! The less he happens to be the embodiment of the Bodhisattva of Compassion, who has a thousand arms and hands, the more he may get pissed off.

The attendant in this story responds three times, and the teacher in seeing this kind of presence of response says, "I thought I had deserted you." I thought I was standing alone in the universe, all one. "But now I see that, originally [the word originally means original mind; original substance is *before thinking*, before evaluating, before checking] you deserted me." This means that you also are like this. That's transmission at that point. I have it; you have it! Mind to mind. Complete here; complete there. Just calling. Just answering.

There is also the point, and I think that's why this story from one point of view is so interesting, that three times calling and three times answering, the attendant is not holding anything. So, each time he comes freshly, as if it were the first time. Without any idea. Without: Why are you bothering me? Without anything! He just comes responding. Wouldn't we all like to be able to live our lives that freshly?

There is a similar story about Zen Master Un Mun. Un Mun had an attendant, and every day for twenty years as the attendant was leaving his room, Un Mun would yell out: "Attendant!" And, as the attendant turned around, the Master would say, "What is it?" For twenty years, the attendant heard this every day and had no answer. But every day he listened! "Attendant!" "Yeah?" "*What is it?*" After two or three months, the attendant knew: Oh, I'm going to get to the door, and this crazy guy is going to call out, "Attendant!" and then I'm going to say, "Yeah?" and he's going to say, "What is it?" After a while, you begin to tune out and turn off as anyone who has studied a little psychology knows. It becomes habituated. For twenty years this guy heard it, listened to it, responded to it, and could not answer it! Then, one day, the story says, he had great enlightenment.

Now, back to the first case. The National Teacher said, "I thought I had deserted you." I thought I was standing alone in the vast universe, all one. Now I see that you also, originally, are also like that. Not holding anything.

The essence of obedience is in that. In not holding anything, and being able to just listen; to just hear; to just respond from the point of view of true hearing. The word *obedience* is related to the term *obaudiens*—thoroughly listening, or obedient. I learned the root meaning of obedience from a little book entitled *A Listening Heart* by a Benedictine monk, Brother David Steindl-Rast, who has been a long-time Zen practitioner. This is a book of talks about the order of Saint Benedict that he gave at various convents to contemplative nuns. One of the first rules of a Benedictine monk is obedience. Obedience really means, according to Brother David, fundamentally, most radically, and most existentially, the development of the capacity to *listen.* In situations such as the Benedictine monastery or in a Zen monastery where there are certain forms and rules, the following of these rules are acts of obedience. They have to do with developing the ability to listen—to listen to yourself, to listen to the environment, to listen to what's going on, inside and outside, without making the mental concept of inside and outside!

The actual structured forms of obedience in a monastic setting—the rules for bowing in a certain way, eating in a certain way, getting up at a certain time, observing silence at certain times—are merely expedient training devices to help one to develop within oneself this fundamental ability to listen and to be responsive. If you understand it in that way, then the narrow forms of obedience do not get deified. If you have an appreciation of what their actual purpose is, you can feel a certain sense of gratitude for those rules and those structures.

Sometimes it happens that something in the rules will "bug" you or begin to irritate you. Why do we have rules? Why are we doing this? Why? At that time you feel anything but gratitude for the rules. If you can recognize that the rule has provoked a reaction where you get stuck, then it is possible to have a sense of gratitude for them. The rules help you to see that.

Obedience is not throwing yourself away and making yourself the lackey of somebody else. One way to help you to listen is to be the attendant, to be the waiter. If you have a lot of pride, for example, then that particular training device will make you listen to that pride and perceive it. It will help you to see that it's getting in the way of just being with the situation. In that sense, it's an expedient device.

Of course, as in the story of Abraham, it's important to look at who is asking you to do a particular thing. For how long are you being asked to do this particular thing? Under what kind of circumstances are you being asked to do this particular thing? Trust must be involved there. Trust does not mean to be a damn fool. It does not mean to blindly go along with something and totally throw away your discrimination. You can put discrimination on the shelf for a while to see and to hear, but if after a while something does not "sit" right, and the feedback does not feel right, then that becomes an abuse of obedience rather than a skillful use of obedience as a training device. One example of this is the infamous Jonestown incident where many of Jim Jones's followers took poison because he said, "It's obedience." That's a total distortion of the function of obedience. There have also been a number of accounts over the past several years of various kinds of abuse—whether sexual exploitation or exploitation of power—within some of the Zen traditions in this country. Basically, obedience has to do with listening, and being able to train in responsiveness. Not holding anything; not attaching to anything; not making any tight-gripped concept in your mind so that you are able to listen, to hear, and to respond. When the bell rings, bonnnnnggg, you hear it! Someone calls, you answer! Someone close to you needs you, you are available to them.

And who is asking? In the story of Abraham, God is asking. Him, Her, It is asking. So, be open, but don't be a damn fool. Any training that is for your unfolding and development will not ask you to be a damn fool.

In *Zen Mind, Beginner's Mind* by Suzuki Roshi, there's a saying: "If you follow what I say too much, I may be very happy, but you won't. If you become a good Buddhist, I may be very happy, but you may not." Being a student means finding what's appropriate for you.

A woman who studied in the Native American tradition and in the Zen tradition told me a story the other day. There were times when the teachers gave some general teaching in a group setting, which she tried to follow but which didn't feel exactly right for her. She tried for a long time and got really bothered by it. Eventually she went to the teacher privately and said, "I'm trying very sincerely to follow your teaching about this particular thing, but it doesn't quite feel right." The teacher said, "Oh, that teaching is not for you!"

You listen to a general teaching, for example, sitting in a meditation hall, and you hear the person who is officiating all fired up that day saying: "Sit like you're sweating blood!!!" And so, you try to sit like you're sweating blood, but that's not appropriate for you. Maybe, in fact, you're an overachiever type and the correct teaching for you is to not sit like you're sweating blood, but to let it be! That also is obedience! This means knowing when to listen to something from outside, and knowing when to listen to inside, in which case you will need to be clear about the difference between internal chatter and the intuitively informing mind.

Q: What is the relationship of Buddha to faith?

A: In Suzuki Roshi's *Zen Mind, Beginner's Mind*, he says that from the Zen standpoint it's absolutely necessary to believe in nothing. He goes further and says that by nothing he means something which has no name and no form, and, at the same time, expresses itself as form and color moment by moment. So, that's one notion of Zen faith, or one way of expressing Zen faith.

An historical reference point regarding faith is Shakyamuni Buddha's enlightenment experience: That each and every thing is from the beginning already imbued with Buddha nature. In Zen terminology that is called Original Enlightenment. Everything already has it. Everything already is complete. Before any cultivation—*already*—each and every thing is imbued with Buddha nature. That's the original point of faith. And, if you sit with that attitude of each and every thing already being complete, then your sitting is not striving after anything in particular. It's just opening to *what is.* THAT becomes the exercise or practice of faith.

So, that is the relationship of Buddha and his experience, and faith in Zen practice. Throughout the history of Zen, various Zen Masters would attempt to pull the rug out from under any kind of faith that was congealing into a particular form. For example, great Zen Master Lin Chi said, "If you kill your parents you can repent to the Buddha. If you kill the Buddha, who can you repent to?" At that time in China there were probably many people practicing a devotional type of Buddhism—doing repentance ritual, and becoming attached to that kind of practice, or something similar. So Lin Chi wanted to shake them out of that. "If you kill your parents, you can repent to Buddha." Just repeat the mantra, *Namu Amitabul, Namu Amitabul, Namu Amitabul, Namu Amitabul.* If you have great faith in that, then you will be taken to Amita Buddha's Western Paradise. But, if you kill the Buddha, then what? Then who? Who will save you then? That's a different kind of faith. That is faith in "don't know."

Or, when standing on top of a flagpole, a hundred feet up in the air, how do you take one step forward? That is another expression of faith. A sense of throwing it all away—even the last vestige. Being open to possibility. Letting go of what is *known and secure.* Standing on top of a flagpole a hundred feet high means holding onto something that feels special and rarefied. Even some state of meditation that makes you feel centered and secure and calm can become a trap of aloofness. So, how do you take one step forward?

Now, that's putting the image into a metaphor that involves life and death. Zen Buddhism uses a lot of life and death imagery as a means of pointing some place. Take one step forward from the flagpole a hundred feet up in the air and you will literally die! So, that takes a lot of faith. But, that means to take a step in any small way—letting go of *knowing* and moving forward one step into *unknowing* and into the area of uncertainty. That requires a certain kind of faith. As you practice with a questioning attitude, at first you might mentally repeat the whole question: What am I? Or, what is true self? Gradually, the question can condense after a while to only "WHAT?" Faith in "*WHAT?*" Only don't know.

Korean Zen Master Hye-Am came to this country when he was over 100 years old. There is a photo of Hye-Am and Zen Master Seung Sahn, who is our Zen Master. They are sitting together as if in conversation, and the caption quotes Hye-Am Sunim. "When you say 'don't know' you've hit the nail on the head." There is a similar statement by a Chinese Zen Master from the T'ang dynasty period. "Not knowing is most intimate" or "Not knowing is closest to it." So, if "don't know" hits the nail on the head, that means faith in "don't know." That's it! It's already hit the nail on the head. Complete! Finished! So, if you were really a superior Zen student (which none of us are), one time you would raise up this question: What am I? don't know!!!! Already completely hit! You've hit the nail on the head! Finished! But, you have to have complete unequivocal faith in that mind and be able to totally support it moment by moment. Most of us do not have the capacity to support that instantaneously, or even to recognize that the first time we say "don't know," *that's it!!!* It's finished! Complete! There is nothing more. We don't recognize it at that moment. So, then we sit there: What am I? "don't know," repeatedly. Then we start thinking about Chicago or dinner etc. Do it again: What am I? don't know. And again. Maybe your mind becomes a little less encumbered and a little less crowded. So, then again, breathing out: don't know. It's an ongoing cultivation. But, if you had some kind of wonderful, complete faith, then the first time you entered into this "don't know" you would be all finished! So, that's faith in "don't know."

Q: As my practice deepens, those habits which have sustained me are falling away. However, when I first started practicing, I felt stronger than I do now. Why is that?

A: I think what you're saying is that especially at the beginning of practice, there is a certain fascination, strong interest, aesthetic or philosophical appeal, or something grabs you for a while. It's not based in belief so much as it is a certain kind of intensity of interest. For a while, you get a sense of everything settling down and being clear. But, if you persist in practice, then, of course, everything begins to come up again. And then you see it even more clearly than previously. And sometimes you see it as worse than before! The garbage in the street *really* stinks then! If your nostrils are clear, the garbage *really* stinks! If you have the luxury of not being so aware, you may pass it by without noticing it. So, that is a phenomenon that goes on in practice. Sometimes practice is not a calm, relaxing experience. You go through many things as you practice, and some of them are not at all calm and pleasant.

Ultimately, stability is the ability to enter into and let go of various situations, and return to a centered place.

Q: Is there a concept of God in the Buddhist traditions?

A: All religious traditions are dependent on the idea of something, usually some form of deity which people see as being outside of themselves, or maybe inside themselves. But, there's some idea or image involved. The kind of faith Zen talks about is *no image; no idea.* Most theologies hold the notion or idea of God as the creator. In Buddhism there is no idea of that kind of creator. We use images; hopefully, they don't use us.

Q: I know of two Zen centers that are dropping all images.

A: At one temple I visited in Korea, the altar had no Buddha. But there was a window that looked out upon a stone stupa that, they claimed, contained a relic of Buddha. Another temple in Korea is on a mountain considered to have strong energy by the indigenous shamanistic tradition. It's a very unusual place. There are many temples and hermitages along the mountain all the way to the top. There's a river that flows down the mountain in a particular kind of way to a pool that is called "Dragon Energy Pool." It's supposed to be a very strong power place. And, at that temple, there is also no Buddha on the altar, but a window looks out on the pool.

You can't get away from form because everything we relate to has some form. Even if you say it's formless, you have already made a form. That's why the Heart Sutra says form is emptiness, emptiness is form. Form is not different from emptiness; emptiness is not different from form. If you understand that all forms are emptiness, that means that each form is a provisional momentary expression of something which is universal in nature. Then you can *use* any form rather than being caught by it. But, if you become attached to a particular form, then you think, "Oh, Krishna is the correct form; Buddha is not." That becomes a problem. You don't understand the true function of form, the true relationship to form. As the Heart Sutra says: Avalokitesvara Bodhisattva, when *practicing* the prajna paramita, perceives that all five skandhas are empty, and is saved from all suffering and distress. Prajna paramita means *practicing* the heart of transcendent wisdom. The heart of transcendent wisdom means that all forms, all five skandhas are empty. Skandha means how all things are composed. The word literally means *heap* or *aggregate*. The physical and mental conglomerates of our experience moment by moment are the five skandhas. So, the bodhisattva perceived that everything was empty and was saved from all suffering and distress.

If you perceive that everything is empty, then you can use anything! Krishna is okay, and Buddha is okay, and Jehovah is okay, and everything is okay because each one of them is *IT*!! Each one is not different from IT! Also, there is a certain equality of principle there. Krishna IS Jehovah, IS Buddha, IS US!!! So, that's a different use of form. Form is okay. Form is not the problem. It's attachment to the form. That's why the Sutra says the bodhisattva depends on prajna paramita, and the mind is no hindrance. That's a wonderful sentence. Depends on this clear seeing. Then mind is no hindrance. With no hindrance, then no fear. Because then you don't need to hold onto something exclusively. Feeling is not a hindrance. Perception is not a hindrance. Nothing is a hindrance. Because everything is open and clear as it is. *Far apart from all perverted views* [perverted views means narrowing something down and forgetting the rest of it] *one dwells in nirvana*, completely.

Q: In some traditions there is the idea of holding onto the teacher until there is a breakthrough. What about that?

A: That is more a notion found in Rinzai Japanese Zen. Aitken Roshi says that in modern Japan, if a Zen student goes to a talk or an interview with another teacher who knows this student is studying with somebody else, he won't mess with him. There's this idea of exclusivity. That's okay, but we don't need to adhere rigidly to it as if it were law. In fact, the old Zen style in China, and even now in Korea to some degree, was for monks to travel around to visit different teachers. A teacher thought nothing of asking, "Where are you coming from?" "Oh, I came from Un Mun." "What did Un Mun teach you?" This immediately prodded the student in some way. So, there wasn't much of an exclusive attachment to a teacher or a methodology, but there was the use of provocation in the interaction between a student and teacher, which helped to push the student along in some way. Now, there were, of course, students who stayed with one teacher for a long time, and others who traveled around a lot, and variations on that. But, this notion of making one teacher a very exclusive and precious thing didn't have the same importance that is seen in some traditions now. However, there was respect and obligation to the teacher.

After having been a student of Kapleau Roshi's, Toni Packard became very interested in the teaching of Krishnamurti. Krishnamurti was an iconoclast. He threw away all forms. One time, one of the teachers in our school was in a workshop with Toni Packard. It was the first time she had met her, and the first time she had come into contact with Packard's style of throwing away all forms. She later discussed this idea with Zen Master Seung Sahn. And he said, "That's okay. But ask her if she is still using her name." It's very hard to get away from form completely.

The gold Buddha on the altar is helpful to a person sometimes. In the last year of my training as a teacher, I was urged to sit with teachers of other traditions. I went to Eido Roshi's zendo to a sesshin. Talk about impressive! He has some Buddha statues that look like museum pieces. This can be aesthetically inspiring and helpful to a person. The form and the appearance or the attitude of the Buddha may transmit something of one's own mindfulness, and to that extent it is helpful. That is what all images are about. In some traditions they are very colorful and bright, as in the Tibetan tradition. In the Korean tradition, very bright primary colors are used. Other traditions may use somber and dark images, and they also are very powerful and aesthetic. Images can be helpful if you don't get attached to them and think that this is the way it has to be!

My teacher gave talks using a circle as a teaching device. He had a diagram : 0 degrees, 90 degrees, 180 degrees, 270 degrees, 360 degrees. Then he would talk about mind at various degrees of the circle. At 90 degrees, this is Karma I. At 180 degrees, this is Nothing I. At 270 degrees, this is Special

Magic I. At 360 degrees, this is Big I. Then he would say, "When you truly perceive this, all the degrees in the circle mean nothing! So, throw it all away!"

Any of these things are helpful up to a point, and any of them may become an impediment.

Q: Will you talk about renunciation?

A: Changing how you do something can be a form of renunciation, and changing your attitude can also be another form of renunciation. You can look at the former as an outer form of renunciation and the latter as an inner form of renunciation. But I don't want to get caught by the words outer and inner!

There is a wonderful saying in *Zen Mind, Beginner's Mind*, the popular series of lectures by Suzuki Roshi. "Renunciation is to accept that everything changes." That is a very simple yet very profound view of renunciation. Renunciation is the acceptance that everything changes. One of the things that develops as you nurture and mature in a sitting practice, is the perception that thoughts come and thoughts go; feelings come, feelings go, sounds from outside come, sounds from outside go, sensations in your body appear, and sensations in your body disappear. You begin to recognize after a while that, moment by moment, birth and death are occurring. Moment by moment, coming and going are occurring; appearing and disappearing are occurring moment by moment by moment.

Even the sense of "I-ness" which seems to be primary, is also perceived as appearing and disappearing moment by moment. It's not as solid as we previously thought it was. So, if you have an experiential acceptance of that and appreciation of that or an awareness of that, then that in and of itself is renunciation. There's no need to make a physical act of renouncing one lifestyle for another lifestyle, or one activity for another activity because clinging to any particular thing and adhering to it and getting stuck in it will not be there. It will not be there because there is a primary sense of "everything is changing, changing, changing, changing." This is not a pessimistic or negative view. It is just a realistic view of how things are. And at the moment that something occurs you may be able to actually enjoy it and experience it fully and completely because you're not trying to maintain it in some particular self-centered way! And, in the next moment—gone! That is an ideal, of course. But as you practice more and more, you may begin to have experiences of that quality.

From the most radical standpoint, renunciation is simply the acceptance that everything changes. But, in some spiritual traditions there are activities that are connected with renunciation. Someone does some particular action, or may give up something, or enters into a particular way of living. These are all forms of renunciation, but primarily they are just facilitating devices.

The fundamental attitude of renunciation is *non-clinging*. With the awareness that everything is transient, you won't cling to anything. You'll enjoy it while it's there, but there will also be an acceptance of its transient nature. That, basically, is the attitude of renunciation in Zen practice. It is not renouncing something for something else.

In the Heart Sutra it is said: No this, no that, no eyes, no ears, no nose, no tongue, no body, no mind, no color. It sounds as though everything is being taken away, taken away. So, what then are you left with? That's a facilitating device to get you to give up, or renounce, every conceptual frame of reference that you're holding onto. And, when you let go of your conceptual frame of reference, then you see. There's just clear seeing. So, that is called *no eyes* because there is no *idea* of eyes. Usually when we're engaged in the activity of seeing, there is a subtle sense of "I am seeing that." So you have three things there: the I over here (subject); the that over there (object); and then this consciousness or activity of seeing. That one act is subtly divided into three. The Sutra cuts those three away little by little. No eyes (subject), no color (which is the thing you're seeing), and no consciousness of eyes (which means the recognition in your mind). So, if those things are cut away as different conceptual pieces, then there is just, the floor is brown! That means "no eyes." That is what this teaching device of negation is about. It doesn't mean you actually take away all of these things and wind up with a big zero. The direction of Zen meditation is to leave your ears open, leave your eyes open, leave your senses open, and experience moment by moment what is right in front of you. This is renunciation.

Trailing Vines

Questions & Answers

℘

Q: Why is there so much physical ritual if it's not as important as how your mind is sitting?

A: The bowing and various forms and techniques are all exercises in mindfulness and paying attention. Some particular way of standing, some particular way of walking, some particular way of sitting, some particular way of bowing causes you to pay attention. Its usefulness is in helping you to facilitate attentiveness and awareness.

In our practices, we put certain limitations on what we do. The purpose is to find freedom within that limitation, as opposed to the idea of freedom through getting away from everything. We find freedom through 100% doing some thing creatively, attentively, and becoming one with it. So, all of those rituals were devised to facilitate attentiveness, and their value and usefulness are within that realm.

What's most important is the quality of your attention. For example, if a person's hands are two inches higher or two inches lower in the formal sitting or walking meditation posture, that's not as important as the quality of attentiveness in keeping the position. In keeping that position with attentiveness, one will experience becoming one with the activity of just sitting, or just walking or chanting.

The great Japanese Zen Master Dogen, who brought the Soto School of Zen from China to Japan around 1200 AD, emphasized that sitting Zen is enlightenment; enlightenment is sitting Zen. His point is that the activity of sitting itself is enlightenment. When you are completely sitting, and there's no conscious idea of self, and you're totally one with the activity—no more analyzing or checking it or evaluating it—that simple activity, whatever it might be, is already the expression of your original nature.

So, the quality of attentiveness is what is most important. To recognize at that moment that inside and outside, subject and object all fuse.

The secondary point is that when we put ourselves under some limitation—like sitting in a particular way, standing in a particular way, chanting in a particular way, or putting on these robes—the aspect of ourselves that doesn't like being put under limitations will appear. We then have the opportunity to take a look at it. There is always a part of us that's looking for a reason not to do something, or that's busy making judgments about something. We make separations in that moment of "why this," "why that?" Why is she chanting so loud? Why is she chanting so soft? It's endless!! And, if you can keep your attentiveness and perceive those "whys" as clouds passing in the empty blue sky, then you are not hindered because you aren't following them. They're just there as part of the bubbling up of different mind waves, and after awhile you'll come to a point where it all settles. Even if it re-bubbles after settling, it will have a different quality than when you are identified with it. When you think that you really have an axe to grind because she is chanting too loud or too soft, then you don't have a prayer in hell at that moment! But when you can perceive those thoughts as a particular form of mind energy, then it has a very different quality. It can become humorous. So, that is the second use for having various forms in our practice.

Skillful teachers over the centuries have developed techniques to help their students. Traditions emerge because some teacher said "do this" and it helped a student. Then when the student became a teacher, he said "do this" because he knew it worked. So a tradition builds. Tradition is useful in a way; you don't have to reinvent the wheel every minute. But, if you are too bound by the tradition and fail to see the essential point behind it, then it becomes dogma and is followed by rote. Its true purpose and meaning is lost. If that continues, it loses its vitality. This is why some institutionalized religions have become just institutionalized religions. People may have lost sight of the original purpose behind some of the traditions.

There are several different styles of practice. One is not necessarily better than the other; each has its place and its time, and its therapeutic function or medicinal effect. For example, a monk decides that he's going to do a ten-year retreat alone up in the mountains. So, on his way to the mountains he passes a farmer and the farmer says to him, "Where are you going? " The monk says, "I'm going to the mountains to do a meditation retreat for ten years." "Oh, that's wonderful. Good luck on your meditation retreat," says the farmer. So, he goes up the mountain and practices for ten years, and then he ends his retreat and comes back down the mountain. When he comes to the edge of the plain, he runs into the same farmer. The farmer remembers him. "Oh, ten years ago you went up there to practice. Now you're coming back. What did you attain?" The monk says, "I attained complete mastery over anger." The farmer says, "Oh that's wonderful! But anger is a very, very difficult emotion in human life. Are you sure that you completely mastered it?" The monk says, "Oh, yeah! Completely! Without a doubt." The farmer says, "Are you sure?" This goes on, back and forth a few times, until finally the dialogue goes like this: "Are you sure?" "LISTEN!!!! I TOLD YOU!"

So, ten years, okay? It's easy to master anger when you're only facing the wall. When you come back down and resume social intercourse, something else gets presented to you. Likewise, when you enter into a community of practice, it acts as a mirror. And certain things emerge that would not when you are practicing alone. Community practice is set up for that; it's one of its functions. For some people problems arise around the structure of the situation. It's very regimented. Everybody has to sit in a particular way. Everybody puts on a robe, walks in a certain way, gets up at the same time, walks around at the same time, bows at the time. All of these rituals, which are really very arbitrary. Why put on a grey robe? We could put on a black robe or a blue robe or no robe! Why bow? Even though they are arbitrary, they have some meaning. And sooner or later, "*I like this*" or "*I don't like this*" mind will emerge.

In a community, one person is in charge of practice, and someone else is in charge of keeping the place clean, so they give orders or directions. And sooner or later, some attitude of "Why are you telling *me* what to do" emerges. But, the basic idea that is stressed is, "Don't make good, don't make bad. Put it all down." Return to your original clear mind. *(Hitting the table)* That is a simple demonstration of original energy point.

So, community practice acts as a mirror, allowing you to see your competitiveness, your checking, your evaluation, and so on. It becomes awareness practice at that time. You see your mind in the mirror of the situation. The purpose of Zen practice is to perceive your mind. This doesn't mean only your *good, holy, or spiritual mind!* Cow dung makes good fertilizer; many things grow in it. This is one of the benefits of group practice. You have to have a feeling of gratitude towards that mirror which lets you see your conditioning. Even in a situation where the activity is simple, your conditioning becomes apparent. At first you are pulled around this way and that way by it, like an ox with a ring in its nose. It can be pulled around every which way. But soon awareness begins to be an aid. The more you can see it, the less you're caught by it. You have to find your center, which is before condition and before situation, and before any idea.

Ordinary Magic

ᓌ

One day a student asked me: Somehow the magic in my life is less and less, but something seems to have replaced it in this practice. Can you comment on that?

It reminded me of a story about Master Hwang Beok, one of the early Zen Masters in China. One time Hwang Beok was traveling around as an itinerant pilgrim monk calling on the famous teachers and monasteries of China. During his travels, he befriended another monk with whom he traveled for a while. One day they came to a river. It had been raining a lot, and the river was extremely swollen. They needed to cross this river but there was no bridge.

As Hwang Beok stood on the bank, the other monk, without hesitation, walked out and onto the surface of the water—like Jesus walking on the water—same style! When he was part way out Hwang Beok said, "If I had known he was that kind of monk, I would have broken both his legs."

I thought of that story when the student used the word magic. It's true that in Zen practice there is no emphasis on the magical or extraordinary. In fact, there is a *de*-emphasis in that the practice itself stresses very ordinary kinds of conditions and very ordinary situations and very ordinary experiences. One of the most well known of the Zen stories is of the monk who came to call on Zen Master Joju. "Master!" the monk said. "I've just entered your monastery. Please give me your teaching." Probably "I've just entered your monastery" is the equivalent of saying "I've just traveled hundreds of miles to come and see you, and I've just gotten here to your monastery, please give me your teaching!" Joju Zen Master asked the monk, "Did you have breakfast?" The monk said, "Yes, I did!" Joju said, "Then, wash your bowls!" The monk had an insight, an awakening. This story stresses the very ordinary. Enlightenment is: After breakfast, wash your bowls.

I think one of the reasons many people feel that their lives don't quite work is because we are pursuing *the magical*. If I had a dime for each time I've heard someone talk about pursuing a relationship in some kind of extraordinary way, how magical it was going to be or should be, or how dissatisfying and unmagical it is, I'd be rich! I think that is something that plagues a lot of us. Looking for the magical in terms of personal relationships, in terms of intimate relationships, in terms of career, in terms of jobs, in terms of so many things. Looking for something extraordinary based on all kinds of expectations that are not quite grounded in the reality of this world.

Of course, what goes up with this type of expectation, comes down! We follow the waves of our karma being pulled by our nostrils. When we come to Zen practice, nothing changes. We still get up in the morning, we still brush our teeth, we still eat breakfast, we still get angry, we still get sad, we still get the same things we get. But, a subtle centering and clarifying process begins to occur and we begin to get a certain sense of stability that isn't lost by exaggerated expectations. In that way our life starts to work because we come more from the authentic center of who and what we are, and that is quite magical in a way very different from what we're used to.

Q: When I meditate using the question "What am I," my experience is something like this: To put it metaphorically, it's like being somewhere and asking a stranger for directions, and instead of answering you, he just starts rambling on about all kinds of crazy things. So I sort of watch him for a long time, while maintaining a sort of detachment. That's what my mind is like in meditation. Is that correct or normal?

A: That's a good analogy. On Saturday mornings we have practice at the Chogye International Zen Center of New York from 8:00 to 10:00 a.m.; that's the one time during the week that I'm here to give individual interviews to people who want them. Yesterday morning a woman came here who had never participated in formal practice before. During her interview I said to her, "Zen practice is understanding your true self. So what are you?" She said, "I don't know." I said, "That's Zen practice—keeping that mind. Ask the question 'What am I' and keep that 'I don't know' attitude. And when it becomes complete, even the sense of 'I-ness' in its usual form is not there. There's just a big sense of 'don't know,'" She thought about this. Then she said, "I thought that meditation was to relax and calm down, but when I ask myself that question, I feel kind of stirred up and uncertain." She said that all this talking starts and all these ideas about "what I am" appear. And she said, "None of them quite answers the question, so I'm left with this uneasy feeling." I said, "Yeah, it's something like when a jet plane takes off. Before it reaches its cruising altitude and speed, there's a lot of rumbling going on. It's a transitional kind of rumbling until it gets to cruising speed. Then it's straight ahead. That same kind of experience happens in meditation. If you are used to seeing yourself through preconceived ideas, or even if you usually just fill up space with a bunch of mental talking, even if it's not really cogent ideas and really well-formed concepts, even it's just blah-blah-blah-blah to fill up something so as not to have a moment of emptiness appear, you stop that with the questioning. Then you're left with a transitional feeling of uncertainty because the world that you had been living in a moment before is not there. At least momentarily, it's a different world."

So, our original stable primary self is there listening to that guy at the crossroads going "yackity, yackity, yackity, yack," and if you can just watch him, after a while he'll shut up, or he'll get tired, or he'll join you! One or the other!

I think one of the reasons some people don't stick with this practice is because this form of questioning can be disconcerting. Some people feel uneasy with it. I think this is a common experience.

One of our members who has been practicing several years now, said that when she first started practicing, that question made her fearful. "I feel like I'm losing everything." Your experience was a little different because you felt like, "Well, I can just listen to all that mental verbiage, even if it doesn't make sense. Maybe every so often I'll say to this guy, 'Yeah, but I want to know the way to such and such place.'" And then the guy talks nonsense, you wait him out and say, "Yeah, but I want to know how to get to there." That's the function of periodically raising the question "What am I?" It acts as a reestablishing of your primary direction and intention.

Q: Is "What is this?" the same question as "What am I?"

A: Same question. "What is this" means: What is this mind at this moment? What is this experience just now? So, if you really have that question, then the usual separation of subject and object in your moment by moment experience drops away. Then there's just a big question: What is this? What am I? What is this road in front of me? What is this existence?

Q: Can you say something about the paradoxical and absurd images that appear in Zen poetry and stories? What are they pointing toward?

A: You see those kinds of images in Zen language. Upside-down images. There's a story about the great Chinese lay teacher Bu Dae Sa. One time he appeared in a Confucian hat, a Buddhist robe, and bare feet. In China at that time, the Taoist monks went bare foot, Buddhist monks wore robes, and the Confucian people wore a particular kind of hat. When asked whether he was Taoist, he pointed to his Buddhist robe. When asked was he a Buddhist, he pointed to his Confucian hat. When asked if he were a Confucian, he pointed to his bare feet. Bu Dae Sa was known for his unconventional actions and sayings. One of his most famous sayings is, "Walking, I ride on the water buffalo. Crossing the bridge, the bridge flows, but the water remains still." This is a famous kong-an. Its imagery is magical and dreamlike, but it has a point. Sometimes you'll have some kind of extraordinary image or some kind of chatter going on in your mind that seems unusual, and it will be an entree into some kind of opening. It catches your attention. Simultaneously, it makes no sense and at the same time, is perfectly clear, so it opens the door to the land of "Just like this." Here is a poem by Zen Master Ma Jo that points toward this.

When you hear the wooden chicken crow in the evening,
you will know the country where your mind was born.
Outside my house in the garden,
the willow is green; the flowers are red.

The first line portrays mystical energy. The second line is about the deep silence and stillness that is the basis of mind. The last two lines suggest that the field of cultivation of this realization is in the realm of returning to the ordinary world and seeing each thing as it is clearly.

Q: One day Zen Master Seung Sahn told the story of the child who looked through the hole and saw all the animals sitting. What would you say about that? I think a lot about it. I can remember a time when I was going through unusual psychic perceptions. I didn't understand what was going on—all these different energies—moods—and images—but I still saw what was happening so clearly. I'm curious what you would say. I guess I think it's "bad," maybe a little crazy. Then I'm reminded it's not really good or bad, it's just a phenomena. But it seems to me that we practice so we'll feel more stable, centered, and grounded.

A: Zen Master Seung Sahn's version of that story is of a mother and little boy who go to a temple. The mother attends a ceremony in the chanting hall. The little boy is not interested in the ceremony so he goes outside and wanders around the temple grounds. He comes to the Zen hall where the monks are sitting inside. All the Zen halls in Korea and China have rice paper walls, so the boy looks through a little pinhole in the rice paper. He sees all of the monks sitting there, and as he watches he sees that all of a sudden one monk turns into a bear, then another one turns into a jackal, and others become lions and tigers, and all kinds of things appear.

Later, with his mother and in the presence of the Zen Master, he says, "I saw these monks turn into lions and bears and elephants and snakes." His mother tries to shut him up, but the Zen Master says, "Yes, that's correct." Our consciousness is changing, changing, changing, changing, and we embody so many different forms of existence. The mind is roaming, roaming, roaming, roaming, like the guy at the crossroads mentioned in the first question. He's changing into a bear, and into a gorilla, and into various kinds of things. But, that's a child's mind! A child would look at it with just a sense of wonder and curiosity and interest. But, if later you begin to be pulled in by those kinds of things in a way that intrudes, interferes, and abuses you, you lose your equilibrium and that's not so good. It's important to establish and practice a central point of being able to stay steady and just watch and let all images come back to the point that is before any of them. Then you may find that you're not so pulled by all of these things.

Years ago I worked in a drug rehabilitation program. My job was to teach meditation and yoga and run some rap sessions. This was before I got into Zen practice. There was a young woman in the program who had done a lot of LSD and had a few breakdowns, and had been diagnosed as schizophrenic and hospitalized. Part of her psychosis was the belief that she had stigmata, which are nail wounds in the hands. In the history of Catholicism there have been a few saints who experienced a strong identification with Christ that produced stigmata. Our group went on a ten-day Yoga retreat that was run by the Yoga institute I was connected with at that time. The retreat was a silent retreat, and every day there was meditation, yoga practice, some talks, and some work. The young woman later told me that during that retreat, she had felt safe enough to allow some of the things she had not allowed to come up since she had left the hospital to resurface in a less intense way. She was grateful for the experience of being able to see some of these things as just mind formations and phenomena and not be pulled into them in a psychotic way. Once you find your center you can not remain frightened because you have a lifeline which allows you to see and keeps you from being pulled and losing your reality base.

Some people become fascinated with unusual images; at first it's interesting and natural, but then the fascination begins to grab them. From a Buddhist psychological perspective, one might say the sixth, seventh, and eighth consciousness, or different mind consciousnessess, are not fused together tightly, or unified—so different things flow in and out. It's something like a radio that keeps picking up other stations along with the one it's tuned to.

None of these things in and of themselves are problems. But if you become attached to them, you may get pulled off center.

Fear and Anger

§

A student of mine told an interesting story. Two frogs are in a large bowl of milk which has very steep sides. They can't get out and will drown eventually. One frog is very intelligent and analytical. It deduces that there is no chance of survival and decides to just give up and drown. The other frog is not so clever and instead feels, I must try no matter what! As it swims and kicks in the milk, the action serves as a churn, and the milk begins to solidify into butter until the frog is able to save itself. There's an important point in this image of transmutation—milk becoming butter—that what was life-threatening becomes life support. It becomes a springboard from which to move forward. One aspect of human structure is emotions. Some of them we consider positive, and some of them we consider negative. But, primarily, emotions are neither positive nor negative. They are a particular energy of our being and a particular activity of our being. So, if we open ourselves to the energies of our emotions, then the possibility of transmutation is there in the experience.

In Buddhism you see these energies represented through the different images of bodhisattvas. For example, in a Tantric Buddhist mandala, whether Tibetan Tantric or Japanese Shingon Tantric, a Buddha sits unmoving in the center. And then there are attendant bodhisattvas. The Buddha in the mandala represents not-moving mind, or still point. The bodhisattvas represent the skillful expression and activity of that still mind.

In the Homage to the Three Jewels chant, there is one section where homage is made to the four universal bodhisattvas. They are: Manjusri Bodhisattva, who represents primal wisdom, or the activity of clearly seeing, or perception. The second bodhisattva is Bo Hyon Bodhisattva, who represents great activity. The third is Kwan Seum Bosal, who represents the activity of mind as universal compassion. The forth is Jijang Bodhisattva, who represents great vows, which means complete stupidity. Just like the frog in the story. Jijang says, according to the legend, "Until every blade of grass enters into final nirvana, I will postpone mine. Further, I will enter into all hells and save all beings, and then I will find my own salvation, but not until all the hell realms are empty of beings." This is the vow of great stupidity.

All of the activities of the bodhisattvas are none other than our own activities: wisdom, great action, compassion, and great vows, or having a direction. When you open yourself to the various energies or activities of your being, then fear emerges, sadness emerges, happiness emerges, anger emerges. If you stay with it and don't push it away, and don't hold onto it and make something out of it, then it is just clear. When you face that not-knowing point, sometimes the transition of going from the familiar to the unfamiliar is like getting on a jet plane to a foreign country. The plane is on the runway and it gets going down the runway, it starts to lift off, and then your stomach drops. At that moment you really don't know. You are leaving what is familiar. Sometimes there is an experience of disorientation. If you can just be with that, then everything becomes open and clear. If you face that rumbling of fear in the pit of your stomach, then a deep stability begins to emerge. Sometimes the image of the churn is used in spiritual schools: The activity of changing milk into butter. But the essential substance never changes. Water, steam, ice, changing, changing, changing form. But, essentially, they are the same and never changing H_2O.

Q: What about anger?

A: Zen practice is two-sided: Understanding my true self, and helping other beings. Understanding my true self and helping beings are not two separate things. In understanding my true self, I recognize my essential inter-connectedness with all other beings, and with the planet and cosmos, everything. This does not have to dawn in some very dramatic and mystical way. But, in very simple ways you can perceive that your true self and everybody else's true self are all not separate. In fact, the root of compassion and empathy which spring forth spontaneously comes from a recognition of that.

If you are attached to anger, if you are angry because you feel attacked, for example, then that's a very personal, self-centered kind of anger. You did this to me, so GRRRRRRRR!!! Zen Masters, being completely human, get angry like anyone else. But, in the traditional Zen stories, anger is always used to help the student in some way. In that sense, anger is not only for "me," it is for all beings. That is bodhisattva anger. That is enlightened use of anger. That is why in the Buddhist literature, bodhisattvas appear in many forms, both benign and wrathful.

Zen Master Seung Sahn used to tell this story: In Korea, a lay woman went to a shaman. The fortune teller told her that her husband was going to die in about 100 days. The woman became distraught and began to act very strange. She then went to the Zen Master: "What should I do?" The Zen Master said, "You should repeat the name of the Bodhisattva of Compassion, Kwan Seum Bosal, over and over and over again, non-stop, 24 hours a day for 100 days! The woman diligently took up the practice, chanting non-stop. In the back of her mind was a vow to save her husband, who worked as a miner. As she practiced, she became weirder and weirder and weirder. Her husband did not know what in the hell was going on! Finally, on the 100th day, some people saw the woman up on the roof, throwing off all of her clothes, standing naked, screaming "KWAN SEUM BOSAL" over and over again. This is not done in Korea, being a very Confucian society! So, the neighbors ran to the mine and called to her husband: "Your wife is on the roof naked, she is completely gone!" The husband came running out of the mine, and just as he got down the hill, the mine caved in.

The bodhisattva reveals himself or herself in very strange and unusual ways. Sometimes it appears in anger, sometimes it appears in madness. But if that anger or madness or sadness affects somebody in some way that is not self-centered, then it is for all beings.

Q: What does the mantra at the end of the Heart Sutra mean?

A: The mantra at the end of the Prajna Paramita Sutra is: Gate, gate paragate, parasamgate, bodhi svaha. Gate means gone. So, gone, gone, gone beyond (paragate). Parasamgate means completely gone beyond. And the last two words: bodhi, which means enlightened wisdom or enlightened being, and svaha, which is a sound with no meaning, which is a seed mantra, is like someone shouting Hurray!!!

There are two aspects of mantra: One is sound, and one is meaning. Mantra as sound reveals the meaning whether you understand the mantra or not. This mantra means: The revelation of the enlightened wisdom which has gone beyond all duality. To go beyond all duality means to go beyond even the duality of here and there. So, the other shore is not the other shore. There is no here and no there. And there is something which is beyond the conceptual separation of here and there. The usual view is that of here being my normal everyday non-spiritual state with all of its defilements. If you think that this state and the state of complete enlightenment (annutara samyak sambodhi) are fundamentally different, then that is not prajna paramita. You have not gone, gone, gone beyond, completely gone beyond, bodhi svaha! If you are still practicing with some idea of getting from here to there, then your practice becomes a tortuous self-betterment exercise!

So, how to make an effort which is not tainted by the notion of here versus there, or the notion of some expectation? How to make an effort simply in this moment without any dualistic idea of gaining something that is over there and is different from what is here? That is very much at the root of what is correct practice. And so, in our school we express that simply as "don't know." What is "don't know"? "don't know!!" Okay? At that moment, when there is just "don't know," there is no dualistic thinking. "don't know" IS "Gate, Gate, para gate, parasamgate, bodhi svaha." If you are in complete "don't know," then at that moment you have attained "gone beyond."

In Zen training, many kong-ans test that point of gate, gate, paragate, parasamgate, bodhi svaha. They test to see if you are still holding onto some dualistic frame of reference. For example, one teacher said, "Above the saddle, no rider, below the saddle, no horse." What is the meaning? One time, Zen Master Man Gong and some of his students went out on a scenic lake in Korea. As they were going across the lake, they looked up. Above the lake there was a beautiful big mountain. Man Gong Sunim said to his students,

"Is the boat moving or is the mountain moving?" If you say the boat is moving, that is a mistake; if you say the mountain is moving, that is also a mistake.

My teacher put a book together a few years ago called *The Whole World Is a Single Flower*. It has 365 kong-ans—one for every day of the year so you can have a big headache every day of every week of every month! In the book, his comment on this story says, "No boat, no mountain, then what???" That's the same as gate, gate, paragate, parasamgate, bodhi svaha. But, some people think that gone, gone, gone beyond means that you take everything away until there is nothing left, or a great vacuum. If you are attached to the notion of the great vacuum, then you already have duality.

No eyes does not mean no eyes, and no ears does not mean no ears! No tongue does not mean no tongue. You have to sit, perceiving with no eyes, sit perceiving with no ears, sit perceiving with no body and with no mind. That does not mean you don't see anything or hear anything, or that your body dissolves into some blissful state where you feel you are totally evaporated.

An eminent teacher said, "The true emptiness of no eyes and no color cannot be found apart from green and yellow." When we sit, there's just a brown floor. Everything becomes one experience, inside and outside, subject and object, all come together. Just seeing, just hearing, just sitting, just walking. Not "I am here and I am seeing there." It's like looking at a wonderful painting in a museum in a nonanalytical way. "AHHHHHHHHHHH." That is "No eyes!" That's gate, gate, para gate, parasamgate bodhi Svaha.

Supernatural Power
and Marvelous Activity

The True Spirit of Practice

℘

(Hitting the table with his Zen stick)

The Temple Rules say, "Understand that you have accumulated bad karma which is like a huge mountain. Keep this in mind as you bow in repentance."

(Hitting the table)

The Temple Rules say, "Our karma has no self nature. That it is created by our mind. If our mind is extinguished then our karma is extinguished. To perceive both mind and karma as empty is termed the 'true repentance.'"

(Hitting the table)

The Temple Rules further say, "We bow to see true nature, and to help all beings."

So, bowing in repentance because we have accumulated a huge mountain of bad karma; perceiving karma as empty is the true repentance; or bowing to see true nature and help all beings. Which one is the highest practice?

KATZ!!!

Light a stick of incense. Put your head and your knees on the floor. 108 x 1 equals 108.

For those of you who don't understand what all of this is about, every morning we do 108 prostrations for our first practice. This practice is referred to as the "small repentance ritual." Zen, like other spiritual traditions, deals with the notion of repentance.

The first time I did bowing practice was in 1975. I had been practicing meditation for about ten years at that time, but I had never practiced formally in a Zen center nor had I ever been to a retreat. Some friends had invited me to a weekend Zen retreat. I was told that we were going to do 108 prostrations first thing in the morning. I didn't know what that meant, so I said, "No problem." Most people doing this practice regularly keep count of the bows, either with a string of beads or mentally. But no one had clued me in on that. Also, at that time I weighed considerably more than I do now— about 40 pounds more—and I knew nothing about aerobic exercise. I had done Yoga postures every day, but that was it. So, we began doing the prostrations, and when we got to about ten or twelve, I thought to myself: We've done quite a few already. And when we got to around 27 I thought to myself: We must be near 108 now. And after that, I gave up all hope and thought: Maybe I'm going to die right here of a heart attack!

Somewhere in that morning I learned something about the spirit of practice.

There is a story related to the saying in the Temple Rules, "We bow to see true nature and to help all beings." It is a classical Zen story about bowing and perceiving true nature. One day, Zen Master Lin Chi was seated on the high seat of the dharma hall, responding to students who came to ask him questions. So, Elder Ting, one of the monks in the assembly, came forward and said, "Zen Master Lin Chi, what is Buddhism's great meaning?" Lin Chi suddenly came down from the High Seat, grabbed Elder Ting, shook him violently, slapped him in the face, and then shoved him away. Elder Ting stood there dumbfounded. He hadn't been expecting that kind of answer! One of the other monks standing next him said, "Elder Ting, why don't you bow?" Meaning, Zen Master Lin Chi has given his teaching, why don't you bow? Ting, without thinking, put his hands together and bowed. At that moment, according to the story, he was greatly enlightened.

So, that is bowing to see true nature. Sometimes, when you are in the 52nd bow or the 78th bow, you may understand Elder Ting's mind at that moment, and maybe you too will see true nature. Seeing true nature is nothing particularly extraordinary or special.

I want to talk now about the real spirit of practice, and how one keeps the spirit of Zen practice alive over and over and over again. I think that spirit is kept alive, vital and sharp through repetition.

Several weeks ago we got the new issue of *Primary Point*, the magazine of the Kwan Um School of Zen. As I looked through it, I found three articles that exemplify the spirit of practice.

The first one is an article that concerns some peace demonstrations in Cambodia. One of the leaders of the demonstrations was Maha Ghosananda, a Cambodian monk. He holds the title of Supreme Patriarch of Cambodian Buddhism, which is an elected position that the sangha there asked him to take. He has been involved with the United Nations, traveling all over the world in his work with Cambodian refugees in France, the United States, and in the refugee camps. He also is a very traditional Theravadin Buddhist monk who has practiced for a long, long time. He has a wonderful warm smile and a very unassuming way about him. The article is about some elections the UN sponsored in Cambodia. There were concerns about disruptions around the elections, so an organization dedicated to peace in Cambodia, made up of monks, students, lay men and women, decided to go on a march for peace. They walked through the territories and finished the march in Phnom Penh, the capital. Maha Ghosananda was at the head of the march. In some of the provinces shooting took place, and in others, intimidation. The people in the villages were told not to come out and greet the marchers, but they did anyway.

The march took about sixteen days. When they arrived in the capitol, there was a three-day Peace Festival. In the morning after the festival, a committee met:

> Tirelessly, the committee of coalition met the following day to plan the next event. When they presented the plan to Maha Ghosananda, he laughed. He said "You all understand very well working for peace! There is no beginning and no end. You must continuously begin again, and never become discouraged." He said also, "Our journey for peace begins today and every day. Slowly, slowly, step by step, each step is a prayer. Each step will build a bridge."

The next article was about three people who were certified as Zen teachers last December at Buddha's Enlightenment Day. The first of these three teachers, Stan Lombardo from Lawrence, Kansas, gave a talk about a poem a friend gave him. The poem is in the style of some of the old Buddhist writings which are referred to as gathas. The poem reads:

> *Whenever the work of saving all sentient beings*
> 	*becomes too much for this present moment,*
> *I vow with all beings to breathe in the grace of the morning star,*
> *And remember that they are really saving me.*

The third article from *Primary Point* which seems to go together with these two is from a talk by Jeff Kitzes, who is one of our teachers in Berkeley, California. In his talk, Jeff said that he was in his early twenties when he first heard the teaching that if you make death your advisor, you will wake up and perceive clearly. Ten years later after hearing that, his father was dying of cancer.

Ten years later, my father was sick with cancer and facing his
own death. He said to me "All my life, I thought I had to hide
who I was. Schmuck!" He realized the futility and waste of spending a lifetime not revealing his true nature to the world. It was
only by facing his own death that he could perceive this fundamental truth.

These three stories in their own way encapsulate the spirit of practice:
that peace begins over and over and over again, that somehow we have to
counteract the energy of discouragement, and that it begins in each step in
each day, over and over again. Maha Ghosananda has a prayer that he begins
by saying:

> *The suffering of the Cambodian people has been very deep.*
> *From suffering comes great compassion.*
> *Great compassion makes a peaceful heart.*
> *A peaceful heart makes a peaceful person.*
> *A peaceful person makes a peaceful family.*
> *A peaceful family makes a peaceful community.*
> *A peaceful community makes a peaceful nation.*
> *A peaceful nation makes a peaceful world.*
> *Amen.*

I think that the point here is not just about doing some kind of peace
work. We bow to see true nature and help all beings, as the Temple Rules say.
Zen practice is the synthesis of our own individual practice, and something
that reaches out from our individual practice into the community in its
broadest sense. But, it is very easy in our own individual practice to become
discouraged over and over again. In a sense, every day we fail to live up to
our highest aspirations, and over and over again, in spite of those failures,
Maha Ghosananda says we should not get discouraged. But we do get discouraged. Then the question is, how do we work with our discouragement?
How do we adjust to our circumstances, how do we use our situation? Sometimes practicing in New York, for example, is very difficult. You can yearn
for a different situation. A woman once said to me that she would like to go
and practice in a country setting. I'd like that, too! But, when you face the
fact that *this is it* for you according to your circumstances and your situation,
then that kind of thinking falls away after a while. Then, choice opens up
within your situation. How do I choose to respond to this? Recently, more
people started coming to the Zen Center. Others, including myself, began
to think, "This place is getting crowded. It's hard to practice in here. This is
not such a good practice place." But, not such a good practice place in some
ways is an *excellent* practice place! Better than a country place with the bull

frogs croaking, and the beautiful sunset, even though that is also a wonderful practice place. Be able to find your practice day by day in whatever situation you are in. Small Zen Center is a small Zen Center; a big Zen Center is a big Zen Center. A country Zen Center is a country Zen Center. A city Zen center is a city Zen Center. But the thing that is constant is: Zen Center! So, find that mind and lift yourself up over and over again with the spirit of trying and sincerity. Then your practice begins to take root and can blossom. If you are always looking for something other than what you have, you are not making the fullest use of what you do have, and then your practice becomes, over and over again, a kind of discouragement.

I like the example set by Maha Ghosananda. Given the situation in Cambodia and the discouragement that one must feel, and knowing that probably one hundred sixteen-day marches there wouldn't put a dent in the situation in one sense, they still try. The strife in that country may continue for a long, long time and yet, in the midst of that, there is the ability to raise up that mind that says: We have to do something. That is the attitude of great courage that is talked about in Zen practice. Facing something that looks hopeless and not being swallowed up by hopelessness, and having the patience to over and over again just try, and try again and again, is an act of heroism. And, of course, that is rooted in a certain faith. There is also a great perplexity here: Why is all of this suffering going on? These three are always present: question, faith mind, and courage mind. These are three aspects of the same thing.

In line with this is the poem mentioned earlier. It speaks about the effort of lifting yourself up over and over again—whether in your individual practice or in some altruistic activity, or in just sitting down to do fifteen or thirty minutes of meditation. Whenever the effort of doing that on your own feels too heavy, or becomes dry and empty in some way, *I vow with all beings....* In our chanting service there is a line at the very end that says: Vowing with all beings to attain the Buddha Way. In the poem there is a vow with all beings to *breathe in the grace of the morning star.* The morning star is what Buddha saw, according to the story, when he achieved his Great Enlightenment. *And remember that they are really saving me.* So, certainly there is the sense of interconnectedness and interdependence and intersupportiveness. That is why it is essential to practice with other people. Even if you are not practicing with people every day, it is important to come together with other people sometimes in order to recognize that there are others trying to achieve this. And even beyond the formal practice situation, recognize that there are others who are trying to do something in this world and for this world. In recognizing that, in some way, we vow together to do this, we find support not just in ourselves but in the perception that we are supported by each other. Otherwise, you may find yourself caught in the illusion of self-sufficiency. That is why the poem says, "I vow to breathe in…." We are always dependent on something outside ourselves from moment to moment. In some sense there is never aloneness, there is always togetherness, and there is always this sense of grace. The grace of the morning star. When Buddha saw the morning star he said, "Now I see that from the very beginning, each and every thing has the awakened nature." That is the perception that there is already an interconnectedness and network that is available. So, to breathe that in and to feel that is to have a sense of grace and salvation that *they are really saving me.*

Saving is an interesting word. The act of saving something means you are, in some way, ascribing value to it. You don't save something that has no value. To save all beings and to be saved by all beings means to perceive the intrinsic value of each and every being and each and every thing. If you perceive that, or some degree of it, then already you are saved by all of them and they are saved by you. This is the recognition of the absolute value of all creation before we ascribe any relative values. That is the second aspect of the spirit of practice.

And the third, of course, is Jeff's point about his father's statement on his death bed: *All my life I lived my life thinking I had to hide my true self. What a schmuck I was!* There is something very sad and poignant in that, but also something illuminating. The sadness, of course, is that his father didn't have this recognition until near the end of his life. There must have been so much suffering in feeling that he had to hide his true self and be something other than what he was. Life is a very, very precious thing. Zen Master Seung Sahn, our teacher and the founder of our school, used to say, "No one guarantees your life!" As an encouragement to practice, it means: You might die tomorrow. Don't treat your life with disrespect or disdain. Treat it as if it were worth saving, as if it had absolute value. And, therefore, encourage yourself over and over again to practice.

There is the idea of using death as an advisor. In one of Carlos Castaneda's books, his teacher says something like, "Always feel as if death is walking next to you, right past the edge of your fingertips." That concept can help you a lot. This teaching is in many traditions. However, if you dwell too much in this idea, then you can get frantic. Without it, you become complacent. So, you need to find the right attitude to use death as an advisor, and couple it with the other two: being very patient and encouraging yourself over and over again to just do something, whether it be in the area of your own formal practice and sitting meditation, or in the area of reaching out to others in some way. No matter what is going on, just be very patient, attentive, and don't get swallowed up in the enormity of the task. The task is always enormous! That is why the bodhisattva vow is also enormous. "Sentient beings are numberless, I vow to save them all!" That is so enormous it is ridiculous, it is absurd. This is why enormous numbers and visionary schemes are used in Buddhist tradition. This serves to wake you up and focus you on the immediate present in the immediate moment and realize that past, present and future are all here now in some way. Then you are not swallowed up by discouragement and the enormity of the task. When you think about getting *clear mind,* it becomes so enormous a task that you think it will take eons to achieve! But, the moment you cease being concerned with it, each moment becomes clear—just as it is. Thinking is not a problem; not thinking is not a problem. Things as they are, are just things as they are.

There is a story about Zen Master Yin-Feng. When he was about to die, he said to the assembled monks, "I've seen people die sitting, and I've seen people die lying down. Have there been any cases of someone who died standing?" One of the monks said, "Yeah, we've heard of somebody dying like that." Yin-Feng said, "Well has there been anything reported by anyone about someone who died standing on his head?" The monk said, "No, we've never heard of such a case." According to the story, Yin-Feng then stood on his head and passed away. The story says that his robe remained well-balanced and that his decorum was perfect. When the monks went to move him to cremate the body, they couldn't budge it. Many people came to see this marvel. Yin-Feng had a sister who was a nun. She bowed down in front of his body standing on its head and said, "Brother, when you were alive you didn't keep the dharma Vinaya precepts. And now that you are dead, you're still confusing people." At that she gave a Zen shout, "KATZ!!!" and pushed over the body. The monks then were able to take the body and cremate it.

There is another story about a Zen student and adept named Layman P'ang. There are many stories about Layman P'ang's wife, daughter and son. The whole family was a Zen family. He studied under two great Zen Masters in China, Ma Jo and Shih-Tou. He asked his first teacher, Shih-Tou, "Who is the person who does not follow the ten thousand things?" The Master placed his hand over Layman P'ang's mouth, and Layman P'ang had an awakening. Sometime later, Layman P'ang returned to visit this teacher. The Master asked, "Since you saw me last, how has your daily activity been?" Layman P'ang said, "If you ask me about my daily activity, I can't open my mouth." The teacher said, "It is because you are like this that I now ask you to say something." So, Layman P'ang presented this verse:

> *My daily activities are not unusual,*
> *I'm just naturally in harmony with them.*
> *Grasping nothing, discarding nothing,*
> *In every place there's no hindrance, no conflict.*
> *Who assigns the ranks of vermilion and purple?*
> *The hills' and mountains' last speck of dust is extinguished.*
> *Supernatural power and marvelous activity.*
> *Drawing water, and chopping firewood.*

The last two lines, "Supernatural power and marvelous activity. Drawing water and chopping firewood," are now a classical Zen saying. The line
about vermillion and purple refers to the officials in Chinese civil service
who wore either a robe of vermillion or purple. Layman P'ang asks who
assigns these ranks? The hills and the mountains are without a speckle of
dust, which means they have no color, no vermillion and no purple, and are
therefore pure and clear.

There is another poem by Layman P'ang which is often quoted:

When mind is as is,
Circumstances are also as is.
There's no real, and also no unreal.
Giving no heed to existence and
        not dwelling in emptiness.
You are neither a saint nor a sage.
Just an ordinary man who has done his work.

(Hitting the table three times)

If you understand these three hits,
then you understand the true spirit of practice.
What is the true spirit of practice?

KATZ!!!

When you open the door to 14th Street,
please watch your step.

Cause and Effect, Expectation, Freedom

The Teachings of Zen Master Baek Jang

℘

(Holding the Zen stick above his head, and then hitting the table with the Zen stick)

Do you see that?

(Hitting the table)

Do you hear that?

(Hitting the table)

Seeing and hearing, are they cause or result?

KATZ!!!

Listen carefully to the following:

There was a monk who studied with Zen Master Ko Sahn. This monk became dissatisfied with his progress and began to travel widely to other Zen Masters and other Zen temples. But wherever he went, he could find nothing that captivated his attention. And wherever he went, he was asked, "Where are you coming from?" and he replied, "From Zen Master Ko Sahn." Everyone said, "Oh, Ko Sahn, he's a very great and unusual Zen Master. You are very fortunate." Finally, the monk turned around and returned to Ko Sahn's place. He decided to interview Ko Sahn one more time. He asked the Zen Master, "You have a very special knowledge of Zen. Why is it that you never revealed it to me?" Ko Sahn said, "When you boiled the rice, didn't I light the match to the fire? When you passed around the food, didn't I also hold out my bowl? When did I ever betray your expectations?" At this, the monk attained enlightenment. What was it that the monk attained?

Tonight I want to talk about three things: cause and result, expectation, and freedom. Cause and result is a central teaching in all schools of Buddhism. In the Zen school it is also portrayed in a very simple, everyday, down-to-earth fashion. The teaching of cause and result is sometimes referred to as "dependent arising." It comes from a very simple statement Buddha makes in one of his early sutras: "Because of this, that. Because of that, this." Because you boiled the rice, I light the match. Because I light the match, you boil the rice. Because you pass out the food, I hold out my bowl. Because I hold out my bowl, you serve food. That's very simple. When the monk heard that, his mind opened up.

There is another aspect to this story. The Zen Master says, "When did I ever betray your expectations?" That is, I think, even more important for us because these talks are not primarily philosophical in nature but are intended to encourage our practice. Expectation in practice is a very, very serious matter. A couple of weeks ago, we had a weekend retreat here, and we sat for three days. The next week, someone came in for an interview with me, and I asked how he was doing, and he said, "When I left the retreat, I felt great, but as the week progressed, I began to notice that I was feeling a little depressed. Then it dawned on me that I had some expectation about what was supposed to come out of the retreat, and I didn't even realize that I was holding this expectation. As the week went on, little by little it began to infiltrate my mood."

Expectation is like that. It exists on so many different levels—this subtlety of our expectation toward our practice and toward the results of our practice. For this reason, it's very important to pay attention to our expectations.

I want to tell you about Zen Master Baek Jang because the notions of cause and result and expectation are emphasized in his teaching. First, a little background on who Baek Jang was, and his Zen development. When he was a young boy, his mother took him to a Zen temple to pay respects to the Buddha. The young boy saw the Buddha statue in front of the temple and pointed to it and said to his mother, "Who is that?" His mother said, "He's a Buddha." Baek Jang said, "His features are very much like a man's. Someday I'll be one, too." So, when he got a little older, he left home and became a monk. First he studied the traditional form or style of Buddhist monk's practice which was available in China at that time. But, gradually, becoming dissatisfied with it, he had heard of the Great Master Ma Jo and made his way to Ma Jo's temple where he was given a job as one of Ma Jo's attendants. Every day when a donor sent some food to the temple, Baek Jang opened the lid of the container and Ma Jo would stick his hand in and take out a rice cake, hold it up to the assembly and say, "What is this?" This went on for two years, every day. Then one day as Baek Jang and Ma Jo were walking together, they heard the sound of wild ducks. Ma Jo said to Baek Jang, "That sound just now, what is that?" And Baek Jang said, "Wild ducks, Master." Ma Jo stood still for a minute. And then he said, "That sound just then. Where has it gone now?" Baek Jang said, "Flown way." Suddenly Ma Jo grabbed hold of Baek Jang's nose and gave it a yank. Baek Jang cried out in pain, and Ma Jo said, "And you said 'Flown Away.'" At that moment Baek Jang had an experience.

When Baek Jang returned to the attendants' quarters, he met another young monk who was also one of Ma Jo's attendants, and started crying. The young monk asked, "Are you thinking of your parents?" Baek Jang said, "No," and continued crying. "Did someone scold you?" "No." "Then why are you crying?" Baek Jang said, "Just now Great Master Ma Jo grabbed my nose and pulled it very hard, and it's still hurting." The monk said, "In what way didn't you accord yourself with the Great Master's mind at that moment that he did this?" And Baek Jang said, "You go ask Master Ma Jo yourself."

The young monk went to the Zen Master's room and said, "Brother Baek Jang was crying in the attendants' quarters. What is it that happened?" Ma Jo said, "Brother Baek Jang understands. You go back and ask him." So, the monk then turned around and went back. He said to Baek Jang, "Master Ma Jo said that you do in fact understand." Suddenly, Baek Jang stopped crying and started laughing. The monk said, "Before, you were crying, and now you are laughing. Why are you laughing?" Baek Jang simply said, "Before I was crying and now I am laughing." The young monk didn't get it.

The next day, the community assembled to hear Zen Master Ma Jo's dharma speech. That day, however, as soon as Zen Master Ma Jo came in and sat in his chair, Baek Jang immediately went to the front and rolled up the prostration mat. Ma Jo then got down from his seat and walked back to his quarters. Baek Jang followed him. Ma Jo said, "Just now, why did you roll up the prostration mat? I hadn't even opened my mouth yet." And Baek Jang said, "Yesterday, you pulled my nose and it hurt." Ma Jo said, "Yesterday, at that time, where did you put your attention?" And Baek Jang said, "Today my nose is not hurting anymore." Ma Jo said, "You have deeply understood yesterday's event."

Baek Jang called on Ma Jo another time. When Ma Jo saw him coming, he held up his fly whisk. (The fly whisk is an emblem of the Zen Master's station.) Baek Jang said, "Do you identify with the function, or do you detach from the function?" (Some translations at this point say, "It is that function, it leaves that function.") These expressions point to the fact that our momentary experiences always have two facets, one of activity and one of quiescence and stillness. So, the activity of this stillness or still point is called its function shining brightly into the world. The stillness itself is the return of function to substance. Baek Jang said, "It is that function, it also returns to that function." So, when he said that, Ma Jo took the fly whisk and returned it to its place. He sat still for a moment, and then he said to Baek Jang, "Later on, when you open your mouth to help people, what will you do?" Baek Jang took the fly whisk and held it up. Ma Jo said, "Do you identify with that function, or detach from that function?" Baek Jang took the fly whisk and put it back in its place. Just then Ma Jo drew himself up and shouted so loudly that, the story says, Baek Jang was deaf for three days. Later on when he was teaching his students, he told them, "This matter of Zen is no light deal."

Baek Jang's Chinese name was Pai-chang. After Ma Jo died, Baek Jang went to Pai-chang mountain. His monk's name was actually Huai-hai, which means Heart Ocean. Pai-chang means Hundred Foot Mountain or Hundred League Mountain. It was a very, very steep mountain. So, actually his name meant Steep Mountain Zen Master. There Baek Jang established a community with the first set of rules for a Zen community. These rules included manual labor as well as sitting meditation. So, in Baek Jang's community everybody worked. Later on, that is what saved the Zen sect in China, because many of the other sects were dependent on patronage, and when Buddhism fell out of favor they were not self-supporting. But the Zen monasteries were self-supporting. Baek Jang was always the first one to get his tools and run to the fields to do work when the work bell sounded. But when he got very old and feeble, the monks tried to convince him not to work any more. He should rest, they said. Baek Jang said, "I have no virtue. How can I ask others to work when I don't?" So, the monks took his tools and hid them. Baek Jang looked for his tools, and when he couldn't find them, he sat down and refused to eat. So, when it looked like he was going to die from his fast, they gave him back his hoe! The famous Zen saying, "A day without work is a day without eating" originated from here.

A monk named Un Am once asked Zen Master Baek Jang, "Every day there is so much hard work in the fields. For whom do you do it?" Baek Jang said, "There is one who requires it." Un Am said, "Why not have him do it himself?" And Baek Jang said, "He has no tools." There is a similar story that makes a similar point. When Ko Bong Sunim was a student in Zen Master Man Gong's monastery, he went into town one day and had too much liquor to drink. When he came back, he was quite drunk. Lying in his room in the temple, he cursed out the Zen Master. "That Man Gong Sunim, his talk is worthless. He's a piece of shit." Man Gong Sunim, walking by, heard this. He slid open the rice paper door to Ko Bong Sunim's room and said, "Ko Bong Sunim, why are you saying these bad things about me?" Ko Bong Sunim looked up in his drunken stupor and said, "Oh, not about you, Zen Master, only about that stinking Man Gong Sunim." So, Man Gong Sunim said, "Man Gong Sunim and me: the same or different?" And Ko Bong Sunim pulled himself up and shouted, "KATZ!!!" Man Gong Sunim slid the rice paper door shut and told him to get some sleep.

This story appears in a book that Zen Master Seung Sahn put together called *The Whole World Is A Single Flower*, containing 365 kong-ans. He gives a little commentary under each kong-an. This story's commentary says:

Ko Bong Sunim sees the world as if it were a small coin. He sees the road as if it were a thread. Buddhas and bodhisattvas are his servants. Man Gong Sunim is like a small baby. Ko Bong Sunim is a great and free person. But, there is one thing that Ko Bong Sunim does not understand. His condition. He only understands his situation. He doesn't understand his condition. (That's a very important point.) So, suddenly a stone girl appears and says, "Ko Bong Sunim, you must get some sleep." And Ko Bong Sunim says, "Yes, ma'am." And he goes to sleep.

This is the same point. There is so much work to do. For whom do you do it? There is one who requires it. Then why not have him do it himself? He has no tools.

One of the most famous stories of Baek Jang's teaching is a kong-an that appears in the *Mu Mun Kwan*, and is the second case, "Baek Jang's Fox." It's kind of a fairy-tale-like story: Every day when Zen Master Baek Jang was to give his dharma speech, the monks would come into the hall, and an old man would also come into the hall with them. When all the monks left, this old man also left. One day, the old man remained behind. Baek Jang asked him, "Who are you?" And he said, "I am not a human being."

This is a very important sentence. Important because it raises the question: What does it mean to be a human being? It is someone who can *fully* participate in the life of being human. If we can't, then we are not human beings. We wander in some other realms: ghost realms, demon realms, god realms, etc. And what is it to attain our freedom as a human being? People wake up to this question in many different ways. Just the other day someone said to me,"I feel like these days that I'm growing, expanding, and becoming more of a person than I used to be. But, suddenly I've discovered that sometimes I am lonely. I used to feel that I didn't need anyone. But now that I recognize I am lonely, I feel a sense of humiliation about my needs. I feel as though I have become human, and yet I am no longer free and detached from my needs and loneliness." As Buddha said, becoming fully human is "no light deal!"

So, this old man said, "I am not a human being. But, a long, long time ago in the time of Kashyapa Buddha, I was the head priest or abbot of this very temple on this very mountain." (In fairy tales you often find two kinds of usage of time and space: "Long ago and far away" and "A long, long time ago in this very place, on this very mountain before the present cosmic eon." Kashyapa Buddha is some mythological Buddha who is said to have lived in some previous cosmic eon. So, how long is a cosmic eon?)

He says, "A long, long time ago on this very mountain, I was the Zen Master." Here on this mountain two Zen Masters stand facing each other. Present-day Baek Jang and olden-day Baek Jang. Sometimes "mountain" means "this body-mind." (Zen Master Lin Chi would sometimes say, "In this mountain of red flesh, there is someone who goes in and out through the senses all day long,") So, in this very mountain live two Zen Masters! But don't think that this story is just about Baek Jang. This story is about you, and you, and you, and me. This is our story because many times, every day we stand facing ourselves.

The old man continued. "And someone asked me, 'Does a greatly cultivated enlightened person come under the law of cause and effect or not?' And I said, 'They do not.' For that I have been reborn a fox for five hundred generations." A fox is universally symbolic of a nature which is crafty, sly, and calculating. How many times each day are we reborn a fox? I remember when I went for an interview with my teacher, Zen Master Seung Sahn, he would sometimes poke me in the stomach with his Zen stick, saying, "You are too CLEVER!" This means too much thinking or too smart, which is a fox's mind!

The old man said to Baek Jang, "You Master, please now give some turning words that will release my consciousness and free me from my fox's body." A turning word means to say something that flips over the basis of consciousness. Baek Jang said, "You ask me the same question." The old man asked Baek Jang, "Does a person of great cultivation come under the law of cause and effect or not?" And Baek Jang said, "Cause and effect are clear." When this old man heard this he said, "I have now attained enlightenment and am freed from my fox's body. Please perform a funeral ceremony for the fox's body as if it were a dead monk." So, after lunch that day, Zen Master Baek Jang had the temple director sound the temple bell in a signal for a funeral. All the monks were surprised because no one had been in the infirmary. They all followed Baek Jang around the side of the mountain to a small cave, and Baek Jang poked out the body of a dead fox with his stick. Then they cremated it and had the funeral ceremony. In the evening, when Baek Jang mounted the rostrum to give the dharma speech, he told the whole story. Just at that time, his number-one disciple Hwang Beok stood up and said, "This old man made one mistake and was reborn a fox for five hundred generations. Suppose someone never made a mistake. What kind of body would they get?" Baek Jang said, "You come forward and I'll tell you." Hwang Beok stood up, came forward, but before Baek Jang had a chance to do anything, Hwang Beok suddenly slapped Baek Jang in the face. And Baek Jang laughed loudly and said, "I thought the barbarian had a red beard, but now I see in front of me a red-bearded barbarian." "Barbarian with a red beard" is Bodhidharma, who was the first Zen patriarch to come to China. That means that Hwang Beok is also in the line of Bodhidharma. So, that is the story of "Baek Jang and the Fox."

Another interesting point in this story of the fox and the old man is found in Hwang Beok's statement, "This old man made one mistake. A single mistake, and he was reborn as a fox for five hundred generations. Suppose a mistake had never been made, then what?" What's a mistake? What's not a mistake? What's correct? What's incorrect? If you perceive moment by moment; if you perceive your correct function, correct situation, correct relationship, then there is no cause, no effect. No birth, no death. You enter the eternal at that moment. But, eternal is different from everlasting. Everlasting means a long time, but eternal is no time: not born. So, if you perceive this moment, there is no birth, no death, no appearing, no disappearing. It's like one complete snapshot. So, from one perspective, cause and effect are nonstop. From another perspective, there's no cause and effect. There is just what is.

It brings up the whole issue of two kinds of freedom. One is this notion of freedom as something that transcends everything. Does the person of enlightened nature fall under the law of cause and effect? The old man says no, he does not; that he is totally free of causes and conditions—any situation—and doesn't have to concern himself with anything. Has anyone seen that kind of freedom? The old man was reborn a fox for five hundred generations because he expressed this kind of freedom. If I had been there at that time, I would have asked him, "If the enlightened man does not fall under the law of cause and effect, then why do you eat every day?"

The other kind of freedom is freedom by becoming one with what is. Does the enlightened person fall under the law of cause and effect? Cause and effect are quite clear. This means moment by moment by moment I attune myself to the situation, to the relationship at hand, to the kind of functioning that is required in that situation. And within that, being in accord with what is, I find my freedom right here in the middle of cause and result. And, of course, Zen practice emphasizes the notion of moment by moment by moment, perceiving what is, and being one with what is and being able to use our particular responses and unique individuality as a way of being in attunement with the world around us.

There are two styles of Zen practice. One is a monk's style of practice and the other is lay life. The monk's style is to put down everything by going to the mountains, living in a temple, and making a very simple life. The lay person's practice exists right in the complexity of everyday life. This requires that you return over and over again to the question, "What is this mind which is perceiving this just now?" Who is the one who goes to work every day? Who is the one who takes care of the children? Who is the one who gets up in the morning and goes to sleep at night? Who is that? If you keep this bright questioning attitude alive, then your everyday circumstances and your original enlightenment come together. That means we must all be very careful and watch our step, moment by moment. This means to use our life as if it were a continuous retreat. Sometimes people ask me, "Have you ever sat a long retreat?" I find myself saying, "Yes, for the last 25 years I've been doing a retreat." But, actually, I never sat a long retreat because I have a family and responsibilities. This has forced me to use the circumstances of my everyday life *as retreat!* The most important question of all is: What am I doing just now?

There is a story about Man Gong Sunim and his teacher, Kyong Ho Sunim. One time Man Gong Sunim went to visit Kyong Ho Sunim on his birthday. Man Gong Sunim said, "Today is your birthday, Zen Master. So, I brought you some presents. Some meat, some wine, and some rice cakes." That's not usual Zen temple food. So, Kyong Ho Sunim said, "It is wonderful that you have come. You're so busy these days. How could you find the time? And where did you get all of these things from?" Man Gong Sunim said, "No, Zen Master, I am not busy these days. These days, I have no hindrance. So, if somebody gives me meat, I eat meat. If somebody gives me wine, then I drink wine. If someone doesn't give me any food, then I don't eat. So, for me meat and rice cakes are the same." (This was the attitude with which Man Gong Sunim spoke). Kyong Ho Sunim said, "Oh, Man Gong Sunim, that's a wonderful mind, but my style is not this way." "Oh, Zen Master, what is your style like?" Kyong Ho Sunim said, "I cannot get freedom. I *want* something." (That is a very important point for all of us to clarify in practice. Here a great Zen Master is saying, "I cannot get freedom; I *want* something!" What kind of want? For who? For me? For you? For my family? For my community? For the whole world? I want something.) "For instance," he said, "sometimes, I want some garlic, but in the temple we don't have any garlic." (Garlic, according to ancient Indian Buddhist teaching is an aphrodisiac, an exciting substance. So, they never cook with garlic in the temple. The monks have to go down the block for it!) "So, I go into town," he continued, "and I buy a bulb of garlic, and then I come back and plant it in the ground. I water it, and after a while it grows up and there is a lot of garlic. Then if somebody wants garlic, I give it to them. That's my style." Man Gong Sunim had an opening all of a sudden, and he bowed to the Zen Master and said, "Zen Master, I'm sorry. Before I didn't understand. Now I understand."

I cannot get freedom; I *want* something. That is the core and root of the bodhisattva path. If you have no wants then you have complete freedom and no hindrance. Someone gives me meat, I eat meat. No one gives me food, I don't eat anything. But there is no intention there. There is no great vow or sense of direction. There is no working within cause and effect to help this world. So, Zen has sometimes an expression that goes like this in the teachings: *(Hits floor with his Zen stick)* Attain your mind which is before thinking. Before name and form. Completely still, quiet and one point. Then, perceive name and form. Use name and form. The sky is blue. The tree is green. Someone gives me meat; meat. Someone gives me wine; wine. Each thing is the truth just as it is. But, that kind of freedom is not the last word in Zen practice. The last word in Zen practice is, "Oh Man Gong Sunim, I cannot get freedom. I *want* something!" So, how do I use my wants?

If you have no want then you can't have any desire. If you have no desire, then you have no feeling. If you have no passion, then you cannot have compassion. How does one light the fire, cook the rice, and turn it into something that everyone can eat? That is our Zen practice.

(Hitting the table)

Do you see that?

(Hitting the table)

Do you hear that?

(Hitting the table)

Seeing and hearing. Are they cause or result?

KATZ!!!

The winter snow is melting deep into the ground.
The spring grass is growing up by itself.

Zen Flesh, Zen Bones, Zen Marrow

ॐ

(Hitting the table)

Is that the flesh of Zen?

(Hitting the table)

Does that reveal the bone of Zen?

(Hitting the table)

Does that get at the marrow of Zen?
What is it that goes to the essence of all three?

KATZ!!!

What are you doing just now?

I want to begin with a couple of short anecdotes. The first is about a famous teacher in China during the very early period of Zen, around 500 AD, shortly after the time that Bodhidharma had come to China. His name was Bu Dae Sa. His Chinese name was Fu; he was referred to as Great Teacher Fu, or Mahasattva Fu. Bu Dae Sa was not a monk. He was a lay person with a wife and family. Bu Dae Sa began practicing Buddhism in his twenties. He worked as a farmer during the day to support his family; at night he practiced very hard and also taught students. He was a social revolutionary and reformer, and periodically he sponsored a non-discriminatory vegetarian feast. (Non-discriminatory meant anyone could come, so many poor people attended.) At that time, China was a Buddhist country, and there was a tradition that anyone who sponsored a religious feast would not be taxed on the money donated to feed the people. So Bu Dae Sa every so often took all of his money and gave a great communal feast, and then he would have no money. Sometimes he sold off his land to give one of these feasts. But the rich people who were his devotees would buy back his land and re-establish him. Bu Dae Sa's action forced the government to look at the social situation and the fact that the peasants were starving.

One time the emperor invited Bu Dae Sa to come to the palace to give a dharma speech on the Diamond Sutra. The Diamond Sutra was one of the main sutras in Buddhism at that time. All of the court gathered in the dharma hall, waiting for Bu Dae Sa to arrive. Finally, he walked into the palace dharma hall past all of the emperor's ministers and courtiers, went up to the dais, mounted the rostrum, took the Zen stick and whacked the rostrum one time *(WHACK!!!)* and walked out of the dharma hall. The emperor stood there dumbfounded. He had organized everyone to come and hear Bu Dae Sa expound on the Diamond Sutra. (You have to understand that this was a period in China before all of those crazy antics started with Zen Masters shouting and hitting people. So, this was a very unusual act at the time.) The first minister said, "Does your majesty understand?" The emperor said, "No, I don't understand!" The minister said, "Bu Dae Sa has completed his exposition on the Diamond Sutra!"

The other story is about Zen Master Hsi-Tang. When Hsi-Tang was a student under Ma Jo, Ma Jo gave him a letter to deliver to the National Teacher. When Hsi-Tang delivered the letter, the National Teacher said, "What does your Master preach?" Hsi-tang just walked from east to west in the hall, and then stood still. That's something similar to *(WHACK!!! Hits floor with Zen stick)* returning to primary point or still point or silence. So, the National Teacher said, "Only that, or is there something else?" Hsi-Tang walked back to the National Teacher and stood still again. The National Teacher said, "That's only what you learned from Zen Master Ma Jo. What do you preach?" Hsi-Tang said, "Reverend, I've already showed you." This is a very important point. It means that when someone is a student, at first they take in the style of the teacher and of what is being established. But, at a certain point, what began as a kind of crude imitation gradually begins to be digested and assimilated and completely owned. And so when the National Teacher asked, "That's only what you got from Zen Master Ma Jo. What is yours?" Hsi-Tang, without hesitation replied, "I've already showed you."

There is a similar story about Zen Master Gu-ji. When Gu-ji taught, he only had one device: He would hold up one finger. So, whenever anyone asked him a question like, "What is Buddha"? Gu-ji would just hold up one finger. "What is the True Way?" *(One finger.)* "Where were you before you were born?" *(One finger.)* With any question, he would just hold up one finger. Gu-ji had been awakened initially by a monk named Chol-ryung. Gu-ji was awakened this way: He was very despondent. Gu-ji called on Chol-ryung and shared his despondency with him, and Chol-ryung suddenly held up one finger. Gu-ji had an awakening.

When Gu-ji was about to die after he had taught for many years using this one finger device, he said, "I learned the one finger Zen from my Master Chol-ryung. I used it my whole life and I never exhausted it." And he held up one finger, the story says, and died.

At a certain point, you get a confidence in what you have taken in, a confidence in your experience, and at that point it ceases to be an imitation or your own invention. At that level of maturity, notions of imitation or your own invention are beside the point. So, someone could similarly say, "I hit the floor my whole life, and never exhausted it."

There is a story about Zen Master Hsi-Tang being visited by another Zen Master. He said to Hsi-Tang, "The sun came up very early this morning," and Hsi-Tang said, "Just at the right time." One time a layman came to call and asked Hsi-Tang, "Is there heaven and hell"? Hsi-Tang said, "Yes, there is." "Do the three jewels of Buddha, dharma, and sangha exist"? And Hsi-Tang said, "Yes, they do." The layman asked many more questions like that, all of which Hsi-Tang answered in the affirmative. Finally the layman said, "Don't you make some mistake, answering that way?" Hsi-Tang said, "Have you previously called on other monks for instruction?" The layman said, "Yeah, I studied Zen under Zen Master Ching-Shan." "Oh? What did Zen Master Ching-Shan say?" The layman said, "Ching-Shan said that none of these that I inquired about exist at all." Hsi-Tang said, "Do you have a wife?" "Yes, I do." "Does Zen Master Ching-Shan have a wife?" "No, he doesn't." "Then that teaching is all right for him." So, the Layman bowed and left.

I opened with the three facets of Zen practice. Zen flesh, Zen bone, and Zen marrow. The flesh of Zen can change quite often and take many different forms. The bone of Zen always remains the same. At the heart of the bone is the marrow where the life's blood comes from. Recently, I saw an article in a Buddhist journal. The title of the article is, "Zen In the Balance. Can It Survive America?" That's a very dramatic title. Quite honestly, I hadn't noticed that Zen was hanging in the balance. But I did notice throughout the winter that when my alarm went off at 5:00 am to get over here to the Zen Center, I felt like I was hanging in the balance! The person who wrote this article walked a fine line, acknowledging that there have always been teachings within the Zen tradition that say Zen can be practiced anywhere and anyone can practice Zen. On the other hand, the article raised some concerns about a tradition that had been established for gaining enlightenment in monasteries in Asia and was perhaps going to get diluted in the United States. The author referred to one American Zen Master who told her, "I don't give a shit about enlightenment." Of course, Zen Masters have always talked out of both sides of their mouths about enlightenment. They say that enlightenment is just an empty name, and then they urge people to practice hard to perceive something. The article also raised the issue of whether Zen was going to be a "non-enlightenment" Zen in America, and whether certain Zen teachings in America were overly concerned with ethics rather than the heart of Zen.

All of this reminded me of a conference I went to several years ago in California. It was geared for psychotherapists who also practice Zen. At that time, several Zen communities on the West Coast were undergoing a lot of turmoil. Many people were confused about Zen in America and the Zen teachers who were here, and about community practice of Zen. One guy who had been practicing in the Japanese Soto line was quite heated up about all of this. He burst out at one point in the discussion, "Maybe shikantaza was a good practice for the monks in the 12th Century in Japan. Maybe it has nothing to do with us here."

Shikantaza means "just to sit." But, if you become attached to that, if you think that sitting means something special and don't understand that it also means not only just to sit, but just to stand up, just to walk, just to talk, just to lie down, just to have a nap in the afternoon, just to eat your lunch when it's time, just to do it moment by moment, if you miss that point, then yes, maybe just sitting was very good for monks in 12th Century Japan.

Zen Master Seung Sahn in his book *Dropping Ashes on the Buddha* says, "Just to have the great question is itself enlightenment." The idea here is that everyone is already enlightened but they don't recognize it. Just to practice is enlightenment, just to sit is enlightenment. Just to do anything completely, without getting caught in some kind of dualistic frame of reference, that's correct practice and the heart and essence of Zen. The forms may change over and over again, but the essence is always constant.

In China around 1200 AD, there was another great teacher in the Lin Chi lineage named Ta-Hui. Ta-Hui had many students both lay and monastic, and he traveled widely and taught people not only in person, but through correspondence as well. It is similar to the letters we see in *Dropping Ashes on the Buddha*, and *Only Don't Know*, so teaching Zen through correspondence is not a new invention. It existed in China as early as 1200 AD, maybe even earlier. Anyway, Ta-Hui's letters have come down to us and were put into a book called *Swampland Flowers: The Letters and Lectures of Zen Master Ta-Hui.* He was very concerned that Zen students not fall into the trap of seeing Zen practice as a cultivation of just stillness. He says in one of his primary teachings that 'Once you have attained some peaceful stillness of body and mind, you shouldn't just rest content at that point because that is a trap which is referred to in the Zen literature as 'the great pit of liberation.'" He doesn't say that peaceful stillness of body and mind is unnecessary either. He has two very beautiful images of this. First is that you should make your mind like a gourd floating on water which can move unhindered and without restraint and enter any kind of situation. It can enter purity or impurity. If you cultivate that mind coming out of your stillness or being supported by stillness, then you begin to have some familiarity with the Zen tradition. The second image is, "If you only cradle the uncrying baby in your arms, what's the use?" If you only cradle the uncrying baby, that means only those parts of yourself that are peaceful and nice and that you're at rest with, and don't cradle the crying baby both in yourself and in the world, then what's the use? Cradle means to hold close or become intimately familiar with, and crying baby means distress, discomfort, and despair within us and around us. That's one of Ta-Hui's fundamental points.

Several other themes come up in his letters. The first is, what is the true vision of freedom? Another one is: How is one to use their condition and situation even if it is dull and dim? How are you to use your own mind and body and circumstances even if you feel like you're a dull, dim-witted Zen student? (That one is familiar to most of us.) Another teaching that he comes back to is: How should one relate to their emotional life? And, how should one gain power in their practice and conserve power and energy?

I will read some excerpts from *Swampland Flowers* and occasionally make comments on them.

We don't have the letters from the inquiring students in this book, all we have are Ta-Hui's responses, but it's fairly clear from the response what the students asked. The first letter is entitled "Where to Escape?" He says:

> Our great Buddhist sages could empty out all characteristics and achieve knowledge of myriad things, but even they did not instantly obliterate what was fixed by their actions, so how could commonplace ordinary people?

This point goes back to an earlier lecture I gave about Baek Jang and the old man who said he had been reborn five hundred times as a fox for giving one answer that was incorrect. You will recall that someone had asked him, "Does an enlightened teacher fall under the law of cause and effect?" and the old man said, "He does not." For that he was reborn five hundred times as a fox. Ta-Hui said that Buddhist sages could see very clearly into things, but even they could not instantly obliterate what was fixed by their actions. This refers to your karma, or what you have done before. You can't just obliterate that in one shot. If sages can't do that, then how can common, ordinary people?

> Since you are one of them, layman, I think you too should enter this state of concentration (I am about to indicate to you). In times past there was a monk who asked an old adept, "The world is so hot, I "don't know" where to go to escape." The old adept said, "Escape into a burning cauldron, into the coals of a furnace." The monk said, "In a cauldron of boiling water or the coals of a furnace, how does one escape?" The adept said, "The multitudes of sufferings cannot reach there." I hope that in the conduct of your daily activities, you will meditate like this. The advice of old adepts shouldn't be neglected.

This sentence, "The multitudes of sufferings cannot reach there," into the heart of the boiling cauldron or the coals of the furnace, makes a distinction between suffering and difficulty. For example, if you are walking along a path and a steep incline appears, or even a mountain that you have to go over, that is an obstacle in the way of your path that presents a difficulty. However, your attitude towards the obstacle is what generates or does not generate suffering. And, in fact, usually, the difficulty encountered is not an obstacle in the path. Fundamentally, it IS the path at that point. There is no path at that point other than this mountain. This is why Ta-Hui says, "Why don't you escape into the furnace?"

> This is my own prescription for getting results. [This means that he himself practices this way, also.] I wouldn't consent to pass it on to you freely unless this Path accorded with you and you were acquainted with this mind. It just takes a moment when the accord [with the path] is crude: being in the boiling water, you don't need to use any other boiling water. If he uses some other boiling water, this makes the person go mad. You must realize this. One moment when the accord is crude—don't look elsewhere, just your daily activities and conduct as a layman.

Just use what you've got. If you look elsewhere than what you've actually got, then you will be making yourself crazy. That's a big problem.

> Therefore the Buddhas and the patriarchs have always gone into the boiling cauldron, into the coals of the furnace, using this medicine to cure birth and death, the great disease that afflicts sentient beings with suffering. They are called the Great Kings of Physicians. [Then he says, now this is important:] I "don't know" whether you believe fully or not, layman. [Do you have confidence in this teaching and do you believe it completely?] If you say you possess a secret method not handed down from father to son, a subtle technique that doesn't use going into the boiling cauldron, into the coals of a furnace to escape, then I hope you'll bestow it on me.

Likewise if someone also has some method today where they think they don't have to go into the furnace or the cauldron, please bestow it on me. I've been looking for it for a long time!

Going a little further with this theme of escape, he says in another letter:

> You report that since you received my letter, whenever you run

into something inescapable amidst the hubbub, you've been
examining yourself constantly, but without applying effort to
meditate. This very inescapability itself is meditation.

That's a very, very important point. This very inescapabiltiy is meditation. Meditation is nothing else but this inescapability. Just opening wide to
what is. To go a little further:

> When you can't escape, you shouldn't exert your mind any fur-
> ther: when you don't exert your mind, everything appears. It
> doesn't matter whether your rational understanding is sharp or
> dull; it has nothing to do with matters of sharpness or dullness,
> nor does it have anything to do with quiet or confusion. Just
> when you can't escape, suddenly you get rid of the cloth bag [of
> illusion] and without being aware of it you'll be clapping your
> hands and laughing loudly. Be sure to remember: if you employ
> the slightest effort to get realization of this affair, then you're
> like a person grasping empty space with his hands—it just helps
> you to wear yourself out.

Picking up on the theme of dimness and dullness, this particular letter
is entitled "Who is in the Way?"

> Your letter informs me that your root nature is dim and dull, so
> that though you make efforts to cultivate and uphold (the
> dharma), you've never gotten an instant of transcendental en-
> lightenment.

This is a common concern of meditators especially when they first
start: My mind is dull; I have too many thoughts. What can I do about all of
this?

> The one that can recognize dim and dull is definitely not dim
> and dull: where else do you want to seek transcendental en-
> lightenment? After all gentlemen of affairs [meaning people in
> the world] who study this Path must depend on their dimness
> and dullness to enter. [We are all very fortunate!] But if you
> hold to dimness and dullness, considering yourself to be with-
> out qualifications [for the Path], then you are being controlled
> by the demons of dimness and dullness.

If you keep holding onto that rather than just accepting it and using it
as an entry point, then you are making something, attaching to something,

and you're stuck in a construction of your own making. That's very different from: I have dimness and dullness. Who is the one that perceives this dimness and dullness? What shape is he or she?

> Since those of commonplace understanding often make the intention of seeking transcendental enlightenment into an obstacle set before them, their own correct understanding cannot appear before them. And this obstacle does not come from outside: it's nothing else but the boss-man that recognizes dimness and dullness.

"Boss-man," that's an interesting translation. I believe that that is the same word as "Master." He then tells a little Zen story:

> Thus when Master Jui-yen was dwelling constantly in his room, he would call to himself, "Boss!" And would also respond to himself, "Yes?" "Be alert!" "I will." "Hereafter, don't fall for people's deceptions." "I won't." Fortunately, since ancient times, there have been such models.

"Models," of course, being lunatics talking to themselves. Our translation of the same story uses the word "Master," but maybe there is something about "Boss" that may be more effective.

> The one who does the arousing isn't anyone else, he's just the one that can recognize dimness and dullness. And the one who recognizes dimness and dullness isn't anyone else, he is your fundamental identity. This is me giving medicine to suit the disease, having no other alternative.... What I said before about depending on dimness and dullness to enter is this. Simply see what the one who can know dimness and dullness like this ultimately is. Just look right here, don't seek transcendental enlightenment. Just observe and observe: suddenly you'll laugh out loud. Beyond this there is nothing that can be said.

There is another one that I want to read here:

> I teach gentlemen of affairs to let go and make themselves dull—this way is the same principle. And it's not bad to get first prize in looking dull either—I'm just afraid you'll hand in an empty paper. What a laugh!

Sometimes when I had an interview with Zen Master Seung Sahn, he'd pick up his Zen stick and poke me in the stomach with it and say, "You are too clever. You must become more stupid!" A similar thing. Just become dim and dull.

In the next piece, called "The Great Affair," he talks about the distinctions between lay practice and monastic practice. And he tries to establish the heart of practice. Though the forms are very different, the essence is the same.

> Work diligently day and night: while eating and drinking, when joyful or angry, in clean places or unclean places, in family gatherings, when entertaining guests, when dealing with official business in your post, when concluding a betrothal—all of these are first class times to make efforts to arouse and alert yourself and awaken.

> In the old days, military governor Li Wen-ho was able to study Ch'an and attain great penetration and great enlightenment while in the thick of wealth and rank. When Yang Wen-kung successfully studied Ch'an, he was dwelling in the imperial Han-lin academy. When Chang Wu-chin studied Ch'an, he was the minister for transport in Kangsi. These three elders are examples of this "not destroying the worldly aspect while speaking of the real aspect." [The next sentence I like a lot.] When has it ever been necessary to leave wife and children, quit one's job, chew on vegetable roots, and cause pain to the body? Those of inferior aspirations shun clamor and seek quietude: thence they enter the ghost cave of "dead tree Ch'an" entertaining false ideas that only thus can they awaken to the Path.... Your study of the Path differs greatly from mine as a homeleaver [monk]. Leavers of home do not serve their parents, and abandon all of their relatives for good. With one jug and one bowl in daily activities according to circumstances, there are not so many enemies to obstruct the path. With one mind and one intent the homeleavers just investigate this affair thoroughly. But when the gentleman of affairs opens his eyes and is mindful of what he sees, there is nothing that is not an enemy spirit blocking the Path. If he has wisdom, he makes his meditational effort right there. As Vimalakirti said, "The companions of passion are the progenitors of the Tathagatas: I fear that people will destroy the worldly aspect to seek the real aspect." He also made a comparison. "It's like the high plateau not producing lotus flowers: it is the mud of the lowly marshlands that produces these flowers. [That's an image that you find very often in Buddhism. The

lotus flower, which is the symbol of awakening and enlightenment, doesn't grow in the high areas. It grows with its roots in
the swampland; in the mud. And so, out of the mud grows up
the lotus flower, the blossom.]

If you can penetrate through right here, as those three elders
that I mentioned before, your power will surpass that of us home
leavers by twenty-fold. What is the reason? We leavers of home
are on the outside breaking in; gentlemen of affairs are on the
inside breaking out. The power of the one on the outside breaking in is weak; the power of one on the inside breaking out is
strong. "Strong" means that what is opposed is heavy so in overturning it there is power. "Weak" means what is opposed is light
so in overturning it there is little power. Though there is strong
and weak in terms of power, what is opposed is the same.

"What is opposed" means your ignorance. What you are trying to cut
through is the same. Essentially what he is saying is, in a monastic situation
everything is simplified and very, very easy for you. So what you are pushing
against doesn't give you much resistance. It's the difference between working
out with a two-lb. weight and working out with a ten- or twenty-lb. weight.
If the resistance is heavier then you gain strength or power. So, essentially he
is saying that the person who is using obstacles as their practice is someone
who gains a certain kind of power.

There is just one more letter I want to read because it deals with emotions. What role do emotions play in Zen practice? How should one relate
to their emotions as a Zen practitioner? The letter is entitled "Feelings and
Affliction:"

I take it your fifth son is not recovering from his illness. [So, the
assumption here is that this guy has sent him a letter, and that
one of his children is extremely sick and maybe close to death
because he mentions death later on.] You had thought that in
this realm the feeling between a father and his son, the flow of
affection over a thousand lives and a hundred ages, would be
impossible…. Nevertheless, it is precisely when afflicted that
you should carefully investigate and inquire where the affliction
arises from. If you cannot get to the bottom of its origination,
then where does the one who is afflicted right now come from?
Right when you're afflicted, is it existent or non-existent, empty
or real? Keep investigating until your mind has nowhere to go.
If you want to think, then think; if you want to cry, then cry.
Just keep on crying and thinking. When you can arouse your-

self to the point where the habit energy of love and affection within the Storehouse Consciousness is exhausted, then naturally it's like water being returned to water, giving you back your original being....

Later he says:

Having entered the world, leave the world completely. Then worldly things are the Buddha dharma and the Buddha dharma is worldly things. Father and son are one by nature: is there such a thing as a father who is not troubled when his son dies and who doesn't think about him, or a son who isn't troubled when his father dies and doesn't think about him? If you try to suppress [such sentiments] forcefully, not daring to cry or think about it, then this is deliberately going against the natural pattern, denying your inherent nature; (it's like) raising a sound to stop an echo, or pouring oil to put out a fire. Right when you're afflicted, it's not at all something alien, and you shouldn't think of it as something alien.

In another letter, just to close this up, he tells someone the story of Bodhidharma coming to China. He says that when Bodhidharma came to China, he called on Emperor Wu, and Wu was at that time a great patron of Buddhism in China. He had built many temples, many pagodas, and had sponsored many monks and nuns, and so he asked Bodhidharma, "I have done all of this. What merit have I gained from it?" There was a teaching in early Buddhism in China that one would gain merit from doing good deeds, and maybe be reborn in one of the heavenly realms. So the emperor asks, "What merit did I gain from supporting all of these Buddhist functions?" And Bodhidharma said, "None." The emperor said, "What is the highest meaning of the holy truth?" And Bodhidharma said, "Emptiness without holiness." The emperor was shocked, and he said to Bodhidharma, "Who is this standing in front of me?" And Bodhidharma replied, "don't know." So, the emperor didn't understand, and Bodhidharma left and went on to Shaolin and sat facing the wall for nine years.

If you want to see real merit right now, don't look for it anywhere else, just comprehend it in "don't know." If you can penetrate these two words, the task of your whole life study will be completed.

(Hitting the table three times)

My task for the evening is now completed. Thank you all for coming.

Please, First Untie This Grass

Interdependency

℘

(Hitting the table with his Zen stick)

The first line of a Zen poem says:
"Good and Bad have no self nature."
Then what kind of nature do they have?

(Hitting the table)

The second line of the same poem says:
"Enlightened and unenlightened are both empty names."
Where do these names come from,and where do they return to?

(Hitting the table)

The third line of the poem says:
"In front of our doors is the land of stillness and light."
Where is the true door to the land of stillness
      and light?

KATZ!!!

This door opens to the Zen Center.
(Points to door of the Zen Center apartment)
Downstairs, two doors open to 14th Street.

The poem just cited has four lines:

Good and bad have no self nature.
Enlightened and unenlightened are both empty names.
In front of our doors is the land of stillness and light.
Spring comes; the grass grows by itself.

    It's Zen Master Seung Sahn's poem; when someone takes the five pre-
cepts, he puts that poem on the certificate. It's a terse encapsulation of the

whole of Zen Buddhist teaching. The first two lines set the stage, so to speak:
Good and bad have no self nature.
Enlightened and unenlightened are both empty names.

To talk about that, I have to refer to some Buddhist philosophy. However, we need to be clear that the purpose of Buddhist philosophy is not to philosophize. In fact, strictly speaking, according to Western standards Buddhist philosophy does not hold together as a philosophic system. On the other hand, you can't call it a theology because there is no god in Buddhism. Buddha said, in talking about himself and his teaching, "I'm the good physician dispensing different medications for different ills." So the essential purpose of any philosophy within the scope of Buddhism is as a medicinal or therapeutic. What it should do is help us to practice and perceive something in a way that we are not perceiving it currently.

So, getting back to the poem. *Good and bad have no self nature.* If they have no self nature, then what kind of nature do they have? According to basic Buddhist philosophy, all things have the nature of *other dependency.* The Heart Sutra says form is emptiness, emptiness is form. This emptiness is sometimes called other dependency. So, good and bad and any other set of categories have the nature of other dependency. Which means that all things have a relational nature. Thich Nhat Hanh addresses the notion of emptiness in his book *The Heart of Understanding.* He says that the concept of emptiness as it appears in the Heart Sutra does not mean non-existence, but that each and every thing is empty of its own self-sufficient nature:

'For example, when I look at this piece of paper that I'm writing on, I don't see just a piece of paper. I see the tree that provided the wood or the pulp that this paper was made from. I see the tree farmer who cultivated the tree from which the pulp of this paper came. I see all the weather that contributed to the tree that provided the pulp for this paper. I see the sun, I see the rain, I see the different seasons coming and going. I see maybe even the table where the farmer who cultivated the tree sat down and had dinner every night. I see his family; and on, and on, and on until within this piece of paper I see almost everything except a piece of paper. This piece of paper is inclusive of all of these things. This is the teaching of the Heart Sutra. Form is emptiness; emptiness itself is form.'

There is another school of Buddhism which explains this in a slightly different way. In the Bell Chant that we do in the morning, there is a small paragraph which says: "If you want to understand all the Buddhas of the past, present, and future, then you should view the nature of the universe as being created by mind alone." The school that uses that teaching is sometimes called the Mind Only School, or Cognition Only School, or Consciousness Only School, or sometimes Just Appearance School. It is sometimes referred to as the Yogacara School because that school was interested mainly in meditation practice. Yoga there means harnessing the mind through meditation to see clearly. When Bodhidharma came to China from India to teach the Zen doctrine, it is said that whenever he referred to a particular sutra or scriptural teaching, he didn't use the Heart Sutra but used a sutra called the Lankavatara Sutra, which is a teaching used in the Mind Only or Cognition Only School. So this notion of Mind Alone seeped into Zen Buddhism throughout its history in China in different ways. It doesn't mean Zen is that school but, rather, that they used certain aspects of it in the teaching of Zen.

In the Yogacara School, there is a teaching which is called the World View of the Three Natures. This means the one world that we all find ourselves imbedded in can be seen three different ways. One is called the Imagined Nature. The second is called Other Dependant Nature. And the third is called the Consummated or Completed Nature. So, this means that we will see what is right in front of us as either imagined in some way or tainted by our imagination, or we will see it in its character of being interdependent and everything depending on everything else. And if we see that clearly, then we see things as they are, and our view then becomes consummated or complete. We recover clear seeing.

There is a simile that is used to demonstrate this teaching. In ancient times in India, magic shows were popular. Magicians set up small road-side theaters. Travelers would stop their journey a while to watch the magic show. And so, this simile goes, the magician takes certain objects, like pieces of wood or pieces of paper, and then through the use of incantation and illusion and maybe a kind of general mass hypnosis of the audience, generates from these pieces of wood and paper the appearance of animals: lions, tigers, bears, elephants, etc. So, the people see the tiger form appearing and are astonished and maybe even frightened. They're frightened because they believe at that moment in what they see. The magician, on the other hand, is quite calm throughout and is not frightened because he sees very clearly the nature of the creative process that is occurring at that moment. And, when the magic show is over, what remains are these pieces of wood and paper, and whatever other props were used on the stage.

The point here, of course, is that the audience has a reaction and becomes frightened based on a belief. And maybe this happens because of a certain attachment to the belief that they are forming at that moment. I think even more important than the fact that they are believing something is the fact that they are having a reaction: an emotional reaction, a behavioral reaction, to what is essentially something that is being imagined.

Sometimes a similar simile is used, that of a stuffed animal. Some stuffed animals look very lifelike. If you go to an expensive toy store like FAO Schwartz and plop down a lot of money, you can get a very lifelike scary stuffed tiger. And sometimes when little children are confronted with the glaring eyes and the fangs and the claws of the stuffed tiger, they become quite frightened. They don't see it as a stuffed tiger; they take it to be a real menacing animal. On the other hand, the same child could be confronted with a stuffed horse and pet it and make friends with it, and really fall in love with it. So, the reaction and the behavior that is then organized around the belief in what this is, is dependent upon the perception. But an adult looking at the same stuffed tiger looks at it very differently. "Oh, that is very well made. It is very realistic. Look at the workmanship that went into that! That's really remarkable." They are taken with the creativity of it, but their belief system is quite different.

In the simile of the magic show it says a tiger form appears. This magically created tiger is not real. What is real are pieces of wood and paper that act as the basis for this creative generation. So, it is easy to see what is what in terms of this three-nature theory. But, there is an important point in this teaching: All who watched the magic show saw the same tiger appear. Enlightened people; unenlightened people. It doesn't make any difference. But, the orientation to what is appearing, and the reactions, understanding and perception of the whole process of appearing is quite a bit different. So, the creative process in the magic show has the nature of being other dependent. It is dependent on a process which is generated through the magician's skill and the props that he uses as his basis. But, the form is undeniably there. Likewise, a stuffed tiger is no less a form than a real tiger.

Our minds operate similarly. Thoughts appear. And these thoughts are, in essence, a creative manifestation and energy amplitude waves of our mind energy. So, in practicing, there is essentially no need to try to get rid of all of these thoughts that appear in our mind. They are the form of our mind. But, the Heart Sutra says: Form is emptiness. So, see the form and have the recognition that these thoughts are not substantive. They are not solid. They are quite transparent. To be able to see that is to recover our clear original vision, our clear original seeing. And the recovery of that is to see and experience our mind as complete, and each and every thing as it is as complete. So, that's a recognition—a re-cognition—of what is already there, untainted by some imaginary overlay.

The third line of the poem is:

In front of our doors is the land of stillness and light.

That is a very important line. It takes us beyond the area of theoretical Zen or philosophy into the realm of practice. Sometimes the five physical senses are referred to as the doors: the door of the eyes, the door of the ears, the door of the nose, the door of the mouth, and the touch sense. There are teachings that say things like "turn the mind light around." But, this poem doesn't say "turn around and look behind your doors." It says, "In front of our doors."

For example, a Zen teacher may give a new student a practice or meditation technique such as: Let your mind rest in your lower belly; breathe slowly and deeply, and just perceive that place. Some people get the idea that they should go inside and stay engrossed in their belly. However, the technique is meant to focus your mind energy if it is scattered and bring it back to a simple sense of centeredness. This is a therapeutic device. It isn't the be-all and end-all of meditation. Also, if you become too attached to that kind of practice of centering in one place and putting your attention there, then at a certain point that attachment will become a hindrance or an impediment to clear seeing.

The other day a woman told me that she had recently gone to a workshop given by Jon Kabat-Zinn, a psychologist who also does a lot of work with people who have chronic pain from on-going diseases. His approach is based on the simple mindfulness practice that is found in most Buddhist schools. When Providence Zen Center was in its infancy, Kabat-Zinn was a student of Zen Master Seung Sahn's for a while. He's become well known and has a clinic affiliated with the University of Massachusetts medical school, and has done a lot of work in pain management. So, this woman went to a workshop that he gave. He taught simple mindfulness meditation, but she said this method was difficult for her because she had trained in the Hindu method that stressed going into a deep state of inner quiet and calmness as its main focus and then perceiving from that point. She said that every time she tried just to be mindful, she began drawing in and losing herself in this inner quiet. She had a conflict between the two approaches.

The poem says, *In front of our doors is the land of stillness and light.* Essentially that means that whatever we are perceiving moment by moment by moment right in front of our sense doors is already of the nature of stillness! Each and every thing is already of the nature of stillness. Now, I know that's a little hard to believe in New York City, but the car horns in the street are essentially *(hitting the table with his Zen stick)* of the nature of stillness. The loud music of the boom boxes that the kids walk up and down the block with is also *(hitting the table)* essentially of the nature of stillness! Each and every thing is already of the nature of stillness. That means essentially that the quality of each and every thing is neither coming nor going. Before coming and before going. Just some still point. Maybe like the apex of the pendulum. Not moving. Also, that still point is not separate from coming, going, birth, death, appearing and disappearing. Absolutely not separate. So, to perceive each and every thing just as it is, is already to be in the land of stillness.

Zen Master Seung Sahn has another poem which has one line in it that says, "After so much suffering in nirvana castles, so joyous to sink into this world." Nirvana essentially means stillness. If you think of nirvana as someplace like a castle on a hill in which you are well fortified, that becomes an entrapment at a certain point. So, after so much suffering in nirvana castles, what a joy to fall back into this world with the car horns blasting and the kids running up and down the street!

Stillness and light; before our doors is the land of stillness and light. Light means shining forth. That means compassionate warmth and compassionate activity. If you don't have stillness then you can't have light. The candle flame is the substance; the light radiating is the function of the flame. So, function means compassionate activity or bodhisattva activity. Some mandalas in the Tantric school depict the five Buddha families, with a Buddha in each circle. Alongside the Buddha stand some bodhisattvas. Buddha means still point or original mind point (not moving), and the bodhisattvas represent the skillful functioning of this Buddha mind *(hitting the table)* in the realm of activity. So, that means bodhisattva enlightened activity.

There's a story about one of the National Teachers in China. Before he was the National Teacher, he was just a simple monk who lived alone in a hermitage. Winter was coming. In China, the Buddhist monks did a ninety-day retreat in winter. So in September or October, this monk went out begging food and provisions to bring back to his hermitage so that when November came he would have supplies for the start of the ninety-day retreat. One day as he was on his way back to his place—he had done pretty well that day and had a big sack of rice on his back and maybe some money—some robbers stopped him and said, "Give us everything you have." They took all his food, all his money, and then they made him take off all of his clothes and lie down on the ground naked on his back. Then the chief bandit had an idea: "This is a Buddhist monk, and Buddhist monks shouldn't kill anything. So let's tie his hands and legs with long grass." So, they did this. And then they left him lying there on his back looking up at the sun completely naked and not moving because he didn't want to rip the grass from its roots because of his vow not to kill. The emperor and his entourage were returning to the palace after their day's hunt when they saw this guy lying in the field completely naked, looking up at the sun. In China, the sun was associated with the emperor, and the emperor, I think, was deemed a descendant of the sun; so taking a sun bath was forbidden. The emperor got pissed off, and he told his captain to go over there and chop that man's head off. The captain went to the monk with his sword drawn and said, "I'm going to kill you." The monk said, "Okay, but first untie this grass." The captain got very confused at that point. "No, I'm going to KILL you!" But the monk's face was just shining, very serene and calm, and he said, "Please, first untie this grass. I shouldn't kill anything." At that point, the captain couldn't kill him. The emperor was waiting and began to get angry. "What's going on?" His captain came and told him, "This monk said 'Killing me is no problem. But, don't kill this grass.'" The emperor got down off his horse and went to the monk. And, when he saw his face shining brightly, the emperor bowed to him and had a recognition: "Today I killed many, many animals, not even for food but for sport. But your compassion is so far reaching that you are even concerned about the blades of grass." He then brought the monk to the palace where he became the National Teacher, or the Zen Master of the court.

So, this is a very famous story about shining brightly.

The last line of the poem says: Spring comes; the grass grows by itself. If you perceive in front of your doors the land of stillness and light, then spring comes; the grass grows by itself. So, I don't understand that line. But if you want to understand it, go ask the trees, go ask the grass, go ask the sun, go ask the moon, go ask whatever you feel will give you a good understanding of the essential meaning of *"spring comes and the grass grows by itself."*

(Hitting the table)

Is this door open or closed?

(Hitting the table)

Is this point stillness or activity?

(Hitting the table)

Is this of the nature of light or of dark?

KATZ!!!

One kind action supports the universe.

Not a Needle is Allowed to Pass;
But Carts and Horses Get Through

Trying, or Correct Effort

℘

(Hitting the table with his Zen stick)

How can you try to approach that?

(Hitting the table)

How can you try not to approach that?

(Hitting the table)

Trying or not trying, which one is correct?

KATZ!!!

Even before the donkey has left,
the horse has already arrived.

Even when the cloud comes in front of the moon,
the moon remains full and bright.

I want to begin by reading two short passages from the record of Zen Master Lin Chi. Lin Chi was one of the foremost Zen Masters in China during the T'ang dynasty; his lineage comes down to us today. In Japan, the Lin Chi Lineage is referred to as the Rinzai Lineage. In Korea, that is the main line also. After some of the stories in the record of Lin Chi, there is a commentary by two other Zen Masters, Kuei-shan and Yang-shan, who talk about Lin Chi's action. Kuei-shan and Yang-shan were teacher and student, but at the time they are discussing these things, their level of maturity in the dharma is fairly equal. In the first story, Lin Chi presents a poem:

> *The Great Way knows no like or different.*
> *It can go West or East.*

Sparks from a flint can't overtake it.
Streaks of lightning would never reach that far.

Kuei-shan asked Yang-shan, "If sparks from a flint can't overtake it, and streaks of lightning would never reach that far, then how have all the wise men from ages past been able to teach others?" Yang-shan responded, "What do you think, Reverend?" Kuei-shan said, "It's just that no words or explanations ever get at the true meaning." Then Yang-shan said, "Not so." Kuei-shan said, "Well, what do you think?" And Yang-shan said, "Officially, not a needle is allowed to pass; but privately, whole carts and horses get through."

The second story is about a visit Zen Master Lin Chi made to Chin-niu's temple. Chin-niu saw him coming and sat down squarely in the middle of the gate, placing his staff across his knees. Zen Master Lin Chi rapped three times on the staff, and then went off to the monks' quarters and sat down in the number one seat. (In China at that time, everything was done according to Hoyle. There was a number one seat, and a number two seat, and you had to "earn" the number one seat. But Lin Chi, newly arrived and knowing the rule, still sat in the number one seat.) Chin-niu came in, saw him, and said, "There are appropriate ceremonies to be observed when a guest and host meet. Where did you come from, Sir, that you behave in this outrageous manner?" Lin Chi Zen Master said, "Oh Reverend, what's that you say?" When Chin-niu was about to open his mouth, the Master struck him a blow. Chin-niu made as though he had fallen down, whereupon the Master struck him again. Chin-niu said, "Today is not my day."

Kuei-shan and Yang-shan discuss this story. Kuei-shan asked Yang-shan, "With these two worthy old gentlemen, was there any winning and losing, or not?" Yang-shan said, "As for winning, they both won all the way, and as for losing, they both lost all the way."

When I opened this presentation, I talked about trying, and I quoted an old kong-an: Even before the donkey has left, the horse has already arrived. Effort, or trying, in Zen is always a problematic and paradoxical issue. This notion of "trying to approach it" comes from a well-known interchange between Zen Master Nam Cheon and his student Joju. Joju says, "What is the true way?" And Nam Cheon responds, "Everyday mind is the path." Joju says, "Should I try to approach it or not?" And Nam Cheon says, "If you try, you are already mistaken." Joju asks, "If I don't try, how can I understand the true way?" That is the student's dilemma. How to try, in what way to try, what is the appropriate way of making effort from a Zen standpoint?

Referring to the kong-an quoted above, a donkey and a horse look very similar. One is a little smaller than the other, but they have similar form. So the meaning in this kong-an might be that the donkey represents the "small" ego-centered self which stubbornly holds onto like and dislike, and the horse represents the "big" self which is free and unbridled. But, the kong-an says, "Even before the donkey has left." Even before we make any effort toward cultivating or perfecting ourselves, the horse is already there! This is the primary point of faith in Zen practice. It is the faith that even before we start to practice, our Buddha nature is pure and clear and full and bright and shining like the full moon. But, that's the official line! Officially, not even a needle can pass through. It is already tight. But unofficially, horses, oxen, cars—everything is passing through. So, to be quite honest, in our practice we spend a lot of time dealing with the donkey. However, it is very important to recognize that even when dealing with the donkey, that effort or that trying has to be rooted in a primary understanding of *already* the horse is here. Already the moon is luminous and bright and clear. That, fundamentally, even when clouds are in the blue sky, the clouds and the sky are not two different things. They are one fabric. Even our distortions, even our craziness, even our getting in our own way is still fundamentally of one fabric with our pure and clear original nature. If we have that primary point, then the efforts that we make are not directed toward something out in front of us.

Joju said to Nam Cheon, "What is the true way?" And Nam Cheon said, "Everyday mind is the path." "Then should I try to approach it or not?" The translation says: "If you try you are already mistaken." But, Joju wants to know if he should try to approach it. If you feel that your goal is something you are going to *approach,* already you have set up an image in your mind of something in front of you that you're attempting to get nearer to. And, of course, the more you try to get closer to it, the more infinite your journey becomes! Because, things can be infinitely long or large or infinitely small. If you cut something in half, and cut those halves again in half, and keep repeating this, you'll never get to the point where you can't continue to cut the halves in half. So, if you start with an image of approaching something in front of you, that will be problematic in terms of the kind of effort that you have to make in Zen practice.

When I first started practicing in this school, our Zen Center was a residential Zen Center. A few people lived here who were available for practice. In 1975 or 1976, the Center moved to a new location and was no longer residential. This meant that in order to have practice in the early morning, someone had to come to the Zen Center early in the morning, maybe 5:00 a.m., to lead practice. And, of course, leading practice meant that you might lead a practice of one because maybe no one else would get up and come that early in the morning. And, in fact, that is what happened. Some of us got discouraged with the whole thing. We wanted to do away with morning practice.

At that time, Zen Master Seung Sahn, the founding teacher of our school, came to New York to pay us a visit. Of course, he had his own idea about our dilemma. He didn't care whether there was one person or one thousand people practicing in the morning. What was most important to him was that someone was there trying! For him, if one person's effort was pure and clear, it saved ten thousand people. At that time, none of us understood what that meant! He was quite firm on that point. So we discussed it with him. We wanted him to see it our way. We were a little whiney: "You know, it's really difficult to get here in the morning…." Finally he said, "Yeah, you can do away with morning practice if you want. But you won't be a Zen Center; you will be maybe a Zen club." Just the way he said it was perfect, just enough of a hint of disdain at the corner of his mouth! It was artful! "And maybe sometimes I'll come here, or maybe I won't. I don't know." So, we all looked at each other at that point, and nonverbally asked one another: Should we do this? Finally, we said, "Okay, we'll set up a schedule. And we will lead morning practice." He said, "Yeah, we try that!" Then he looked us dead in the eye and said, "Try, try, try for ten thousand years nonstop."

Around the time of our meeting with Zen Master Seung Sahn, the popular "Star Wars" movies were playing. For those of you who missed the Star Wars trilogy, they were science fiction movies with a somewhat spiritual tone to them. In the second movie, there were a group of people called the Jedi knights, who were modeled after kung-fu or martial arts masters. They had an inner power that they could direct. There is a guru-like main character, a Jedi master whose name is Yoda. The young hero of the movie goes to a distant planet to find this Yoda in order to study with him. The hero wants to save the universe from the Dark Force.

This Yoda is a little old crumpled-up guy. He has the young disciple stand upside down in a hand stand, and while in this position, Yoda has him practice mind control. The disciple's task is to raise his space ship out of the swamp that it fell into when he landed on the planet. He struggles with the task and fails, but Yoda tells him to do it again. The disciple says, "Well, I'll try." And Yoda says, "Either do or don't do. Don't try." This "do or don't do" and Zen Master Seung Sahn's "try" are different expressions of the same spirit. Opposite words but the same spirit. Do or don't do. Try, try, try for ten thousand years, nonstop. The intent is to do it wholeheartedly.

In the second story about Lin Chi mentioned earlier, Yang-shan said that when those two old birds won, they both won completely, and when they lost, they both lost completely. That means when you do something, just do it. Success or failure, it doesn't make any difference. Just do it completely. That's "try." That's correct effort.

A few weeks ago, a new copy of "*Woodfish*," our Zen Center newsletter, came out which contained an excerpt of a talk of mine along with two articles. One article, written by a visiting student from Lithuania, was about the struggle to establish a Zen center in Vilnius, Lithuania. The other article, written by Ruth Forero, a senior dharma teacher at Chogye International Zen Center of New York, was about our Zen Center in Zabreb, Croatia. She went to Croatia as part of a social work group to help health professionals there who were dealing with victims of violence and rape. When I read these two articles, I thought: These are more inspiring than the Zen Master's article! They were both about trying. Really, really trying.

The article about Vilnius Zen Center is a wonderful metaphor for anyone's establishment of practice. After our late Zen Master Su Bong visited Vilnius, some students there decided that they wanted to have a Zen Center. So, they started practicing in a vacant room in a public or government building where one of the members was the night watchman. They didn't have any meditation mats or cushions so they each brought a blanket and a pillow from home. One woman's grandmother, when she saw her going out with the blanket and pillow repeatedly, said to her, "I'm sorry your boyfriend is so poor!"

When they could no longer practice there, they moved to another place next to a locker room near a public pool. But that got a little too noisy; the keys to lockers clanked all the time. Then they moved to a school, but the kids looked in the window all the time. They then found an old dilapidated building or house, and made a bid on it to the government. They won the right to use it and began to fix it up. What makes this interesting is that part of the work, of course, was demolition and part of the work was construction. Our individual practice is like that. We start out by finding a little bit of a place within ourselves to establish practice. But it is rather shaky in the beginning; it comes and goes and comes and goes. And then, if we persist with that, after a while maybe we find a house that we can begin to establish within ourselves. But the roof might be in tough shape and needs to be propped up, and there is a bunch of junk in there that needs to be taken out. You see that kind of imagery even in the classical Zen teaching, the series of pictures called the "Ox Herding Pictures" that represent the same kind of spirit of establishing practice. The first one is where you see the footprints of the ox. Then you catch a glimpse of the ox. Then you maybe get the ox by the reins. Then, later you are able to ride the ox. And so forth and so forth and so forth. The ox, of course, is a symbol for mind, so the pictures represent training the mind. Starting a Zen Center in Lithuania with all that was going on at the time was very difficult. But difficult or easy, it doesn't make any difference if you want to do something. You just do it. If you live in a troubled country, you "don't know" if it is difficult or easy; you have nothing to compare it to! It's just what it is. Sometimes too good a situation is not such a good situation. Sometimes a more difficult situation is a better situation.

The other article was about the Zagreb Zen Center which took root in the living room of a Zen practitioner's family home! Ruth traveled to this

Zen Center, and practiced there a few times. You can imagine the difficulty
this must have presented. Not only must it have been physically difficult—
with the turmoil and savagery that was going on around there—but keeping
enough of a centered mind to still have some kind of basic spiritual direction
is very, very heroic, and very inspiring.

Of course, you don't have to go to Croatia or Bosnia to face the inner
turmoil of whether or not there is any spiritual truth in the world. You can
find that kind of turmoil right here in New York City any day of the week.
Bosnia is right here, and right here is Bosnia. At the same time, the situation
in New York City is not equal to the situation in Bosnia and Croatia. We
each find our own inner crisis in different ways in terms of starting practice
and sustaining practice, and keeping the continuum of practice going. In
fact, real practice begins for many people when they have to face that inner
crisis of doubt about whether any of this means anything or not.

There are three basic elements in Zen practice. One is establishing
your own center. The second is having a sense of direction, i.e., a clear intention. The third is having a clear perception or cognition according to time,
situation, and relationship, or seeing things just as they are in the moment.
And those three are all embodied in the word "try." If you try, then you will
find your center. You try whether it's good or bad; whether it's successful or
unsuccessful; whether it's sunny or cloudy; whether it's a war zone or a peace
zone. You just keep trying. Then you find your center. It's like the unmoving
apex of a pendulum.

Direction means that what you do isn't just for yourself but is connected also with something that is more inclusive than just "I." Or you
begin to see "I" as being more inclusive than just this small self-centered
"self." That's having a direction.

If you have a center and a direction, then you stop clinging and holding onto your ideas and opinions and your constructions. At that point, you
may begin to see much more clearly what is appropriate for this time versus
that time. What is appropriate for this place versus that place. What is appropriate for this relationship versus that relationship. Those three elements
are all together in that one word "try" or making an effort. And, of course,
effort is not just making a formal effort in formal practice. Effort also means
"What is correct trying in terms of relationship to other people as well."
This is referred to in Buddhism as the bodhisattva Path—the path of self-
lessness, or of compassion and warmth and love.

The Lotus Sutra is one of the main scriptural teachings in Buddhism.
It's an imagery-filled method of teaching that's rather fantastic. The world
that is portrayed in the Lotus Sutra is one where Buddhas and unusual beings appear frequently and repeatedly.

There are different realms and different worlds that people travel back
and forth to and from. Towards the end of the sutra there is a little story

about a bodhisattva named Never Despise. In this story, things cease being visionary and fantastic, and become more simple and human. The story is told by Buddha to a celestial bodhisattva named Greatly Accomplished, who is visiting him along with a number of other disciples. Buddha says, "Greatly Accomplished, many, many, many, many thousands of aeons ago, there was another Buddha. After his teaching had been expounded and he passed away, little by little the purity of his teaching began to tarnish. And when his teaching entered into the degraded stage, many of the followers of the Buddha's teaching became arrogant and very attached to the words of the sutras and not to the spirit of the teaching. At that time there was one simple, simple man, who, whenever he met anyone, no matter how arrogant they were, would bow to them and say, 'I dare not disparage you or despise you, because you will become Buddha.'" He didn't study scripture or practice in a formal sense, but everywhere he went he just bowed to everyone he met and said those words. Some people began to get pissed off at him. When they saw him coming, they called him "Never Despise." And they threw stones and sticks. And he would back up to an appropriate distance and bow. The story goes on and on, but because of the great power he attained through this simple practice, he lived a long time. All of those other arrogant people wind up going to the hell realms for many æons.

The Buddha ends the story by saying, "So, Greatly Accomplished, do you know who that bodhisattva Never Despise was?" "No." "He was myself in a former age. And do you know who all the disciples are who are here now partaking of this teaching of the Lotus Sutra? They are all of the arrogant ones at that time who threw sticks and stones, and have now come here after many lifetimes to this place to receive the teaching."

That's sutra style: some huge length of time which is always connected with the present. The meaning is that the attitude of Never Despise is Buddha; Buddha is Never Despise. The moment of Buddha mind is the momentary experience of not contracting yourself with arrogance. There is an expression, "That one pushes my buttons." At the moment you feel your buttons being pushed, rather than reacting with arrogance, or pushing the other person out, or withdrawing, try to see that reaction at that moment and be open to the situation. That is the bodhisattva spirit of Never Despise. That is seeing that there is something more to this than what you have narrowed it down to.

A friend of mine, who does Tibetan Buddhist practices, went to a weekend workshop which taught a practice called "receiving and giving." You imagine that you are voluntarily taking on all of the negativity of everybody else, and that you are at the same time sending out positive feelings toward these same people. In the traditional visualization practice, for example, you think of someone you feel is very negative. You visualize him perhaps with a black cloud rising out of him, and then you breathe in all of his negativity, and then send it back to the person as golden light. But, there is a danger in that kind of practice; you may come close to martyrdom. You have to be careful with that stuff. However, at the moment that you come face to face with someone you feel negativity from, or someone who pushes your buttons, if you can at that moment be open to their presence, then that is, in a sense, taking them in rather than putting up walls. And, if you can be open to them, then you can be open to your own reactions and you can see what you are constructing, and how you are narrowing down the interactive relational field between the two of you. So, that is what is suggested in this fable of the bodhisattva Never Despise.

There is one more story that I would like to tell. In Japan a few hundred years ago, Zen Master Hakuin revitalized the Rinzai Zen tradition there. Hakuin had a reputation for being a very pure character. And, in the neighborhood where he lived and had a small temple, there were some merchants. One of these store owners had a daughter who was in her late teens. It was discovered that she was pregnant. So, the parents kept after her, "Who is the father of this child?" She would not tell them at first, but finally she said, "The father of this child is Zen Master Hakuin." The parents were furious and went to Hakuin's place and confronted him with this. All Hakuin would say was, "Is that so?" Some months later the baby was born, and by this time Hakuin's reputation was completely ruined. But that didn't seem to bother him too much. The parents brought the baby to Hakuin and told him that he had to take care of it. He accepted the baby. He got milk from the neighbors, and took care of the baby for a number of months. Then finally the girl could not contain herself any longer, and she said with a lot of regret and remorse, "The Zen Master is not the father of my baby." So, the parents, with a lot of humility and regret, went to Hakuin and apologized profusely, and asked for the baby back. Hakuin very readily gave up the child, but all he would say to their apologies and regrets was, "Is that so?"

(*Hitting the table*)

TRY

(*Hitting the floor*)

TRY

(*Hitting the floor*)

TRY
Which one of these three is correct?

KATZ!!!!

One kind action embraces the entire universe.

Putting Out Wares in the Marketplace

௪

(Hitting the table with his Zen stick)

Do you realize this through effort?

(Hitting the table)

Do you realize this without effort?

(Hitting the table)

Do you realize this through an effortless effort?

Which one of those three is the correct path to
realize this?

KATZ!!!

Early in the morning, the bell rings. There is sitting and chanting.
In the marketplace people are already putting out their wares for the
day's work. So, officially, my talk is now finished!

How do you encourage someone to practice? There is a famous saying
of Bodhidharma: Fall down seven times; get up eight times. How do you
encourage someone, including yourself, to renew their resolve when it waiv-
ers, or, how do you re-intend something? And, thirdly, how do you help
both yourself and others to clear away erroneous ideas, misconceptions and
attitudes regarding practice?

These are very important considerations for one who pursues a spiritual or Zen path. And, I think it is especially important for us because Zen is
very new in this culture and was introduced to Westerners by people who
had practiced in monastic settings. Although Zen practice did not exist only
in monastic settings throughout the history of Zen in Asia, in the last few
hundred years or so the mainstay of keeping Zen tradition alive in countries
like Japan, Korea, Vietnam and China has been in a monastic setting. So,
not being a monastic myself, and never having been a monastic, nor am I
particularly interested in becoming a monastic, I've always been interested
in finding traditional texts that go back hundreds of years which bring forth
that spirit of Zen which is unencumbered by some particular cultural setting

like monasticism or lay life. How is the essence of Zen incorporated into one's particular lifestyle or vocation?

In an earlier talk I mentioned a book called *Swampland Flowers* which is the teachings of Zen Master Ta-Hui. There is another book called *Zen Letters: The Teachings of Yuan-wu*. Yuan-wu was Ta-hui's teacher.

Yuan-wu and Ta-hui are very closely connected with the Korean Zen tradition. Yuan-wu and Ta-hui lived around 1000 to 1100 AD. At that time in Korea, there was a very great Zen Master named Chinul. There is another figure several hundred years earlier, Won Hyo, who is also a very famous indigenous Korean monk and teacher. Chinul never went to China to meet Ta-hui, but he got hold of some book of Ta-hui's. It might have even been *Swampland Flowers* or some of his letters. Chinul was greatly influenced by Ta-hui's style of teaching. Ta-hui used the practice of taking hold of one big question and using that one big question to practice with. Ta-hui had written about this method, and Chinul was very taken by the way he had presented it.

Ta-hui's teacher, Yuan-wu, is most famous for a collection of kong-ans called *The Blue Cliff Record*. At that time in China, the *The Blue Cliff Record* was circulated widely and read by the intelligentsia. They got so engrossed in the literary aspect of it that they missed the heart of the Zen teaching in it. So, Ta-hui took his teacher's book and burned it, saying, "Only one big question." The *Zen Letters of Yuan-wu* are different in style from *The Blue Cliff Record*. They are much more direct and simple and practical and not so obscure as the talks from *The Blue Cliff Record*. I have picked out sections from three of the letters to use as a basis for this talk.

The translator's titles of the letters are, "Make Enlightenment Your Standard," "The Original Person," and "Right in Your Own Life." They were written to fellow Zen teachers, and to monks and lay students of his (both men and women). The climate in China at that time was very cosmopolitan, so Yuan-wu had many lay students.

In the first letter, "Make Enlightenment Your Standard," Yuan-wu begins by saying:

> Fundamentally, this great light is there with each and every person right where they stand. Empty, clear through. Spiritually aware; all-pervasive, it is called the 'scenery of the fundamental ground.'

The first sentence, "...this great light is here with each and every person, right where they stand," means: just where you're standing right now; just where you're sitting right now. This fundamental great light is there. *(Hitting table with his Zen stick)* Already. That is the initial and primary point of faith in the Zen tradition. Just where you are sitting and standing right now. *(Hitting table)* That's it! Already! That's "Good News" as they say in the Christian tradition. That means you are already saved. The essence of this light is empty, clear through. So, you cannot form any idea about it. There is nothing sticking to it. Empty, clear through. But, spiritually aware, and all-pervasive it is called the *scenery of the fundamental ground.* What is the scenery of the fundamental ground? *(Hitting table)* Only that? Or is there something else? In spring, the grass covers the ground. In fall, the leaves.

Yuan-wu continues:

> Sentient beings and Buddhas are both inherently equipped with it. It is perfectly fluid and boundless, fusing everything within it. It is within your own heart, and is the basis of your physical body, and of the five clusters of form, sensation, conception, motivational synthesis, and consciousness. It has never been defiled or stained, and its fundamental nature is still and silent.

The first paragraph I quoted is the basis of primary faith. This second paragraph is the basis of compassion. This great light is flowing into each and every thing fluidly. So, in a square container, it becomes square. In a round container, it becomes round. There is a line in the Morning Bell Chant that says, "Each and every dust particle fuses with the next. Each and every moment all interpenetrate." If everything is in some way boundless as Yuan-wu says, fusing everything within it, then what is within me is within you. What is within us is within them. What is within one group of people is within another group of people. In some way, what one does to another is done also to one's self. This is the basis of Great Action and Compassion. And, fundamentally, its nature is still and silent, and at the same time fluid and pervading everything.

A few paragraphs later, he says:

> The most important thing is for people of great faculties and sharp wisdom to turn the light of mind around and shine back, and clearly awaken to this mind before a single thought is born. This mind can produce all world-transcending and worldly phenomena. It is forever stamped with enlightenment. Your inner heart is independent and transcendent and brimming over with life. As soon as you arouse your conditioned mind, and send errant thoughts moving, then you have obscured this fundamental clarity.

Here he begins to talk about method: "The most important thing is to turn your mind around and awaken to *this mind before a single thought is born.*" Zen Master Seung Sahn is very fond of using the expression, "Before thinking mind." The technique that these two old guys in China used was referred to as Hua T'ou, or in Korean they say hwadu. This means the "word-head," or more broadly, the moment or absolute moment before words and speech appear. So, how do you turn your mind around and grasp hold of this moment before a thought is born? How does one do that? If you look into yourself, then already you are questioning *"What am I?"* What is mind? That is referred to as the "word-tail." The word-head is what results when you turn around and have that kind of question: What am I? (Become like a simpleton, completely stuck with no words or answer; that's the "word head.")

> If you want to pass through easily and directly right now, just let your body and mind become thoroughly empty. It is vacant and silent, yet aware and luminous. Inwardly, forget all your conceptions of self, and outwardly cut off all sensory defile-ments.

We are always holding so many ideas about ourselves. Who I will be in the future. Who I was in the past. Who I am right now. Who I want others to see me as. And on and on and on. That is all conception. "In-wardly, cut off all your conceptions of self. And outwardly, cut off all sensory defilements." At the same time that we make up all kinds of pictures of ourselves, we also make up all kinds of versions of the world. This "cutting off all sensory defilements" doesn't mean stop hearing, seeing, feeling, sens-ing. What is a sensory defilement? Senses are originally clear and empty. But as soon as we make up some duality, then there is something not clear in them. The Heart Sutra says, "No eyes, no ears, no tongue, no body, no mind. No sight, no smell, no taste, no touch, no object of mind, no realm of consciousness." This means that when we divide things into "over here is the seer, and over there is the thing seen, and in between is this process of see-ing," it is defiled. Because essentially, it is not separate, it is all just non-separate. You can't even say it is all one.

We have this teaching that says "Don't make anything." So, inwardly forget all conceptions of self. That means don't make anything; don't hold anything; don't attach to anything. A little while ago, I ran into a translation of a text that mentioned "habitual fabrications." It's probably a translation of the Chinese character for the opposite of "Don't make anything." I looked up this word "fabricate" in the dictionary. There were a few different defini-tions. The first one said, "To make or manufacture." Well, we have some great manufacturing plants going on here in our heads! The second one said, "To make by combining parts; to assemble." So, to "fabricate" means to make by combining parts or to assemble. What we do is pick up these bits and pieces of information and views, and out of these bits and pieces we assemble some sense of what we tell ourselves about the world. And we tell ourselves what we are about! This becomes an assemblage. The third definition of "fabricate" is "to invent." So, we may assemble by combining parts: My mother said this; my father said this. Or, we invent. And for any gaps in the story, we make up some version of what we imagine it should be.

Yuan-wu says, "If you want to pass through easily and directly right now, just let your body and mind become thoroughly empty. It is vacant and silent, yet aware and luminous. Inwardly, forget all your conceptions of self, and outwardly cut off all sensory defilements." So, how do you forget all of your conceptions of self? "What is my true self?" Do you forget them in the moment that you grab hold of the question "What is my true self?" For a split second, you do. Then, you bring out the pre-fabricated stuff. So, over and over again, you have to let go of that! This means returning over and over again to that mind which is before thinking, before concept, before any held opinion. "When inside and outside are clear all the way through there is just one true reality. Then eyes, ears, nose, tongue, body, and conceptual mind, form, sound, smell, flavor, touch, and conceptualized phenomena, all of these are established based on that one reality." It doesn't say to get rid of any of these things. It just says you have to perceive all of this as it is based on this one reality. "This one reality stands free, and transcends all of the myriad entangling phenomena. The myriad entangling phenomena have never had any fixed characteristics. They are all transformations based on this light."

That is an important point. The mandalas that hang on the walls in some temples are a big circle, and inside the very colorful circle are many different images of Buddhas, bodhisattvas, gods, demons, and many other images. They are designed in such a geometric way that they pulsate when you look at them. That is the formal or traditional mandala. The mandala also is organized around a unifying principle. So, it is a big circle and in the center is a centralized point that everything radiates from and returns to. "The myriad phenomena have never had any fixed characteristics." This means that nothing in the phenomenal world is fixed and substantive, nor does it have an identity of its own. It is all transformations of this one brightly shining light which is before thinking, before inside and outside, before subject and object. We are always story-telling to ourselves! One time I sat a retreat and for hours I talked to myself. Talking, talking, talking. I couldn't stop it. Finally, I said to myself: "Are you that lonely that you have to be entertaining yourself?" Then it stopped. When you stop telling stories to yourself, then the brightly shining world that is all just transformations of the same basic principle emerges. The sky is blue, and the grass is green. The dog is barking, "Woof, woof," the cat is meowing, "Meow." That is the great mandala. All just radiating out as it is!

Things have never had any fixed characteristics of their own. Everything is changing. And, everything is an active, pulsating mandala. That means the whole universe is brightly energized. When you come to that, Yuan-wu says, "You will be brimming full of life." Because every story that we tell ourselves to maintain this view is a narrowing down or inhibiting of our basic energy principle which can radiate out brightly!

Going a little further Yuan-wu says, "You must awaken to this mind first, and afterwards, cultivate all forms of good." So, first get some sense of "What is my true self?" And then, practice all forms of good. He then goes on to ask, "Haven't you heard the story of the Bird's Nest Monk?" And he tells a traditional Chinese story about this monk. He made his home in a tree as though he were living in a nest. That is why they called him the Bird's Nest Monk. He became very famous and people came to him for his teaching. He spoke to them from his tree perch. One time a military man called on him. He said, "Bird's Nest, what is the true teaching?" And Bird's Nest said, "Do what is right, and don't do what's wrong." The man got pissed off and said, "That's the kind of simple teaching you would give to a three-year-old." The Bird's Nest Monk said, "Yeah, a three-year-old can hear that, but even an eighty-year-old can't practice that."

The letter continues: "Thus we must search out our faults and cultivate practice. This is like the eyes and the feet depending on each other." This is a very nice image. Here are two aspects of practice: looking into oneself and recognizing this original mind, and doing something in the world out of that recognition. So, he says this is like the "eyes and the feet depending on each other." On the one hand there is insight and seeing into something. At the same time, there has to be action. The feet cannot move without the eyes seeing or else you bump into something. Also, no matter what the eyes see, you cannot go forward and realize it unless the feet move toward it. That is his point here. They depend on each other. "You must keep this mind balanced and equanimous. Without deluded ideas of self and others, without arbitrary loves and hates, without grasping or rejecting, without notions of gain and loss. Go on gradually nurturing this for a long time. Perhaps twenty or thirty years." Steady, consistent practice over long periods of time is a recurrent theme in his writing.

"Whether you encounter favorable or adverse conditions, do not retreat or regress. Then when you come to the juncture between life and death, you will naturally be set free and you will not be afraid." Do you want to practice something for your reincarnation? You don't have to visualize being reborn in celestial Buddha fields. You don't have to practice some technique of drawing the energy up your spine and sending it out the top of your head. All you have to do is to gradually nurture this mind for a long time, perhaps twenty or thirty years without retreating or regressing. Then when you come to the juncture between life and death you will naturally be set free. "As the saying goes, truth requires sudden awakening. But the phenomenal level calls for gradual cultivation." So, he makes a distinction between sudden awakening and gradual cultivation.

He says to first awaken to yourself then do good for others. It isn't necessary to follow his advice in a sequential order. Sometimes you may have a sense of what to do to be helpful in a situation. Sometimes your center is not yet clear or strong enough to know what to do in a particular situation. In that sense, Yuan-wu is saying first cultivate your own center. First, find your own truth point or primary point, and then you will be in a position to be helpful in the world. But that does not mean that you should wait until you have some huge realization before you offer a hungry person a slice of bread!

He ends this letter with what I feel is a wonderful sentence. "Make enlightenment your standard, and don't feel bad if it is slow in coming. Take care." So, what is enlightenment? One section in *Dropping Ashes On the Buddha*, by Zen Master Seung Sahn is entitled "Wanting Enlightenment." He makes the point that there is a difference between desire and aspiration. Aspiration is desire without self-centeredness. So, if you practice with this kind of spirit, if enlightenment comes, that is fine. If enlightenment doesn't come, that is also fine. That is itself enlightenment! So, here Yuan-wu says to make enlightenment your standard and don't feel badly if it is slow in coming.

The next letter has the same theme within it. I will just read a little bit of it. It's called "The Original Person." "The great teaching is basically quite ordinary. It is easy to enter for those with sharp faculties and quick wits and broad penetration who don't use their intellectual brilliance to try to comprehend it." So you need quick wits, but if you use your intellect you will miss it. Sometimes when you go in for an interview, a Zen Master will take his stick and poke you in the stomach. (At least the Zen Master I had did that!) And then he might say, "You're too clever! Must become more stupid!" Yuan-wu says a few paragraphs further, "If you are equanimous towards everything including the ultimate ungraspability of mind itself...." This is an important point towards practice. When some people pick up the kong-an "What am I" or "What is this," or whatever the primary question is, they try to get hold of something. Here Yuan-wu says that if you keep balanced toward everything, including the ultimate *ungraspability* of mind itself, then there is *nothing* to get hold of! And at that point where there is *nothing* to get hold of, you must keep calm and balanced or else you will burn yourself out. Yuan-wu continues, "So if you keep equal towards everything including the ultimate ungraspabilty of mind itself, and your conditioned mind fades away and spontaneously comes to an end, then perfect illumination of inherent nature appears whole without needing any contrived efforts to make it." Without making any contrived efforts to make it.

There is a wonderful story of Zen Master To-an. To-an was traveling around visiting other temples dressed in the regular clothes of a traveling monk. At one of the temples, he asked a monk about the Zen Master of the temple. The monk said, "The Zen Master of this temple is one of the greatest monks in all of China. Every day he does one thousand prostrations. He only eats one meal. He hasn't left the temple in twenty years, and he is always sitting in meditation." To-an said, "Well, he sounds like an extraordinary person. I can't bow one thousand times a day, but my mind is never lazy. I can't eat just one meal a day, but I never desire food. I can't stay in any one place for very long, but wherever I go, I find no hindrance. I can't sit meditation for too long, but my mind never gives rise to thinking." The monk said, "I don't understand you." To-an said, "You go inside and ask your Master." The monk went inside, and a few minutes later the Zen Master came running out and prostrated himself on the ground in front of To-an and said, "Thank you for opening my mind. Before, my practice was only focused on myself with a bunch of contrived efforts. Now I see something different. Please let me become your student." To-an said, "No, no, no. You don't need to become my student. Only keep the mind you had when you were bowing just now."

(Hitting the table three times)

Thank you all for listening.
Are there any questions?

Q: During our practice when you told us to ask ourselves the question "What am I?", there was part of me that thought and tried to come up with an answer. Then there was another part of me which was, I think, the part that I ended up listening to, which was just to hold the question there somehow. I could come up with all sorts of answers, but I guess I just would like for you to talk about that part of it—the part that just sits with the question.

A: How to do it. The methodology of it. This is an unusual technique compared to what we're used to in our usual approach to learning something. That kind of question in Zen practice is called hwadu. It literally means the *head of speech.* The words of the question are the question's tail, but the mind that results from asking the question is the *head of speech,* or the *word-head,* or the *moment before thought.* The moment before name and form appear. When you raise up the question using the words *What am I?,* it's like a finger pointing at something. So, if the finger is pointing at the moon, don't keep looking at the finger, look at the moon! The state of mind that results from having that kind of question is like the moon. It's the head of speech. Before speech. If I say to you "What are you?", what can you say? *(The questioner was silent and looked puzzled).* Yes, that mind!! That's the head of speech. When we ask this question, we direct ourselves toward it and, of course, lose it over and over and over again! The main thing, then, is to keep coming back to that subtle feeling of unanswered question, or perplexity, or curiosity, or a certain kind of uncertainty about the actual nature of myself.

Ultimately, when the question has become complete, there are no words there, no speech. No name. No form. Just a wordless sense of *don't know*. But, that is difficult to sustain in the beginning. Then we back up to ways and means of facilitating that and stabilizing attention enough so that you can stay with it. If someone could hear that question one time, and have that mind and just stay with it, they would never need to say the words "don't know" again. If your mind is moving a lot, you can periodically mentally just say the words "don't know" to re-tune yourself with that attitude. The moment you "don't know" with sincerity, it's as if you have put down a huge bundle. All thoughts, all concepts, all opinions. Temporarily, you have let go of them. Or, if you need a little more structure, if your mind is very discursive, or you need a narrower focus to keep your attention in check, then pay attention to your breathing. Let your mind rest just below the navel. That is the body's center of gravity, and it is where your breath originates from. In Asian countries, this part of your body is referred to as *energy garden*. This place is the root of your vitality. So, it has a certain kind of focusing power. If you breathe out from there, you can use your breathing to stabilize your attention. If you need it, you can do that with each breath. If you don't need it, you can throw it all away. Also, after a while, it may get mechanical, so you may have to arouse some edge of curiosity. What am I? For example, you can inhale *What am I*, and breathe out *don't know*. If you're not going to use your breathing, if you're going to sit letting your breath just take care of itself, then periodically you'll raise up the question *What am I?* Sometimes the words will just condense themselves into just one word *What?* That will be enough to give you an edge of curiosity. And then you'll have the feeling of not knowing. Having that feeling of not knowing is like the moon in the sky. It gives you a vantage point. Having established that, thinking will come, thinking will go. Feelings will come, feelings will go. It doesn't make any difference. Just let it be. But, if you lose it and start to get pulled away by thinking and feeling, then again you'll have to re-establish it.

Q: Can you say something about integrating practice into your lifestyle if your life is such that you have to use ideas a lot everyday?

A: Thinking or conceptualizing or intellectual functioning per se are not the problem. Human beings have intellectual functions the same as they have physical functions, emotional functions, and various other functions. That is not the problem. The problem is when you begin to see and attach and hold on to those functions as if they were the whole story. That's when it becomes difficult.

If a job requires you to use your intellect, that's a job. If you're clear, then you can use your intellect very clearly to help someone. If you're a teacher, you're helping your students; if you're a physicist, hopefully what you're engaged in helps this world in some way. That's not a problem. The question is: Can you use that clearly?

When you raise up a primary question such as *What am I?*, or, *Who am I?*, and the question becomes 100%, there's just a wordless sense of not knowing. At that moment you touch a place which is before thinking, before name, before form, before speech, before words. Don't know. We sometimes refer to that as "primary point." So, that "don't know" mind, or that primary point, is sometimes referred to as "clear like space."

This means that it is clear like a mirror. It doesn't mean you space out and go somewhere! If your mind is clear like a mirror, then if red comes it's red at that moment, if white comes, it's white at that moment. If nothing comes, it's just empty mirror. This means that when you're doing something and you're not holding anything or making anything or attaching to anything, then you're just doing it! Inquiry in activity means you are one with your activity.

The words of the question are sometimes referred to as "the finger pointing at the moon." That means, *what am I?*, or any question, is like a finger pointing at the moon. If you look at the moon, you can't keep looking at the finger. The finger becomes irrelevant. So, the moon is like the question's head. The finger, or the words of the question, is like the question's tail. One points you toward the other.

If you keep holding onto the words of the question when you're seeing the moon, it's like saying, "Oh, there's the moon, there's the moon, there's the moon...." It becomes silly. At that moment there is just the moon. Of course, in our practice we lose sight of the moon over and over again. When that happens, you take out the finger and use it.

So, essentially, in practice this means being able to use what you have without hindrance. To use your thinking, your emotions, your physicality—to use all of these things. That's the final meaning of the phrase from the Sutra; *no eyes, no ears, no nose, no tongue, no body, no mind.* No eyes means, simply, "Oh, the wall is white!" At that moment of just seeing, there is no sense of "I am over here looking at a wall that is white." That's clear functioning.

Pierce the Target, Draw the Bow

Joyfully Alive!

ℰ

(Hitting the table with his Zen stick)

Layman P'ang said, "Difficult…like taking a handful of sesame seeds and throwing them at a tree and trying to get them to stick."

(Hitting the table)

Laywoman P'ang said, "Easy…like touching your nose when you get out of bed in the morning."

(Hitting the table)

Their daughter said, "Not difficult; not easy…like the tips of a hundred blades of grass, the patriarchs' meaning is clearly evident."
If you make one of those correct, you go to hell like an arrow. If you make none of those correct, you're also making a big mistake. So, what is correct then?

KATZ!!!

When the alarm clock rings, quickly get up. If somebody is hungry, give them something that is nourishing and sustaining.

In my last talk I read from a selection of Yuan-wu's letters. In his letters, there are a number of themes that emerge to which he repeatedly returns. One of the themes is the contrast between taking it easy, thereby allowing some spontaneous emergence to occur, versus doing strong practice over a long period of time. Another theme is the notion of inwardly letting go of all ideas of self, and outwardly letting go of all ideas related to the objective world. He plays with these ideas back and forth because the medicine of one moment may not be the medicine of another moment— the medicine for one student may not be the correct medicine for another student.

The letter I began with at the end of my last talk is called, "The Original Person," and I will now expand further on it. The first sentence is, "The great teaching is basically quite ordinary. It's easy to enter for those with sharp faculties and quick wits and broad penetration who don't use their intellectual brilliance to try to comprehend it." A little further on Yuan-wu says, "If you are equanimous towards everything, including the ultimate ungraspability of mind itself, and your conditioned mind fades away and spontaneously comes to an end, then the perfect illumination of inherent nature appears whole without needing any contrived efforts to make it." Mind IS essentially ungraspable and ungraspability IS the essence of mind. Take care not to get too tense about that. It reminds me of our tradition of the "don't know" attitude, or the not-knowing mind. We emphasize this teaching, but there still is a tendency to want to make something out of this "don't know." I had a friend years ago who first introduced me to the Kwan Um School of Zen. He practiced with us for a while after introducing me into all of this stuff, then he dropped away. Once or twice a year, I'd get a call from him and we'd chat. Sooner or later he'd come around to the question, "So, this 'don't know mind.' What is that?" Then six months or a year would go by and he would call me again, and he'd say, "So, this 'don't know mind.' What is that?" This went on for years. I got a call from him the other day. It's close to twenty years now since I started practicing in this school. This time, however, he didn't ask me about "don't know mind." I think something occurred for him; he may have finally realized this "don't know mind" in some way. But, for years, he wanted to grab hold of something. What is "don't know?" This was his question over and over again to me. *(Hitting the table with the Zen stick)* "don't know." "But, what IS 'don't know?'" *(Hitting the table)* "don't know." "But, what is 'don't know?'" That can become a big sickness. Be careful.

"If you maintain equanimity towards everything...." including mind itself, "and your conditioned mind fades away...." This is the mind of ideation, the mind of holding opinions of one kind or another, the mind that forms judgments about things. This "conditioned mind fades away and spontaneously comes to an end." This is a beautiful image. This is like clouds in the sky. This mind just fades away if an attitude of equanimity is kept. Let the clouds come and fade away. There is no need to get into pushing them out of the way because clouds essentially do not have much substance to them! They will fade away on their own. Your thinking will fade away on its own. Your conditioning will fade away on its own. So, if you allow this conditioning to fade away like clouds in the sky, it will spontaneously come to an end, "then perfect illumination of inherent nature appears whole without any need for contrived efforts to make it."

Too often we grab hold of a technique or an approach, or go from one teaching to another in some contrived attempt to make something happen. But, if you look at some of the basic Zen teaching, you can see there is not much of an attempt at contrived pushing. For example, when the Second Patriarch came to see Bodhidharma, he stood in the snow and Bodhidharma ignored him. According to the legend, he finally cut off his arm. Bodhidharma then said, "What do you want?" The patriarch-to-be said, "My mind is not at rest. Please, Master, give my mind rest." So, Bodhidharma said, "Take out your mind and give it to me, and I will put it to rest." The Second Patriarch said, "When I look for my mind, I cannot find it." Bodhidharma said, "Then I've already given your mind rest." There is not much contrivance there!

There is another similar story. A monk said to an eminent teacher, "How can I be free and unfettered?" The Zen Master said, "Who put your mind in chains?" Who puts your mind in chains? Who is putting my mind in chains at this moment, the next moment, the next moment? If you perceive that "WHO," then freedom spontaneously emerges. Not much contrivance there. On the other hand, if you think that these stories point to some notion that there is no necessity for practice, then you have missed their intent. One has to practice, but with an attitude of noncontrivance or nongrasping as a background attitude. So, hard practice, easy practice; it doesn't make any difference. But, if your practice is not informed by a basic notion of "don't make some kind of contrivance out of this" or "don't make a 'thing' out of this," then sooner or later you will be led astray, and your practice will become subtly materialistic.

In another of his letters, in terms of a different kind of attitude towards practice, Yuan-wu says:

> This thing is there with everyone right where they stand. But, only if you have planted deep and strong roots in the past will you have the strength in the midst of worldly truth to be able to push entangling objects away. You must constantly step back from conventional perception and worldly entanglements and move along on your own and reflect with independent awareness. Cleanse and purify your karma of body, mind, and mouth, sit upright and investigate reality until you arrive at subtle insight. Right in your own life, detach from conditioned views. Abandon deep-seated conditioning and erroneous perception that has been with you from time without beginning. Smash the mountain of self to pieces.

This is a pep-talk. Here he says to "smash the mountain," and in the other he says to just take it easy, no problem. So, which is the correct way to practice? Should you smash the mountain of self to pieces, or should you just let the clouds in the sky pass by until they come to an end spontaneously? That is a very interesting question. How should one practice? Is the strong-effort style correct; is the no-effort style correct? Can you merge the two? How? That is a very important point.

Moving along a little further, Yuan-wu talks about compassion which is based upon fearlessness:

> If you are in opposition to anything, then this creates duality. If you take a step further, not a single thing is established. After that you are quiet and properly attuned and you clearly see the original person. Your whole being is liberated, and at peace. You are forever without any possibility of retreating or regressing. You attain fearlessness, and with expedient means based on this fearlessness you can rescue sentient beings.

So, he links the notion of fearlessness and compassionate activity, which he calls "rescuing sentient beings."

There are a couple of stories in our tradition that I like to tell which relate to this notion. Zen Master Seung Sahn's teacher, Ko Bong Sunim, traveled around and stayed at various temples. One time, he came to a small mountain temple. The abbot of the temple asked Ko Bong Sunim if he would stay there for a day or so and just watch over the temple while he went down the mountain to take care of some business in the town below. So, Ko Bong Sunim said that would be no problem. After the abbot left, a woman came up the mountain to the temple. She told Ko Bong Sunim that she had come to have a memorial service performed for one of her dead relatives. (In Korea, on the anniversary of someone's death, the relative comes to the temple with a rice offering, and the temple monk performs a chanting service.) So, Ko Bong Sunim said, "No problem, we can have the memorial service." However, Ko Bong Sunim had only trained as a Zen monk and not as a chanting monk. That is a different style. But because the woman wanted so badly to have a memorial service, he said, "No problem." He took up the moktak (the wooden instrument with which we chant) and started chanting. He knew a little bit of the beginning of this particular chant. But after two or three minutes he'd just about exhausted what he knew of it. In his youth he had studied Taoism for a while and had learned some Taoist chants. So, he segued into the Taoist chants without any hesitation or embarrassment. When he ran out of the Taoist chants, he went back to the Buddhist chant and finished the ceremony. The woman bowed and thanked him, and started home. Halfway down the mountain she ran into the abbot on his return to the temple. Now, this woman had been a nun for some time in her early years, and she had reentered the world and raised a family. She was quite familiar with what the liturgy should sound like. The abbot asked her, "Where are you coming from?" "I just came from the temple. We had a memorial service for my relative." The abbot was confused. "Who performed the memorial service?" She said, "That monk who you left to watch the temple." The abbot said, "That monk is a Zen monk. He doesn't know the liturgy." And she said, "I know. It was wonderful." That is expedient means based on fearlessness.

There is another story about Ko Bong Sunim's grandteacher, Kyong Ho Sunim, who lived in the 1800's into the early 1900's. Kyong Ho Sunim was living in a small hermitage with his student Man Gong Sunim, who acted as his attendant. A leprous woman appeared at the hermitage begging food one day. (At that time, leprosy was a frightening disease, and lepers were considered outcasts.) As the story goes, Kyong Ho Sunim took her into his hermitage and spent two or three days with her in his bedroom. Man Gong Sunim brought his Master food, and realized after a while that he brought food for more than one person. When he realized that Kyong Ho Sunim had a woman in his bedroom with him, Man Gong Sunim looked at Kyong Ho Sunim kind of inquisitively and said, "You're my teacher, and I don't check or evaluate your behavior." But there was kind of a questioning attitude like, "What's going on here?" And Kyong Ho Sunim said, "This woman presented herself and I could see that she had lost all sense of human feeling, and so I invited her to stay with me for three days." That's also expedient means based on fearlessness.

In some lesser way, we also practice that in our school. Shortly after a person becomes a member of the Zen Center or formalizes their relationship with our tradition by taking the five precepts, they are invited to give a dharma talk. The person gives a talk whether or not he or she is confident or scared to death! It doesn't make any difference, inhibited or not, they still give a fifteen or twenty minute talk. Sometimes people in the audience feel embarrassed for the person or feel an intense discomfort. I remember feeling that myself! On occasion, Zen Master Seung Sahn comes to New York and gives a dharma talk, or more exactly, answers questions from the audience after the student's talk. And, at the end of a student's talk, Zen Master Seung Sahn will always say, patting the student on the back, "Wonderful talk." Of course, he probably doesn't even understand half of what they say because his English is so limited. But, that doesn't make any difference. What he's responding to is the heart it takes to come up here and present a talk. Good, bad, or indifferent, doesn't make any difference. You did it! That is training in fearlessness.

Inch by inch we stick our toe in the water of that fearlessness. But that is a wonderful experience. You begin to realize that whatever mistake you might make or whatever imperfection you might present, is not the big deal that you often make it into in your mind! Most of us believe that our short-comings will be cast in concrete, and perhaps even a tag will be hung on the cement marker, like "Fool!" or "Idiot!" or whatever the dreaded name may be! There is a feeling that this will be very very permanent, that whatever I do will be solidified and named and will exist for æons! But in Yuan-wu's letter the point is made: "Your conditioned mind fades away like clouds and spontaneously comes to an end." If you perceive that these things are not substantial like cement blocks, that they are much more like clouds floating and dissolving, then a certain kind of possibility of fearlessness emerges. This doesn't mean that you don't necessarily feel butterflies in your stomach. Or that you don't feel uncertain. Fearlessness in this sense means that you go ahead and do it anyway with a perception that none of this stuff is solid like cement. That is a very important practice point—perhaps the most important practice point: Recognize this and just do something over and over and over again.

After a student gives a few dharma talks, Zen Master Seung Sahn might say, "Soon become dharma teacher necessary!" This means that you will be given a long robe, and you know that you "don't know" your ass from your elbow in terms of what Zen practice is really about. In your mind you've got this image of somebody training for twenty or thirty years in a Zen monastery where everything is very austere, and you've only been practicing maybe a year or two, and are just beginning to be able to sit still. And suddenly, now you are a dharma teacher! At that point, you may feel you cannot do this. But, bit by bit, some kind of encouragement towards the direction of fearlessness emerges. Of course this isn't limited to a Zen organization. Such experiences present themselves to us every day of the week in some fashion or other. So, we need to encourage ourselves to see that none of this stuff is so substantive that we have to be afraid of it.

Moving on to another one of Yuan-wu's letters, this one is called "Self and Things." "All the myriad things are neither opposed to nor contrary to your true self. Directly pass through to freedom, and they make one whole. It has been this way from time without beginning." He is saying that all the phenomena in the world are neither opposed nor contrary to your true self. If you pass directly through to freedom, you and the world make one whole, not separate. In another letter he says to someone else, "Abandon the deep-seated conditioning and erroneous perception that has been with you since time without beginning." He says that, on one hand, you have been one with the universe, and on the other, you have been caught by deep-seated conditioning and erroneous perception. That means that "time without beginning" *(Hitting the table with the Zen stick)* is right here and now, moment by moment by moment. At any particular moment, on one side is: You and the universe have never been separate. Right next to that, like two pictures flashing in and out in one big circle is: All of your conditioning and ideas about separation of self and other, inside and outside, good and bad, etc. Both have existed since time without beginning. That means right within your erroneous perception you may perceive this wholly unified self and world at any particular moment over and over again.

He says, "The only problem is when people put themselves in opposition to it, and spurn it and impose orientations of grasping or rejecting, creating a concern where there is none. This is precisely why they are not joyfully alive."

Zen Master Hyang Eom addressed his students one day saying, "This matter of Zen is like a person up a tree. His hands are tied behind his back, also his feet are tied and bound. He hangs from a branch by his teeth...."

A very striking image! Hands are the means by which we get a grasp onto something. Also, we manipulate and move things around with our hands. So, the possibility of grasping anything or moving it around and manipulating it is cut off in this story. Feet are also tied and bound. Feet are the appendages with which we get a stance and solidify ourselves and find our place. Yuan-wu has advised us to stay balanced, even towards the ultimate ungraspability of mind itself. This means, in some sense, there is no particular stance. We try, though, over and over again, to form some stance as if it were going to endure. We act as if our position is the enduring position.

Returning to the story, Hyang Eom said, "At that moment, someone under the tree asks the hanging man, 'Why did Bodhidharma come to China?'" There are probably other things that one might be more concerned about at that moment! But this question actually refers to Bodhidharma's trip from India to China to reveal mind-to-mind transmission, or Zen mind. So, this question means, "Please reveal to me the teaching of the Zen tradition and help me find out how I can attain clear mind."

Hyang Eom continues: "If the person in the tree keeps his mouth closed, he evades his duty or obligation to help this seeker down below who is sincerely asking for help." Some translations of this story say the person in the tree will be killed if he evades his duty. Other translations say he's as good as dead. On the other hand, if the person up there opens his mouth, he'll fall. It's a very high tree, and it is a long way down. So, if you are this person in this tree, how will you stay alive?

Our practice is an encouragement to stay alive and vivid and clear. How do you stay alive? Yuan-wu says, "If you're not grasping or rejecting, then this is precisely the point where you will become joyfully alive." So, if you want to be joyfully alive, then you must perceive the following question: How do you stay alive in whatever you are doing? At each moment, we may find ourselves at an impasse between the novelty of the emerging phenomena and our fixed categories related to our known past. At that time, how do we meet the challenge of the moment and stay alive rather than closing down and deadening our experience?

One time I was leading a retreat, and someone came in for an interview. I presented a kong-an to this person. She had been practicing for a while, and understood intellectually the meaning of the kong-an. She said to me at one point, "You want me to demonstrate something, don't you?" I said, "Yes, so why not do it?" And she could not bring herself to demonstrate the point in the kong-an. She felt stuck in a place where she could neither go forward nor backward. "You want me to come alive and demonstrate something here about this point!" Finally, I asked her, "Would you feel terribly embarrassed if you gave this demonstration?" She said, "Yes, I would."

That is a big, big problem for many of us. At the moment something calls to us to "come alive," or to take a step forward and step into the world, we shrink up and withdraw. And at that moment, in some way, we deaden ourselves, inhibit ourselves, and hold back the joyful, free flowing of our life energy. That energy which could flow into compassion, warmth, helping ourselves and helping others in this world. Please try to stay alive!

(Hitting the table)

Does that express sameness or differentiation?

(Hitting the table)

Does that express neither sameness nor differentiation?

(Hitting the table)

Does that express both sameness and differentiation?
If you say any of those, that's a big, big, big mistake.
Why?

KATZ!!!

If you want to catch the lion, then you must enter the lion's den.
If you want to pierce the target, please draw the bow.

Play It Again, Sam

The Spirit of Repetition

§℘

Zen Master Un Mun took his stick and hit it once on the platform. Then he said to the assembly, "All sounds are the Buddha's sounds, and all forms are the Buddha's form, but when all of you hold up your bowl of food, you hold a bowl view. And when all of you stand up to walk, you hold a walking view. And when all of you sit, you hold a sitting view. How you all go on this way!" And he chased them all out with his stick.
So. (*Holding up his Zen stick*)
Can you see this?

(*Hitting the table*)

Is that Buddha's form?

(*Hitting the table*)

Do you hear that? Is that Buddha's sound? Sound and form, seeing and hearing all come from where?

(*Hitting the table*)

Is that Buddha's original brightness?

KATZ!!!

The sun has already set over the western mountains.
The moon is rising in the east. In the country at this time of year, the crickets are silent.

In this talk I will return to the letters by Zen Master Yuan-wu. I'm going to read a few lines to use as a jumping-off point. In my last talk, I ended with this paragraph from one of the letters entitled "The Original Person":

You're forever beyond any possibility of retreating or regressing. You attain fearlessness, and with expedient means based on this fearlessness, you can rescue sentient beings. You must continue this way without interruption forever. This is the best.

In another letter entitled "Right in Your Own Life," he says toward the middle of the letter:

> You should spend twenty or thirty years doing dispassionate and tranquil meditation work. Sweeping away any conditioned knowledge, and interpretive understanding as soon as it arises, and not letting the traces of the sweeping itself remain either. Let go on that side, abandon your whole body and go on rigorously correcting yourself until you attain great joyous life.

In a letter called "Self and Things" he says:

> Time and again I see long-time Zen students who have been freezing their spirits and letting their perceptions settle out and clarify for a long time. Though they have entered the Way, they immediately accept it as a single device or single state, and are now rigidly holding to it and won't allow it to be stripped away. This is truly a serious disease. To succeed it is necessary to melt and let go and spontaneously attain a state of great rest.

That last line seems to be particularly important, "to succeed it is necessary to melt and let go...."

I think you can see the first two phrases are similar. The first one says you should go on this way forever. The second one says you should do about twenty or thirty years of dispassionate practice, sweeping, sweeping, sweeping until even the traces of the sweeping are gone. Now, how do you get rid of the final traces of the sweeping? That is an interesting question. What do you use to sweep away the sweeping? And, in both of the letters he's talking about a long time—not being concerned with the amount of time it takes. You should go on this way forever, just practicing; just practicing. Twenty, thirty, forty, fifty, sixty, years. Twenty, thirty, forty lifetimes. It doesn't make any difference. Just keep sweeping until there is not a trace left of even the sweeping. Then joyous life appears. Sounds good to me! The third quote is about letting it all melt and letting go. There clearly is something about the spirit of practice in these three quotes.

A couple of weeks ago, I got a letter from a person in Philadelphia asking about meditation practice. Over the last year, he had read books on meditation and tried various methods. He tried Tibetan, Nichiren, Zen meditation and so on. He finally settled on practicing counting his breaths. But then he came across Kapleau Roshi's book *The Three Pillars of Zen*, where he found a statement that went something like this: "If you want to attain enlightenment, then you can't just practice counting your breath." The book advised picking up a kong-an and working with that if one were seeking enlightenment. He was a little confused at this point. How should I practice, he asked. Should I just keep counting my breath, or should I use a kong-an?

This raises a question about the advisability of directing one's self towards some notion of enlightenment to begin with. And, will that interfere with practice at some stage? And, does it not interfere with practice in its purest form when one is looking for something called enlightenment?

Last weekend we had a three-day retreat. When it came time to end the evening at 9:45 p.m. on Saturday in order to resume the next morning at 4:30 a.m., I told the people, "It's said that the period between 12:00 midnight and 2:00 in the morning is a very special practice period because at that time a special kind of dharmic energy is present and accessible to people if they are receptive to it. I think we should all go to bed from 10:00 p.m. to midnight and get up and sit from midnight to 2:00 a.m. and then go back to bed. If anyone thinks they can't do that, then you're excused." Of course, no one had the "chutzpah," as they say in Yiddish, not to attend after that speech! The next day at the end of the retreat, during the circle talk, someone commented, "I am a salesman by profession, and I listened to you last night, and you're a pretty good salesman." He said, "When I got out here at midnight, and we started sitting, I began to wonder: Where is the dharma energy? It certainly isn't over here on this cushion! Maybe it's over there with Ken or somewhere else!"

It is true that many traditions say that certain periods of the day are more advantageous for practice, and it is usually the time when there is a juncture between day and night or between one day and the next. Not only Zen and Buddhist tradition teaches this. You also find it in the Jewish Cabalistic tradition, for example. What is more significant than whether anyone felt the dharma energy or not, is the fact that they were willing to go beyond what they normally think of as what they can and cannot do, and tried. Most of us are very attached to sleep and a number of other things that we don't recognize. On some level we believe that we can't make it without a certain amount of these things. And, in that belief, we narrow down the realm of our possibilities. As Yuan-wu says, "At a certain point, you just have to let it all melt." Whether anyone got dharma energy or did not get dharma energy between 12:00 and 2:00, more important was the aspect of, "Yeah, I'll try this, and just see." That is the quality of experimentation and taking a leap, and not being attached to any particular result. Dharma energy comes? Great. Dharma energy doesn't come? That is also great. Enlightenment comes? Wonderful. Enlightenment does not come? That is also wonderful. In fact, that is enlightenment!

This does not ignore the fact that at some point along the path some-one may have an unusual experience that is labeled an "enlightenment expe-rience." But, in the broader perspective of practice, that is not so sustaining as the experience of, whatever comes, "wonderful." Ram Dass told a story that relates to this. He gave a lecture at a university auditorium, and in the front row there was an elderly woman sitting and crocheting. Ram Dass talked about non-attachment and the non-duality of existence and letting go and just being, and all of the profound Vedantic and Buddhist notions that he is greatly in love with and has spent his life cultivating. After com-pleting his talk, people came up to speak with him. The woman whom he had noticed crocheting during the talk came up to him and said, "Oh, you understand that, too, huh? Do you knit, too?" (Meaning, I spontaneously grasp these truths that you just talked about during my knitting sessions.) That is the spirit of practice. She had just sat there crocheting. She had come to spirituality late in life. It was a big discovery for her.

There are a couple of stories about some of my favorite jazz piano players that also exemplify this spirit of practice. One is about Bud Powell, who, along with people like Dizzy Gillespie and Charlie Parker, revolution-ized the jazz scene in this country in the late 40's. One day some musician friends came to call on Bud at his house. It was summertime, and the door was not locked. They came in and found Bud sitting at the piano playing "Embraceable You," an old standard tune from maybe the 1930's. He played "Embraceable You" over and over. After a while, the guys got a little disinter-ested, so they went out and bought a jug of wine or pot or something, hung out, got high and goofed around for a couple of hours. Then they decided to go back and hang out at Bud's house again. When they got back, Bud was still sitting at the piano playing "Embraceable You."

A friend of mine, jazz pianist Barry Harris, told me a similar story about Thelonious Monk. At one time Barry lived in the same house with Monk. One day, Monk sat down at the piano and played a very old tune, "My Ideal," another one that goes back maybe to the 20's or 30's. He said Monk just played the melody to "My Ideal" over and over again. In jazz, you usually play the melody and then improvise. But Monk just played the melody over and over and he got deeper and deeper into playing the melody of this tune. Maybe he even began experimenting with the harmony behind the melody.

Those two stories have the spirit of practice in them. When we talk about Zen practice, we are not talking about practicing something in order to do something else. Like in music, you practice scales in order to be able to play a piece later. Or you practice some exercises to get in shape to run the race. Something like that. That is practice directed toward something else that is not practice. In Zen we use practice in a different way. Like the prac-tice of medicine. That means much more of an ongoing way of living and being. A cultivating of a particular way of perceiving in the world. These two stories are interesting also because of the titles of the tunes. One guy plays "Embraceable You." If you are really going to practice the Zen Way, then you have to embrace the Way, and the Way has to embrace you. To keep practice alive, you have to encourage yourself over and over again to embrace the Way and let the Way embrace you. The other tune is "My Ideal." One of the dangers in practice is that we set up these ideals, or some idealized version of how we should be or how we should practice. We sometimes construct an image in our mind of some idealized version of ourselves, sitting up in our head somewhere, and then we proceed towards trying to attain that idealized version of ourselves which, of course, we never quite attain because we never quite live up to it. It always gets just a little higher, a little higher and a little higher. Suzuki Roshi says in one of his talks in *Zen Mind, Beginner's Mind,* "If the gap between where you are and your ideal is too great, you will commit suicide." He says that practice is much more like "baking bread. You should strive of course to make a good loaf, but the spirit of practice is there in the making of each loaf of bread." Rather than striving toward some great ideal. This is the Bodhisattva Way. To in some way make a sincere effort to express ourselves and be ourselves in each moment, moment by moment by moment ongoingly.

Zen Master Ko Bong, my teacher's teacher, gave a talk and said, "When gold is in the ground it is bright. If you put gold into a hot furnace, gold is still bright. Before it went through the furnace it could not be used to make anything. Also, when in the furnace it cannot be used. But after it comes out of the furnace, we can use it to make many things: a ring, earrings or a hair pin." In the Mahayana path, or bodhisattva tradition, there are the Six Paramitas. These have the literal meaning of Transcendent Acts. In practicing the paramitas, one does something in a transcendent way. But, transcendent does not mean to go to some other place which is transcendent of this place. What it means is that, in practicing the paramitas, one's actions transcend duality. If you do something that transcends the dualistic way of approaching things, then that is the paramita or transcendent act. If you do something in a non-dualistic way, then this very place is a very different place! So *(hitting the table)* here at this point you transcend.

What is the furnace that you put the gold into? The furnace is the paramitas. One is generosity or the transcendent act of giving or being generous. Another is ethics or morality, the transcendent way of being an ethical or moral person. Then there are the paramitas of patience, zeal, meditation, and prajna (the wisdom transcendent view). For example, the generosity paramita is the act of giving something without thinking of "over here is the giver, and over there is the one given to, and here is the process of giving." If you let go of giver, given to, and process as three separate things, then you transcend. And then the action is a unified action of giving without holding anything, or any notion of "Aren't I special for giving?" That is dana paramita or generosity paramita. Suzuki Roshi said, "To give something is to be non-attached. But actually to be non-attached is already to give something." When you are not clinging to subject, object, and making all of these dualities, then that non-clinging way of being is a generous, open way of being. This is the generosity paramita.

If in giving or receiving you do not hold on to any notion of duality, and just have a clear action towards the giving or the receiving, then that is the precepts paramita because your clear action kills duality. The Sixth Patriarch said, "Don't make good and bad. At that moment what is your Original Face?" So, if you give or receive without any notion of good or bad, then the action is clear. Giving is clear; receiving is clear. That cuts off good and bad. That is the precepts or ethics paramita. Transcendent ethics means that you respond to what is correct.

The third paramita is patience paramita. Ko Bong Sunim said, "If something is bothering you, and you can be forgiving towards that, then inside you get a sense of satisfaction and pride of a particular kind. And pride is something like a plant that grows in water. The roots are not in the ground, so they can float freely anywhere." That is patience paramita. If you are forgiving to those things that bother you then you can float freely. He adds, "Just be careful with this pride, not to become too indulgent."

His view of the meditation paramita is:

> If when you see different things your mind is not moving, then that is the meditation paramita. And when you see things and realize that everything comes into being (whole countries, whole civilizations), stays for a while and then fades away, from the biggest to the smallest, and the most simple object to the most complex... if you have this view that everything comes into being, maintains itself for a while, and then gradually fades away, then that is the practice of the prajna or Wisdom paramita.

He says one more thing: "The sun is in the sky whether clouds are in front of it or not. Whether gold is in the ground, or gold is in the furnace, or gold is in the earrings, it still is all just gold." This is called the diamond paramita. Diamond in Sanskrit sometimes is referred to as vajra, which means "adamantine." The diamond paramita is the one that all the others come out of and return to. That is the basic point of faith in practice. When gold is in the ground, still gold. When you put it in the furnace, gold. When you take it out of the furnace, gold. From the very beginning to the very end the point is that there is something which does not change in the midst of all of these changes. That is the diamond paramita. It is more fundamental than all the rest of them *(hitting the table)*.

Here is a story about practice. A student came to Zen Master Hyang Bong and asked, "Master, please give me your dharma." Hyang Bong said, "My dharma is very expensive!" For the sake of clarification before going on with the story, the word "dharma" has several connotations that all fuse together. In one sense, dharma means "teaching." At the same time, dharma connotes "path." Dharma also sometimes means "phenomena." So, each and every phenomenon is called a dharma. The whole meaning is that the teaching and the path ultimately are in each and every phenomena. Usually, when a student comes to a teacher asking, "Master, please give me your dharma," this means "Please give me your teaching." When Hyang Bong said, "My dharma is very expensive!" the student said, "Oh, how expensive is it?" Hyang Bong said, "How much do you have?" The student reached into his pockets and took out what he had. Hyang Bong said, "My dharma is much more expensive than that. But even if you could produce mountains and mountains of gold out of your pockets, still my dharma is more expensive than that!" The student went away and practiced for some time.

Months later he came back with a little confidence, and again he said, "Master, please give me your dharma. I'll give you my life!" Hyang Bong said, "Even if you gave me your thousands and thousands of lives, my dharma is still even more expensive than that." The student went away again a little dejected, but fired up about continuing practice. He practiced more and began to get a recognition: "Oh, the basic Zen dharma is mind dharma." He had a little opening. So, he went back to Hyang Bong. "Master! I'll give you my mind!" Hyang Bong said, "Your mind is a stinking pail of garbage, and even if you offered me all of the minds in the universe, still my dharma is more expensive than that!"

Now, the student was really dejected, but he went away again and sat for a long time. After a while, he had another recognition—that the whole universe is empty. So he went back to Hyang Bong and said, "Master, now I understand how expensive your dharma is." And Hyang Bong said, "Oh, how expensive is it?" The student shouted, "KATZ!!!" And Hyang Bong said, "No, more expensive than that!"

Now the guy was really in deep despair, but he went away again and was determined to practice. One day, he had an awakening. He realized, "Oh. The truth is in each and every thing. The sky is blue; the grass is green." He went back to Hyang Bong and said, "Master! Now I understand your dharma!" "Oh, then what is it?" The student said, "The sky is blue; the grass is green." "No, my dharma is even more expensive than that!" The student at that point got angry and said, "I don't need your dharma! Take it and shove it up your ass!" Hyang Bong didn't seem to be fazed by this in the least and laughed. This made the student even angrier, and he started to walk towards the door. Just as he got to the door, Hyang Bong yelled to him, "Hey!!!" The student turned around. "Take good care of my dharma." The story ends by saying: At that, he attained.

That is a very important last line. "Take good care of my dharma." What does that mean? In one sense there is the notion of obligation to the teacher. There is also the notion of cultivating attention and mindfulness. What is your teaching? Attention. And after that? Attention. And after that? Attention. But, there is a difference between just cultivating attention and mindfulness as an exercise in keeping a certain sharpness to what we perceive and do and a complete spiritual practice. The first is in the realm of being artful, and it has a certain value. But, if something is to be truly a spiritual practice based on attention, attention, attention, then it is not just paying attention—it is "to take care of" with attentiveness. This means take good care of the water. Take good care of the air. Take good care of the trees. Take good care of your fellow human beings. Take good care of the animals. Take good care of my dharma.

(Hitting the table three times)

Take good care of yourselves.

Nothing

(Hitting the table with his Zen stick)

Is this costly or is it free?

(Hitting the table)

Is this full or is this empty?

(Hitting the table)

If you say both, that's only your intellectual understanding.
If you say neither, then where is this neither pointing towards?

KATZ!!!

Un Mun said, "Hear sound, perceive the Way. See color, get enlightenment. The Bodhisattva of Compassion comes with some cash in hand and buys sesame cakes. Letting them go, she exclaims, 'Oh, they've become ordinary dumplings.'" If you don't understand the bodhisattva's magic, then go around the corner to the Chinese noodle shop and watch the woman making dumplings.

In my last dharma talk, I told the story of Zen Master Hyang Bong's student who kept asking Hyang Bong for his dharma. The Zen Master's reply was always "My dharma is too expensive" to the student's repeated and sincere attempts to "receive" the dharma. This continued until one day, anger arose in the student, and, storming out, he exclaimed, "You can take your dharma and shove it up your ass!" At that, Zen Master Hyang Bong called out, "Hey!" The student turned around, and Hyang Bong said, "Take good care of my dharma!"

So, just how expensive is it to practice this way? If you go back to Un Mun's speech, it does not sound very expensive. But to hear sound and perceive the Way, you may have to give up a lot. To JUST hear and to JUST see, you might have to let go of quite a bit of stuff.

There is one case in the *Mu Mun Kwan*, a collection of forty-eight kong-ans, which relates to this point. The name *Mu Mun Kwan* has several translations. "Mu" means no; "mun" means gate; "kwan" means barrier. When I was in Korea I bought a calligraphy which says,"Dae Do Mu Mun," meaning the "Great Way has No Gate." "Dae" means great; "Do" means way. So, *Mu Mun Kwan* sometimes is translated as "gateless gate." Sometimes it's translated as "no gate pass"; and in other translations it may be "no barrier." In the Kwan Um School of Zen version, translated by Zen Master Seung Sahn, the title of the first edition is "No Gate Pass," but in a recent second edition the title is "No Gate Checkpoint." An interesting word, which relates to this point.

When you travel from one country to another, you come to a border. There is a barrier called a checkpoint where you have to show your papers. At one time you had to do that in Europe. So, "no gate" infers that if you perceive that originally there is no hindrance and everything is free and open, then there is no barrier. But, Mu Mun set up forty-eight cases as checkpoints to see how firmly you can hold this sense of "the Great Way has no gate." And, of course, Zen style is the crossing over from one territory to another beyond the checkpoint.

The particular case I'm referring to is the Tenth Case in "The Gateless Gate." It is called "Cheong Sae Is Poor." The translation reads:

A monk named Cheong Sae said to Zen Master Cho Sahn, "I am poor and destitute. Please help me." Cho Sahn said, "Cheong Sae!" "Yes, sir?" "It is as if you have already drunk three cups of the best vintage wine in China, and yet you say that you have not even wet your lips".

Another translation goes: A monk once said to Zen Master Cho Sahn, "I am poor and destitute. Please Zen Master, make me rich. Cho Sahn said, "Venerable Cheong Sae?" "Yes, Master?" Cho Sahn remarked, "Having tasted three cups of the best wine in China, you still say that your lips are not yet moistened."

In Mu Mun's compilation, he also has after each case, a short commentary. Well, not really a commentary; it's more like a few comments to poke you in the stomach. It is very terse and jabbing, and then a poem. Here the poem says:

Poor like Beom-Dan
Energy like Hwang-Du [a courageous, great general]
Even without ideas,
Dare to challenge the rich and powerful.

Or, another translation says:

His poverty is like Hantan's.
His spirit is like that of Kou.
With no way to earn a livelihood,
He dares to compete with the richest of men.

The last lines of the two versions are quite different. "Without ideas," and "With no way to earn a living." If you have no ideas, then you have nothing.

There are a number of points in this case. The first one is "poor and destitute." The second point is calling the monk's name and the response, "Yes, sir." And the third point is, "It is as if you have already drunk three cups of the best vintage wine in China, and yet you say that you have not even wet your lips."

There are a few ways to look at the first point, "poor and destitute." "Poor" means I have nothing. But to say you have nothing is to have something. That is already a problem. Some dust comes from this nothing. So, maybe this monk has plenty of nothing! Poor, coming with no idea of "I-ness" or property or possessiveness, and because I am coming with all of that, I perceive that everything is nothing. But to say nothing is to make something. In Zen dialogue there is a challenge: "Why do you make nothing?" Some translations use the word "alone" instead of poor.

"Destitute," of course, has a few different connotations. Destitute means to have no resources. It also has the connotation of being abandoned and deserted. If I am abandoned and deserted, that means I have no one to lean on. I have nothing to support myself with. Having left all of my previous ideas and notions behind, I come to a crossroads with none of the familiar stuff I have been using to lean on and get support from. So, that is a crisis. Poor and destitute and abandoned.

You can look at this phrase in a number of ways. Perhaps the monk is challenging the Zen Master. "Master, I am poor and destitute! Please help me!" That means I have come with nothing; now, what are you going to do? It is a challenge and an invitation perhaps. Or, this is my situation, Zen Master: I have let go of everything and feel like there is nothing. This is a moment of crisis. Many traditions talk about it. For example, the Christian tradition refers to this crisis as the dark night of the soul. You come to a place where there is nothing. Everything has been left behind. It's as if you have been abandoned, deserted. And you have no resources to lean on. Nothing to get a grasp of. So, maybe that is this monk's situation and he is sincerely asking the Zen Master, "This is my condition; please help me take one more step forward." Or, maybe he is saying, "I am completely empty. I am ready to receive what you have to give." At that moment the Zen Master just yells out his name, "Cheong Sae!" "Yes, sir?" That is very important. In that "yes" is everything. That is not "yes" as compared to "no." It is the "yes" of responsiveness. "Cheong Sae!" "Yes!" In that one word is the opening, or the seed, of compassion. In that one word "Yes" is sangha, our connection with each other, and with everything.

The other day I was on the bus. I was trying to get my talk together in my mind and was thinking about this line, "Yes, sir!" I happened to look up at the advertisements and saw a promotion called "Poetry in Motion." There was a poem by e.e. cummings:

> yes *is a world,*
> *and in this world of* yes
> *lives, skillfully curled,*
> *all worlds.*

So, this one word *yes* is a cornucopia of possibilities. To be able to respond with that kind of spirit without holding back is to have no hindrance. And, in a certain sense, to have Great Courage. It is very difficult to live from that point of *yes*. However, it is more difficult not to live from that point of *yes*. That is the dilemma we find ourselves in so often. Trying to make things safe or more secure or familiar, we hold back that "yes, sir," and evade, in that moment, our true responsibility. Response and ability—the ability to be responsive. Yes!

So, Zen Master calls out, "Cheong Sae!" "Yes, sir!" "It is as if you have already drunk three cups of the best vintage wine in China. Why do you say you have not even wet your lips?" That means, this nothing that you are talking about is just now responding to me in the form of "yes." This nothing that you are talking about is hearing me call your name. This nothing that you're holding on to is also seeing and moving and interacting and responding. So, why do you say you are so poor with all that you have? Go watch the woman make dumplings around the corner! Initially, it is a little intoxicating to recognize that this nothing IS seeing and hearing and tasting and smelling and responding and doing all of these things. So, when you get that recognition, don't get dizzy and lose your balance!

The story I just told you is a Zen-style teaching. It is very quick, very terse. There is a teaching parable in The Lotus Sutra which makes the same point using a different style. The parable is about a young son who left his father and wandered widely. He began to forget where he had come from and who his father was. He hired himself out in menial labor to support himself wherever he happened to be. His father never gave up on him. He looked for his son in various places, but could not find him. Eventually, the father settled down in a city and became quite wealthy. He had many holdings, money, jewels, servants; he lived like a king. The son stayed away for ten, twenty, thirty years. Then, at a certain point, without knowing it, or intuitively, he began to head back towards the country where he was born. Eventually, he came to the city where his father lived. When he saw the father's house, he thought, "Maybe I can get some work here. So, I'll go and see if I can hire myself out." As he came to the open gate, he saw the father sitting in the courtyard in a huge chair like a throne. He was laden with gold and jewels and had many servants around him. The whole thing looked so grand that the son got afraid. He thought, "This is not the place for me. If I stayed here, maybe they would press me into servitude and I wouldn't have my freedom." And so, he started to leave. But the father saw him, and, never having forgotten his son, he immediately recognized him. He told one of his servants, "Go and get that man and bring him to me." The servants went to get him, but the son was frightened because he felt that he didn't belong there, and tried to flee. So they grabbed him and brought him forcibly. He said, "I haven't done anything. Why are you taking me in this way?" And he thought to himself, "Maybe they will throw me in jail, and maybe they will kill me." When they brought him in front of the great man, he fainted. The father understood the condition of his son's mind and how poor he had become. He had him revived and let him go on his way.

This parable illustrates an interesting point about practice. When some people first start to practice Zen, they come to a place that looks at first very appealing and enticing. But before long a notion comes up about freedom—being hindered and impinged upon, and maybe even pressed into servitude. Such things may arise when you come into the Zen Center. Notions like, "Why do we have to wear these robes?" "Why do we have to bow at a certain time?" "Why do we have to chant that stuff?" Why, why, why? "Who wants to do all of that? I read these books about Zen; they talk about unhindered, unfettered, unrestrained." So, the person doing all of this questioning really has a fear of losing him or herself in some way.

In the parable, the son went away from the house and found his way to a small village. He felt more comfortable there and hired himself out. But the father had devised an expedient means. He sent two of his servants dressed up in funky-looking clothes to seek out his son and offer him a job at double his present wages.

"Expedient means" is a phrase in Buddhism that means Buddha's teaching is one lie after another! You tell one lie to cause someone to start doing something positive for themselves, and when they start doing that, you tell them another lie to get them to go further. That is expedient means.

So, here the father used an expedient means. When the job was offered to him, the son asked what kind of job they wanted him to do. He still thought of himself in a very small, humble way. The servant said, "Well, the job we have for you is shoveling a pile of dung." So the son said, "Okay." He returned to the father's house with them and became a shit shoveler! And, he was very happy doing his job. He was given a little hut outside the main compound which suited him fine. And day after day he did his job.

One day the father looked out the window and saw how pitiful his son looked. And so he devised another expedient means. The next day, he put on old clothes and took a shovel and went out to work beside his son. He said to the son, "You must work very hard here, and if you do, you can count on me. I am like your father and I have many riches and many holdings here, and you can have whatever you need." So, the son thought that was nice, and little by little he began to feel more comfortable. For many years he continued his job as a shit shoveler, even though the father gradually let him know of his riches and let him participate in some of the more important activities. But, still, inside, he had a feeling that his identity was really there in the dung. That is where he felt he belonged.

Here is another point about practice. If you hold on to a notion of yourself as small and not a part of the abundance of what is, that is an impediment and a hindrance. In the Zen tradition we say that everything from the very beginning is imbued with awakened nature. This is a point of basic faith or basic confidence that informs our style of practice. You see it expressed in various ways in different religious traditions. For example, in some Tibetan meditations the person visualizes some Buddha or bodhisattva and then identifies with the deity, and feels: I am this Buddha or I am this bodhisattva. Not: I am this poor shit shoveler who does not belong here! Or, in the Soto Zen tradition, shikantaza, or the practice of just sitting, is to manifest your Buddha nature. To just sit is to sit as Buddha and to manifest it. If you lean towards attaining something out in front of you rather than manifesting yourself, then that is killing the Buddha. If you can just completely sit with a basic confidence and a basic faith, then that is a manifestation of your inherent Buddha nature. And in the kong-an or Lin Chi tradition, there is a saying that "Just keeping the great question is itself already enlightenment." What am I? Don't know. That "don't know" is full of all possibilities. What you know is very small. What you "don't know" is very very wide. So, just to have that great question is already enlightenment. But we don't always recognize that. After we practice for a long time, one day we wake up and, "Oh, this is enlightenment! Before, I thought this was all shit shoveling, and that someday I was going to clear the field out, and then realize. But, no, from the beginning there is enlightenment. What am I? don't know. It has been like that from the start. Maybe from before the start. I just didn't recognize it."

So, here is the son with the father. This has gone on for many years now. The son was in his father's house, and maybe filling the job of steward by this time. But the guy still viewed himself as belonging outside the main compound and that really he was still just a dung shoveler. The father at that time perceived that soon he was going to die. He called everyone of importance to his place. By this time the son had begun to feel a little differently about himself. He was kind of weary of his former attitude. The father announced, "This fellow who has been working here all of these years, he is my biological son, but in his youth he ran away, and wandered widely and then returned. But he didn't know who he was. But I recognized him. So now I announce to everyone that I give all of my belongings to him." The son said, "I never expected this."

This is Zen practice. So, better look at what you're expecting to happen!

(Hitting the table with his Zen stick)

If you heard that, did you enter the Way?

(Holding the Zen stick overhead, then hitting the table)

If you saw that, did you get enlightenment?

(Hitting the table)

What is it that goes beyond these two?

KATZ!!!

Please offer somebody a helping hand. Take care of yourselves.

Compassionate Activity

ॐ

(Hitting the table with his Zen stick)

If Buddha had not seen the morning star,
would he have been called blind?

(Hitting the table)

If the Bodhisattva of Great Compassion does not hear the cries of the
world, would she be considered deaf?

(Hitting the table)

If the Buddha had not opened his mouth, and moved his tongue for
forty-nine years telling one lie after another, would he be considered
mute?

KATZ!!!

Wonderful to see all of your faces here again.
Please listen carefully to the dharma talk.

My opening remarks allude to two things. One is Buddha's Enlightenment, which is celebrated at this time of year in most Buddhist countries
throughout the world. The other is a story in *The Blue Cliff Record* which
also appears in the *Record of Un Mun*, or Yun Men, as the Chinese say. I will
read two versions of the story. The case is sometimes referred to as "Hyeon
Sa's Guiding and Aiding Living Beings" or "Hyeon Sa's Three Kinds of Sick
People."

One day Zen Master Un Mun gave his dharma speech and cited the
following story of Zen Master Hyeon Sa. Hyeon Sa said, "The old venerables
everywhere keep talking about making use of anything to guide sentient
beings. If all of a sudden they encountered someone with the three illnesses,
how would they deal with him? Since he is blind, he won't see their picking
up the gavel or raising up the whisk. Since he is deaf, he won't hear their
most eloquent words. And since he is mute, they may want him to speak,
but he cannot. So, how would they deal with him? If they cannot guide him,
then the Buddha's teaching has no spiritual use." The monk asked Un Mun
for instruction on this matter. Un Mun said, "Bow." The monk bowed and

rose up. Un Mun poked him with a stick and the monk drew back. Un Mun remarked, "Well you are not blind!" Then he told the monk, "Come closer." The monk stepped forward, and Un Mun then said, "And you are not deaf." Then Un Mun held up his staff and asked, "Do you understand?" And the monk said, "No, I don't." And Un Mun remarked, "Neither are you mute." At that the monk attained an insight.

The version from *The Blue Cliff Record* goes: Hyeon Sa, teaching his assembly said, "The old adepts everywhere, all speak of relating to things for all people. If they unexpectedly encountered three kinds of sick people, how would they relate to them? With a blind person, they could pick up the gavel or raise the whisk, but he would not see. With the deaf person, he would not understand the samadhi of words. With the mute person, if they had him speak, he would not be able to speak. But how would they relate to such people? If they could not relate to these people, then the Buddhadharma has no miraculous effect."

So, these old adepts all speak of relating to things for all people, or we might say, acting selflessly. This means that if someone is skillful, he can use anything or any situation to help someone according to their need. So that's in accord with the bodhisattva path, or the path of compassionate activity. To relate to all things, or to use anything or any situation to help all beings. And, the little preamble to this story says, "He breaks the golden chains." This refers to the teacher that can best respond to each situation. "Golden chains" refers to the precepts, Buddha's teachings, and anything that is in accord with the regular tradition. So, it is golden, and it is wonderful! And yet, still it is a chain you can become too bound up in or attached to. Even that, he breaks!

In the story about Zen Master Kyong Ho Sunim, he took a leprous woman into his little hermitage for three days. When his attendant looked confused about his actions, Kyong Ho Sunim said, "When I first saw this woman begging alms, I could see that because of the way that she related to herself as a leper, there was almost no human feeling left. And so, when I saw that, I took hold of her, and invited her into my room for three days."

My dharma brother, Dae Gak Sunim, who is the abbot of Furnace Mountain Monastery in Kentucky, told this story to a Catholic priest or monk from Gesthemene Monastery which is nearby. Hearing the story, the Catholic Priest exclaimed, "Oh, Kyong Ho Sunim even renounced his holiness!" This is what the old adepts meant by relating to things for all people: Using ANYTHING, even themselves, in some way only for all people.

The question goes on to ask, if they unexpectedly encountered the three kinds of sicknesses, how would they be able to relate to each one? If they raised up the gavel, the blind person would not see. If they spoke eloquently even in the deepest meditation and the words poured forth as samadhi words, still that person would not hear it. And if they needed feedback from a mute person, the mute person could not speak. So, how would they help such a person?

There are a number of meanings that we can find in this image of blind, deaf, and mute. Of course, the blind, deaf, and mute are none other than ourselves. The first meaning is that in meditation states which are deep, calm, quiet, drawn inward, and peaceful, the person no longer sees anything! Nor does that person hear anything! If a bomb went off nearby, the person in this meditation state may not even hear it! And even the mental verbiage, which usually goes on non-stop, has all subsided into this profound quiet. So, that person is deaf, blind and mute in a sense. But it is not blind, deaf, and mute in the Zen sense.

Hyeon Sa ends his query with the statement, "If he could not relate to such people, then the Buddhadharma has no miraculous effect." Miraculous effect in the Zen tradition is a little different from other traditions! In Christianity, Jesus is always curing some blind person or raising someone from the dead. He does a lot of miraculous things. In the Zen tradition, there are a couple of examples of "miraculous effect." One is the time Zen Master Hwang Beok traveled with a companion. At a swollen river, the companion walked on the water to cross. Seeing this, Hwang Beok exclaimed, "If I had known that you were THAT kind of fellow, I would have broken both of your legs!" So, that's what he thought of miraculous effects! On the other hand, Layman P'ang said, "My miraculous meditation power is chopping wood and hauling water. My deep samadhi is when I am hungry, I eat; and when I am tired, I sleep."

This business of blind, deaf, and mute is a little tricky. I once co-led a workshop at Providence Zen Center with an M.D. who is active with ACOA (Adult Children of Alcoholics). I led the guided meditation for the group, which was made up of professional nurses, social workers and other people in the helping professions who work with addiction. Many of them had never practiced Zen before, but most of them had practiced some kind of meditation. I gave simple meditation instructions: Sit straight, place your hands left on top of right with the thumbs lightly touching, gently look at the floor in front of you, and then ask yourself, "What am I?" So, we practiced for about ten minutes, and then I opened the floor for discussion to see if there were any questions or comments about this practice. One woman raised her hand and said, "I don't practice meditation to stare at the floor! I practice meditation to look inside myself and realize my true self." In a sense she was correct; we don't practice meditation to stare at the floor either! But, there is this thing of being attached to internalization, and quiet, and stillness—and that becomes like another Golden Chain, or like gold dust in your eye. The gold dust is very valuable. However, it can blind you just as the dust from the floor can blind you. Being attached to this gold dust is another meaning of blind, deaf, and mute. In the Zen tradition, we call this "falling down in emptiness," or "attached to emptiness." It is not yet complete. On the other hand, there is a saying that goes, "Though it fills his eyes, he doesn't see form. Though it fills her ears, she doesn't hear sound. Manjusri, the Bodhisattva of Wisdom, is always covering his eyes. Kwan Seum Bosal, the Bodhisattva of Compassion, is always covering her ears." This means to SEE as if blind or to HEAR as if deaf. That is to perceive that there is only one unified activity. The temple bell goes off at a distance, and though it fills her ears, Kwan Seum Bosal does not relate to it as a sound out here somewhere. Even calling it sound at that moment is not relating to the experience. For her, there is no sense of a hearer, hearing, or a heard. There is just one complete, full, round experience. This is Zen deafness or Zen blindness. Buddha said, "Though I talked for forty-nine years, I never said a word."

There is a kong-an that says, "The whole universe is on fire. Through what kind of meditation can you escape being burned?" It is asking, how do you relate not only to something beautiful that you see or something interesting that you hear, but to the whole world that is on fire? How do we relate to pain, to suffering, to sorrow, to injustice, to inequity, or to things that we don't like? Essentially, can you become one with any situation, pleasant or unpleasant, rather than trying to get away from it?

I had an interesting experience today. While I was at home, I lit a stick of incense, and the smell was wonderful. When I got on the bus to go to work, a person, perhaps homeless, got on the bus. Her clothes had a very strong musty odor. She sat down right next to me. So, here I am coming from this wonderful incense smell, and my mind started to move toward aversion. I thought, "Should I get up and change my seat?" And then I thought: "Oh, this is just another kind of incense! What is your problem? Can you sit here and just be with this!" (I can't say I completely overcame my aversion or impulse to pull away!) So, when it fills your eyes but you don't make it into form, or it fills your ears and you don't make it into sound, then that is the Buddhadharma having miraculous effect. Zen mind is everyday mind.

Which brings us to the story of Buddha's enlightenment. According to one story, Buddha was sitting in meditation, and he was in a state which is sometimes called Ocean Seal Samadhi. This means his mind was serene, calm and open, like the great ocean without any waves. The image is one of the ocean reflecting the entire cosmos in it. Not only does it reflect everything, but it may absorb anything that is put into it. (We have learned, however, that the ocean cannot absorb quite everything and anything that we put into it! This story is before plastics and hazardous waste!) So, Buddha was sitting in this completely even and still Ocean Seal Samadhi, completely open. And early in the morning as he arose from this state and looked up at the morning star, in that moment the openness and serenity came together with his perception of the star! And he had his great awakening: "Now I perceive that each and every thing from the very beginning has the Buddha or Awakened nature."

When Buddha was born, the palace seer told the King, "Your son will either become a great king or a world teacher." The King was not interested in his son becoming a spiritual teacher, so he did his best to shelter him from seeing anything that would cause him angst. It is said that he lived in the lap of luxury. But, at one point, he went out with his charioteer and saw four things that disturbed him and got him percolating. One day he saw a sick person; another day he saw an old and decrepit person; on another occasion he saw a dead body; and on a fourth occasion, he saw a monk or a renunciate.

It is hard to imagine that he had never seen any of these things before. I'm sure in the palace he saw sickness and old age and death. I think the meaning of this is that, even though these things were there, he never SAW them! But now, they began to have an impact on him, and he began to awaken to a questioning: "What is the meaning of human existence?" What is this?

The prophecy foretold that the son would become a king or a world teacher. Of course, this is not just a story about the historic Shakyamuni Buddha. It is a story about each and every one of us in some way. A choice is implied here. You may become a "king" or a "world teacher." A king is someone who lives in a palace and is concerned with such things as acquisition and protecting his boundaries and his territory, and perhaps also intruding on someone else's boundaries. My notion of a palace is some kind of fortress. So, living within a fortress and relating to the outside world from a fortified and limited position with an acquisitional nature is the choice of materiality. So, that is the king in the story. The world teacher, on the other hand, means to be unbounded, to be open and to move freely in the world.

Those who take the five precepts in the Buddhist tradition are given a bib-like cloth called a kasa to wear over their robe. The kasa contains lines that point to the four corners—the east, west, north, south—as well as up and down, which represents the entire world. The other representation of the lines is that of a farmer's field with rows of things planted in it. To put on the kasa means to carry the whole world and cultivate the Way. That is a vow or intention.

In taking the precepts one is saying, "I am carrying the whole world." But, that is not something new at that moment or something added on. It is what is referred to in the health insurance industry as a "pre-existing condition." When you apply for health insurance you fill out a questionnaire which asks, "Have you ever had a heart problem, kidney problem, or have you ever been to see a psychiatrist?" If you check off any of these things, it is referred to as a pre-existing condition which the insurance company won't pay for until a certain amount of time passes because you're bringing it with you into their plan. Putting on the kasa and vowing to carry the world is an awareness and an acceptance of a pre-existing condition. To think that we are not already carrying the world in some way, is an illusion and delusion. This is what is meant by blinding ourselves to a very important fact, and is the third meaning of blind, deaf, and mute.

We see a lot of blindness of this kind these days. People who don't recognize they are interconnected and interdependent with the rest of society and with things far beyond the scope of their narrow existence—whether this existence be their family or their country. And there is a lot of deafness because too many people don't listen very well to each other. It would be nice if some people would be more mute! This would allow themselves and others to be. The point is, when we put on the kasa it is just a wake-up call to something that is already there. We are already deeply and intrinsically interconnected with each other and with the whole world. In our practice, its purpose, like any vow or intention, is to wake us up to anything which is, in essence, a pre-existing condition. We may have ignored this condition temporarily, but to see it again is to open our eyes and to cure ourselves of blindness.

We are always faced with the choice of a materially limited existence based on not seeing clearly, not hearing clearly, and not speaking clearly, or one in which we open up and recognize that in our own particular way we are, each and every one of us, world teachers. That, in interacting with the world on a daily basis, we all are in some way already Buddhas and bodhisattvas. Seeing this, our responsibility becomes clear!

Buddha saw these four things: sickness, old age, death, and someone who had answered the call to find out who and what they are. He decided that this is what he must do, and so he left the palace, practiced hard, and then had the experience of seeing the morning star. Buddha's enlightenment was a complete experience in which something universal, vast and wide, based on equality, came together in one clear perceptual point: the star.

One day, Un Mun quoted dharma teacher Seng-zhao who said, "All individual entities are without difference, yet, one must not stretch the duck's legs and shorten the crane's, level the peaks and fill up the valleys, and then think that they are not different." In The Record of Un Mun, there is a footnote to this which seems to come from another teacher's writing. The translation reads: "Though the duck's legs are short, to stretch them would make it suffer. Though the crane's legs are long, to cut them shorter would make it sad. Thus: what is long by nature needs no cutting off. And what is short by nature, needs no stretching." Here is the essence of Zen mind and Zen attitude. What is by nature long, needs no cutting off, and what is short by nature, needs no stretching. This means that when you sit in meditation, do not cut off anything, and do not stretch and expand on anything. When we think that the duck's legs need to be lengthened and the crane's legs need to be shortened, we are caught up with image. And, when we come back to our simple practice of "What am I? don't know," in that "don't know" we are before any image. We are allowing the duck's legs to be the duck's legs, and the crane's legs to be the crane's legs. And we are all odd ducks! Appreciating that fact and allowing it to be is the essence of compassion towards ourselves and others. Our practice is rooted in that, begins in that, in the middle is that, and in the end it is JUST that.

(Hitting the table)

Did you see that?

(Hitting the table)

Did you hear that?

(Hitting the table)

Do you have something to say about that?

KATZ!!!

Happy Holidays, and a wonderful New Year to everyone.

The Last Word

Goal Or No Goal?

℘

Q: Is the goal of practice to achieve a certain state of mind?

A: If you assume a particular state of mind as a goal, you will direct yourself towards that particular state of mind, and at a certain point that will become an impediment.

Zen practice is a practice in the true sense of the word. Practice is a way of being and a way of functioning. Being and becoming. So, no particular state of mind becomes the thing to direct yourself toward. Instead, an ongoing perception and activity of "what is just now?" becomes the *way*. We have a tendency to form some idea of a particular state of mind, or a particular right way versus a wrong way. This points to an habitual attachment to language and ideas connected with language.

The old Zen Masters often used techniques that pulled the rug out from under someone who was attached to any particular state of mind or any particular idea or concept of what *should* be. This is seen over and over again in stories in the Zen tradition.

For example, there is a story about Chinese Zen Master Joju. During his travels as a pilgrim calling on different teachers and monks, he came upon a hermit. He asked the hermit, "Do you have it? Do you have it?" And the hermit held up one fist. Joju said, "The water is too shallow to dock here," and he walked away. Some time later, he came upon a second hermit and asked, "Do you have it? Do you have it?" And this hermit also held up one fist. Joju said, "Wonderful! You are a great man! Free to give life and take life! I bow to you!"

So, same question two times: "Do you have it? Do you have it?" What is *it*? What kind of goal is that? And the monks answer by just holding up one fist! What is that? Is it good? Is it bad? Is it right? Is that wrong? Is that being? Is that non-being? Is that life? Is that death?

This story became well known and was used as a kong-an in the later Zen tradition. The question asked at the end of the story is: Joju approved of one, and disapproved of the other; what is the meaning of that?

There is another similar story about Zen Master Poep An, who was several generations after Joju. One day, in Poep An's monastery, he was about to give his dharma speech before the noonday meal. The entire assembly was there. Suddenly, Poep An pointed to the bamboo blinds in the windows. Two monks simultaneously rose and rolled up the blinds. Poep An said, "One has got it, and one has lost it." Again, later generations picked up that story and asked: Why did Poep An say "One has got it; one has lost it?" What is the meaning of that? Same action, same time, same injunction, and yet he says, "One has got it, and one has lost it."

We find the clue in another story. Zen Master Ma Jo taught, "Mind is Buddha; Buddha is mind." Everyone practiced that. Then one day (who knows what the circumstances were: perhaps everyone had gotten so attached to that practice they felt they had it now, that this was the way!), Ma Jo said, "No mind; no Buddha."

If you can express something that goes to the heart of these stories, then you've perceived something that transcends ideas of good or bad or notions of particular goals. These kinds of devices have been used to try to direct people to perceive something before their conceptual minds taint the basic "just as is-ness."

If one can say there is a goal in Zen, that goal is to perceive the basic suchness or basic fact of things. That means coming back to your center which is before all ideas and concepts, and perceiving your correct relationship moment by moment by moment. To become one with your situation. But, even to say *to become one* already taints and puts dust on the mirror!

What's most important in the Zen tradition is the development of practice. So, if you hold onto some idea of a goal, or even of no goal, then you are missing the main point. If, however, you let go; then all of this talk becomes irrelevant. Then there just is *what is*.

Q: If there's no goal, then why do you come here?

A: It's my job.

Glossary

§∂

Blue Cliff Record: (Chinese: Pi-Ye-Lu; Japanese: Hekigan Roku): compiled in 1125, one of the most important collections of kong-ans, still in use today.

Bodhidharma: the first Zen patriarch, he reputedly came from China in 520 A.D. and sat for nine years facing a wall at Shaolin temple.

bodhisattva (Sanskrit): *bodhi* means perfect wisdom or prajna, and *sattva* means a being whose actions promote unity or harmony; one who vows to postpone the still bliss of enlightenment in order to help all sentient beings realize their own liberation; one who seeks enlightenment not only for oneself but for others. The bodhisattva ideal is at the heart of Mahayana and Zen Buddhism.

Buddha-nature: that which all sentient beings share and manifest through their particular form; according to the Zen school of Buddhism, the Buddha said that all things have Buddha-nature and therefore have the innate potential to become Buddha.

chugpi: a wooden stick used to designate the beginning and ending of sitting and walking meditation.

dharma: basically, Buddhist teaching, but in wider sense any teaching or truth.

dharma teacher: an older student who takes an additional five precepts and accepts the responsibility to teach new students about Zen practice.

five precepts: ethical guidelines taken to formalize the student's relationship to the teaching.

interview: a formal, private meeting between a Zen teacher and a student in which kong-ans are used to test and stimulate the student's practice; may also occasion informal questions and instruction.

karma (Sanskrit): "cause and effect," and the continuing process of action and reaction, accounting for the interpenetration of all phenomena; thus our present thoughts, actions, and situations are the result of what we have done in the past, and our future thoughts, actions, and situations will be the product of what we are doing now. All individual karma results from this process.

KATZ!!!: the famous Zen belly-shout; its proper use is to cut off discriminative thinking.

kong-an (Korean) *kung-an* (Chinese), *koan* (Japanese): literally, "a public notice issued by the government"; in Zen practice, kong-ans are the recorded sayings, actions, or dialogues of Zen Masters with their students or with other Zen Masters. They are the core of Zen teaching literature. As a tool in practice, they are used by a Zen Master to test the intuitive clarity of a student's mind, or to bring a student from thinking back to "don't know." There are approximately 1,700 kong-ans.

Kwan Seum Bosal (Korean): literally, "One who perceives the cries of the world" and responds with compassionate aid, the bodhisattva of compassion.

mantra: sounds or words used in Zen practice to cut through discriminating thought so that the mind can become clear; in some practices, mantra is used to induce various kinds of insight.

moktak: a gourd-like instrument used to set the rhythm during chanting.

Mu Mun Kwan: usually translated as "The Gateless Gate," was composed in 1228 by the monk Mu Mun Ekai (1184-1260). This is a collection of forty-eight kong-ans and is usually studied before *The Blue Cliff Record*.

samadhi: a state of intense concentration or absorption.

sangha: in the Theravada tradition an assembly or brotherhood of monks; in the Mahayana and Zen traditions, the community of all Buddhist practitioners; may also refer to a family of students under a particular teacher.

satori: the experience of spiritual awakening and becoming clear; enlightenment.

skandhas (Sanskrit): the five aggregates which make up human existence: form, feelings, perceptions, impulse and consciousness.

Soen Sa Nim (Korean): "Honored Zen teacher," a Zen Master.

sesshin: see Yong Maeng Jong Jin.

transmission: formal handing over of the lineage succession from teacher to student.

Yong Maeng Jong Jin (Korean) *Sesshin* (Japanese): literally, "valorous or intrepid concentration," sometimes paraphrased, "to leap like a tiger while sitting." In the West it is a two- three- or seven-day silent retreat involving thirteen hours of formal meditation practice a day. Participants follow a schedule of bowing, sitting, chanting, eating, and working, with an emphasis on sitting meditation. During the retreat each participant has interviews with the Zen teacher.

Zen Master Wu Kwang

ℰ

Zen Master Wu Kwang (Richard Shrobe) started practicing with Zen Master Seung Sahn in 1975 and has been associated with the Chogye International Zen Center of New York for many years. He was certified as a Ji Do Poep Sa Nim (dharma master) in 1984, and received dharma transmission on August 1, 1993.

From 1967 to 1972, Zen Master Wu Kwang studied intensively with Swami Satchidananda, living with his wife and children for four years at the Integral Yoga Institute. He has a Master's degree in Social Work and did four years of postgraduate study in Gestalt, including training with Laura Perls. He has been director of a drug program, and has served as an instructor in psychiatry, and Gestalt therapy.

A former piano player, his undergraduate training was in music, and he also studied with jazz pianist Barry Harris. Currently he has a private practice in psychotherapy, specializing in the Gestalt approach. He lives in New York with his family.

$\wp$

Primary Point Press is the publications division of the Kwan Um School of Zen, a network of centers under the spiritual direction of Zen Master Seung Sahn and senior teachers. For more information about the School, including lists of the Zen Centers and Primary Point Press titles, and a sample copy of the journal *Primary Point,* please contact:

The Kwan Um School of Zen
99 Pound Road
Cumberland, Rhode Island 02864-2726 U.S.A.
Telephone (401) 658-1476
Fax (401) 658-1188
Internet kwanumzen@compuserve.com
www.kwanumzen.com